Lorenzo Cantoni and Stefano Tardini's absorbing introduction considers the internet as a communication technology; the opportunities it affords us, the limitations it imposes and the functions it allows. From music to gaming, information gathering to eLearning, eCommerce to eGovernment. *Internet* explores:

- the political economy of the internet
- hypertext
- computer mediated communication
- websites as communication
- conceptualizing users of the internet
- internet communities and practices

Lorenzo Cantoni is Professor of the School of Communication Sciences at the University of Lugano in Switzerland. His research interests lie in the overlap between communication, education and new media, from computer mediated communication to usability, eLearning to eGovernment.

Stefano Tardini is the executive director of the eLearning Lab of the University of Lugano in Switzerland. His research interests include computer mediated communication, eLearning, virtual communities, cultural semiotics and argumentation theory.

ROUTLEDGE INTRODUCTIONS TO MEDIA AND COMMUNICATIONS

Edited by Paul Cobley *London Metropolitan University*

This new series provides concise introductions to key areas in contemporary communications. Each book in the series addresses a genre or a form of communication, analysing the nature of the genre or the form as well as reviewing its production and consumption, outlining the main theories and approaches that have been used to study it, and discussing contemporary textual examples of the form. The series offers both an outline of how each genre or form has developed historically, and how it is changing and adapting to the contemporary media landscape, exploring issues such as convergence and globalisation.

Videogames
James Newman

Brands
Marcel Danesi

Advertising
Ian MacRury

Magazines
Anna Gough-Yates

Youth Media
Bill Osgerby

News
Jackie Harrison

Cyberspace
Mike Ledgerwood

Internet
Lorenzo Cantoni and Stefano Tardini

INTERNET

*Lorenzo Cantoni
and Stefano Tardini*

Routledge
Taylor & Francis Group

LONDON AND NEW YORK

First published 2006
by Routledge
2 Park Square, Milton Park, Abingdon, Oxon, OX14 4RN

Simultaneously published in the USA and Canada
by Routledge
270 Madison Ave, New York NY 10016

Routledge is an imprint of the Taylor & Francis Group

Transferred to Digital Printing 2010

© 2006 Lorenzo Cantoni and Stefano Tardini

Typeset in Perpetua and Univers by
Florence Production Ltd, Stoodleigh, Devon

British Library Cataloguing in Publication Data
A catalogue record for this book is available from the
British Library

Library of Congress Cataloging in Publication Data
Cantoni, Lorenzo.
 Internet/by Lorenzo Cantoni and Stefano Tardini
  p. cm. – (Routledge introductions to media and
 communications)
 Includes bibliographical references.
 1. Internet. I. Tardini, Stefano. II. Title.
 III. Series.
 TK5105.875.I57C365 2006
 004.67′8 – dc22   2005036062

ISBN10: 0–415–35225–8 (hbk)
ISBN10: 0–415–35227–4 (pbk)
ISBN10: 0–203–69888–6 (ebk)

ISBN13: 978–0–415–35225–3 (hbk)
ISBN13: 978–0–415–35227–7 (pbk)
ISBN13: 978–0–203–69888–4 (ebk)

To our families

CONTENTS

ILLUSTRATIONS

FIGURES

TABLES

SERIES EDITOR'S PREFACE

There can be no doubt that communications pervade contemporary social life. The audio-visual media, print and other communication technologies play major parts in modern human existence, mediating diverse interactions between people. Moreover, they are numerous, heterogeneous and multi-faceted.

Equally, there can be no doubt that communications are dynamic and ever-changing, constantly reacting to economic and popular forces. Communicative genres and modes that we take for granted because they are seemingly omnipresent – news, advertising, film, radio, television, fashion, the book – have undergone alarming sea changes in recent years. They have also been supplemented and reinvigorated by new media, new textualities, new relations of production and new audiences.

The *study* of communications, then, cannot afford to stand still. Although communication study as a discipline is relatively recent in its origin, it has continued to develop in recognizable ways, embracing new perspectives, transforming old ones and responding to – and sometimes influencing – changes in the media landscape.

This series of books is designed to present developments in contemporary media. It focuses on the analysis of textualities, offering an up-to-date assessment of current communications practice. The emphasis of the books is on the *kind* of communications which constitute the modern media and the theoretical tools which are needed to understand them. Such tools may include semiotics (including social semiotics and semiology), discourse theory, poststructuralism, postcolonialism, queer theory, gender analysis, political economy, liberal pluralism, positivism (including quantitative approaches), qualitative methodologies (including the 'new ethnography'), reception theory and ideological analysis. The breadth of current communications media, then, is reflected in the array of methodological resources needed to investigate them.

Yet the task of analysis is not carried out as an hermetic experiment. Each volume in the series places its topic within a contextual matrix of production and consumption. Each allows readers to garner an understanding of what that communication is like without tempting them to forget who produced it, for what purpose, and with what result. The books seek to present research on the mechanisms of textuality but also attempt to reveal the precise situation in which such mechanisms exist. Readers coming to these books will therefore gain a valuable insight into the present standing of specific communications media. Just as importantly, though, they will become acquainted with analytic methods which address, explore and interrogate the very bases of that standing.

ACKNOWLEDGEMENTS

We are very grateful to all the people who helped us in making this volume possible: special thanks to Eddo Rigotti and Paolo Paolini, for all what they have taught and continue to teach us; to Daniele Alberzoni, Lara Bachmann, Davide Bolchini, Luca Botturi, Marco Farè, Fabiana Giulieri, Isabella Rega, Sibilla Rezzonico, Maria Grazia Silvaroli, Chiara Succi and Luca Triacca, for their contributions, remarks and suggestions (we are pretty sure we have forgotten somebody: please, forgive us – in the internet era, memory is sometimes lacking, but not gratitude!).

Without the proposal, careful reading and thoughtful suggestions by Paul Cobley, this book wouldn't be in your hands. Thank you also to Kate Ahl, Katrina Chandler, Sarah-Jane Fry and Susan Leaper for their patience and irreplaceable support.

FIGURE
ACKNOWLEDGEMENTS

We are indebted to the people and archives below for permission to reproduce photographs. Every effort has been made to trace copyright holders, but in a few cases this has not been possible. Any omissions brought to our attention will be remedied in future editions.

FIGURES

1.1 An S-curve represents the rate of adoption of an innovation over time.
Reprinted with permission from Fidler, R. (1997: 15) *Mediamorphosis. Understanding New Media*, Thousand Oaks, CA: Pine Forge Press.

1.2 Stages of the innovation-decision process.
Reprinted with the permission of The Free Press, a Division of Simon and Schuster Adult Publishing Group, from DIFFUSION OF INNOVATIONS, Fourth Edition by Everett M. Rogers. Copyright © 1995 by Everett M. Rogers. Copyright © 1962, 1971, 1983 by The Free Press. All rights reserved.

1.4 Centralized, decentralized and distributed networks.
Reprinted from Baran, P. (1964) 'On distributed communications', Memorandum RM-3420, RAND Corporation; available at: www.rand.org/publications/RM/RM3420/
Awaiting permission.

3.1 The memex as it was imagined and described by Bush.
Reprinted from Bush, V. (1945) 'As we may think', in N. Wardrip-Fruin and N. Montfort (eds) (2003) *The New Media Reader*, Cambridge, MA; London: The MIT Press, 37–47; originally published in *Atlantic Monthly*, 176 (1): 101–8; and in *Life*, 19 (11), September 1945; available at: www.ps.uni-sb.de/~duchier/pub/vbush/vbush-all.shtml.
Awaiting permission.

6.1 'On the Internet, nobody knows you're a dog.'
Reprinted from *The New Yorker*, 5 July 1993, p. 61.
Awaiting permission.

6.3 Continuum of online learning applications.
Reprinted with the permission of UNESCO from page 22 of *National Strategies for E-learning in Post-secondary Education and Training* by A.W. Bates, © UNESCO, IIEP, 2001.

TABLES

1.1 ITU DAI definition 2003.
Reproduced with the kind permission of the ITU.

1.2 ITU DAI results 2003.
Reproduced with the kind permission of the ITU.

1.3 A typology of internet governance issues.
Reprinted with permission from *Political Science Quarterly*, 119 (Fall 2004) 477–98.

6.2 Internet business models.
Reprinted from Rappa, M. (2004) 'Business models on the web', *Managing the Digital Enterprise*, available at: www.digitalenterprise.org/models/models.pdf.
Awaiting permission.

6.3 How often participants commented on various issues when evaluating the credibility of websites.
Reprinted from Fogg, B.J. (2002: 23) *Persuasive Technology: Using Computers to Change What We Think and Do*, London: Morgan Kaufmann.
Awaiting permission.

ABBREVIATIONS

ACM	Association for Computing Machinery
ARC	Augmentation Research Center
ARPA	Advanced Research Projects Agency
AWARE	Analysis of Web Application Requirements
B2B	business-to-business
B2C	business-to-consumer
Bcc	blind carbon copy
bps	bits per second
CAI	Computer Assisted Instruction
CAL	Computer Assisted Learning
CALL	Computer Assisted Language Learning
CBT	Computer Based Training
Cc	carbon copy
CERN	Conseil Européen pour la Recherche Nucléaire – European Organization for Nuclear Research
CMC	Computer Mediated Communication
CRM	Customer Relationship Management
DAI	Digital Access Index
DNS	Domain Name System
DTD	Document Type Definition
EPOS	Electronic Point of Sale
FPS	First Person Shooter
FTF	Face-to-Face
G2B	government-to-business
G2C	government-to-citizen

G2G	government-to-government
GBDe	Global Business Dialogue on electronic commerce
HAM	Hypertext Abstract Machine
HCI	Human Computer Interaction
HON	Health On the Net
HTML	HyperText Markup Language
HTTP	HyperText Transfer Protocol
HTTPS	HyperText Transfer Protocol Secure
ICANN	Internet Corporation for Assigned Names and Numbers
ICR	Intelligent Character Recognition
ICT	Information and Communication Technology
IDM	Interactive Dialogue Model
IEEE	Institute of Electrical and Electronics Engineers
IETF	Internet Engineering Task Force
IP	Internet Protocol
IPTO	Information Processing Technology Office
ISO	International Organization for Standardization
ISOC	Internet Society
ITU	International Telecommunication Union
LAN	Local Area Network
LIH	Lost In Hyperspace
LMS	Learning Management System
MMORPG	Massive Multiplayer Online Role Playing Games
MMS	Multimedia Message Service
MOO	MUD Object Oriented
MRF	Machine Readable Format
MUD	Multi User Dungeons [sometimes Multi User Domains]
NCSA	National Center for Supercomputing Applications
NLS	oNLine System
npc	non playing character
NSFNET	National Science Foundation Network
OCR	Optical Character Recognition
OPA	Online Publishers Association
P2P	peer-to-peer
PC	Personal Computer
PDA	Personal Digital Assistant
RIAA	Recording Industry Association of America
RPG	Role Playing Game
RSS	Rich Site Summary
RTS	Real Time Strategic Game
SGML	Standard Generalized Markup Language
SMS	Short Message Service

SSL	Secure Sockets Layer
TBDL	Technology Based Distributed Learning
TCP	Transfer Control Protocol
TEL	Technology Enhanced Learning
TOC	Table of Contents
URL	Universal Resource Locator
VoIP	Voice over IP
W3C	World Wide Web Consortium
WAI	Web Accessibility Initiative
WAN	Wide Area Network
WCM	Website Communication Model
WWW	World Wide Web
XML	Extensible Markup Language

INTRODUCTION

You switch on your computer in the morning and connect to the internet. You have to check immediately if your colleague has sent you the file s/he promised: you open your mailbox and look through the new messages: it's OK, your colleague's message is there, with the file attached. You open the attachment and check it: it's good work, you just need to make a few changes in order to deliver it to your client. You can make them later. Now you check the other messages in your inbox: some newsletters, a couple of spam messages you immediately delete ('Some spam messages can always pass the anti-spam filter!'), one message from a friend of yours who invites you to go to the cinema ('Unfortunately, I planned to play a session of *Ultima Online* tonight'), and finally some work messages from your colleagues and clients. You immediately reply to the few messages that require an urgent answer, make a phone call to answer verbally to an e-mail, then check your agenda: the video conference is at 11.00; you therefore have some time to finish writing a report you have to deliver by tomorrow.

Once the report is completed, you have still a few minutes before the video conference: why not have a look at the latest news? You rapidly browse through some newspapers' websites: they all give prominent space to the incredible triumph of Liverpool Football Club in the Champions' League final over A.C. Milan. 'Yes, it was indeed an incredible match!' you think. 'Let us see how the Liverpool F.C. official website celebrates the triumph.' You connect to the official website, www.liverpoolfc.tv: unsurprisingly, the website enthusiastically celebrates the success. On the website you find an interesting link to download the ringtone of the team's official anthem, 'You'll never walk alone'. You decide to download it and set it as the main ringtone of your mobile phone. After the download, you become curious to know more about the song: you connect to your favourite search engine and make a search typing in the phrase: 'You'll never walk alone'. As an answer, you get back more than 300,000 results. Among them, you find on the first page an interesting website that explains the history of the song and reports its original lyrics; you bookmark it in order to get back to it easily later on.

It is now the time for the video conference: it is a web conference, so you connect to the assigned Universal Resource Locator (URL), set your web-cam and your speaking and audio apparatus. The conference is very interesting: the speaker is good at catching your attention; you interact, ask questions, give feedback, chat with other participants, and so on. You also share with them the documents the speaker is showing, editing them as you go along, and have a 'web safari' under the direction of the speaker.

After the conference, before going to lunch, you want to talk to your partner, who is abroad for a semester of study: you open your messenger, check if s/he is online, and write a message, inviting her/him to an audio conversation via messenger. Hearing her/his voice is definitely better than simply writing text messages! While talking to her/him, you suddenly remember that tomorrow is her/his birthday: you buy a present for her/him online, to be delivered when s/he comes back from the university to her/his home college.

You check your mailbox again: you have some new messages, but none of them is urgent; you decide to process them in the afternoon and go to lunch. Before leaving your office, you load onto your iPod the music files the podcasting service you have subscribed to has downloaded onto your computer.

While going to lunch, you reflect upon how the internet has become a massive part of your life: you could not even imagine living and working without it. And to think that only a few years ago you wrote academic essays without even knowing of the existence of the internet, that you lived most of your life without it, and – frankly – did not miss it. Yet now the internet thoroughly suffuses your life.

As a matter of fact, the internet is one of the newest and most powerful communication technologies, and is rapidly spreading worldwide. It is no doubt changing in depth the way we interact and communicate, both in everyday life and in our professional activities; it is changing our social life; the way we conceive of ourselves and our relationships with the others; the way we learn; the way we buy;

the way we take care of our health; the way we interact with the civil services, and so on.

However, an important clarification should be made immediately: it is not the first time a new communication technology has arisen and caused some changes in a society, nor will it be the last. Every communication technology – from writing to letterpress print, from the telegraph to the personal computer (PC) – has always brought along larger or smaller changes in the society, organization or community in which it has been adopted. The internet is no different in this respect. Thus, when considering the changes the internet has brought about in our social life, we must be aware that this new and powerful technology is somehow only a further step in a long process of development of the so-called 'technologies of the word', which started with the invention of writing and will have further and unpredictable developments even after the internet. Of course, the internet can be considered as a milestone in this long process, like few other technologies, since the changes it brings along are no doubt deep and thorough.

From this perspective, the current volume seeks to provide an introduction to the internet as a communication technology, stressing the communication opportunities it offers, the limitations it imposes and the uses it allows, rather than just its technological aspects.

Chapter 1 introduces the internet in its context, both from a sociological and historical perspective. The processes of diffusion of new technologies in societies and organizations are first presented; a brief history of the development of the main communication technologies from the invention of writing to the spread of the internet is then provided, along with a taxonomy for the analysis of these kind of technologies. Finally, the internet in its actual context is presented from the point of view of the main political, economical, legal and ethical issues it raises.

Since the internet is a communication technology that cannot be accessed without hardware – currently computers, palmtops and mobile phones, although this might change as technologies converge – there is a need to consider the kind of communication facilitated by such hardware and the software it employs. In Chapter 2, the main features of Computer Mediated Communication (CMC) are therefore presented: the different tools for communicating online, the characteristics of the settings and of the language they rely on, and a brief overview of the basic technical aspects concerned.

Chapter 3 deals with a fundamental concept in internet communication: hypertext. In fact, this concept is at the very origin of the rise of the web and of the internet generally; furthermore, this concept has a theoretical importance as well, since it has challenged the very concept of 'text'. After a general definition of hypertext, the chapter addresses it from the point of view of ancient rhetoric in order to gain a better understanding of the communication it engenders. Finally, a brief history of the hypertext is sketched.

Chapters 4 and 5 are devoted to one of the most used and known objects on the internet: websites. They are presented not just as technological artefacts, but rather from the point of view of communication, on the basis of the Website Communication Model (WCM). In Chapter 4, the issues related to the contents and services offered by a website, to the tools that allow the access to it, and to the publishers who design, build, manage and promote it are presented. Chapter 5 deals with the users of websites and web services, addressing the issues of web promotion, usability, analysis of websites' usages, internet search engines and the ecological context of a website.

Finally, Chapter 6 presents in more detail some social practices that have been particularly challenged by the spread of the internet: mass communication, community building, education and learning, economy and commerce, politics and government.

1

THE POLITICAL ECONOMY
OF THE INTERNET

The internet is no doubt one of the newest and most powerful instances
of information and communication technology (ICT). Yet, what does it
mean to call the internet an instance of 'communication technology'?
Communication can be defined as an exchange of signs that produces
a sense, i.e. an exchange of messages. The basic nature of the messages/
signs that are exchanged in a face-to-face (FTF) communication event
tends to be oral/acoustic: basically, communication relies on the consequence that a physical fact (mainly, a piece of sound) refers to a
non-physical fact, i.e. a piece of meaning, a linguistic value (Rigotti and
Cigada 2004: 23–31; see also Bühler 1982; Clark 1996; Jakobson 1960;
de Saussure 1983). We can conceive of an FTF conversation as the most
basic form of human communication; in a communicative event such as
a conversation between two friends speaking and facing each other, no
recognizable technology is involved, although language is itself a medium:
communication just occurs by means of spoken language (and – of course
– by means of the speakers' phonatory and auditory systems, i.e. mouth,
tongue, vocal chords, ears, and so on; and by means of the air as well,
where sound-waves spread through). But as soon as we move away
from an FTF conversation, human communication takes place under the
mediation of some kind of technology: it can be mediated through writing – the basic form of communication technology – or through different media, such as radio, telephone, a video-conference system, chat,
television, and so on.

In a broader sense, a technology is everything purposely created by humans for a well-defined goal (*ad artem*). A technology of communication is a technology created in order to support, to facilitate, to foster and to enhance communications. In this sense, the sense of human communications, whatever is invented, created or used in order to support communication is a communication technology, or, after Ong, 'technologies of the word' (Ong 2002).

At the risk of sounding clichéd, the internet was not invented by anybody who woke up one morning and said: 'Let's have an internet!' It did not arise from a 'zero context'. So, with this in mind, and to avoid the common mistake of thinking that for the first time in the history of the world a new communication technology has brought along important social changes, it is crucial to understand the context in which the internet has spread and the historical stages that led to its invention. The internet, in fact, emerged in a context where other communication technologies pre-existed, which have their own role and their own history, which in their turn have taken the place of other technologies, and so on.

This opening chapter therefore presents the context in which the internet has emerged and is spreading from both a sociological and historical perspective. Presenting the details of this context is crucial if we are to avoid the pitfalls of imagining that the internet's development is unique in the history of communications and believing that the internet developed as a technology divorced from other social factors. Furthermore, any serious study of the internet needs to proceed from an acknowledgement that the internet carries with it the heritage of a number of forms of communication that preceded and coexist with it. The first section (1.1), then, deals with the relationship between technologies and society in order to reveal the mutual influences between them; the second section (1.2) provides a historical overview of the development of the technologies of the word; then a taxonomy for the analysis of the technologies of the word is presented, which proves to be very useful with regard to the internet as well (1.3); in the fourth section (1.4), the history of the development of the internet is briefly sketched to show where the present interests, patterns of ownership and struggle for control of the internet have come from; finally, the present context from where the internet is spreading is described, along with an introduction to the main political, economic, legal and ethical issues it throws up (1.5).

1.1 COMMUNICATION AND TECHNOLOGIES: A SOCIOLOGICAL PERSPECTIVE

As we have indicated, the internet is not the first communication technology to have appeared, nor has it developed in a socio-political vacuum. In this section we are going to focus on the close relationship between communication and technology from a sociological perspective. In particular, we will introduce the most relevant ideas from diffusion theories, i.e. those theories that explain how technological innovations enter a community of people (1.1.1), what are the possible attitudes of people towards new technologies (1.1.2), and what is the process that leads a technology to be (or not to be) adopted and to spread within a community (1.1.3). Then we will focus on the appearance and diffusion of new communication technologies in particular, analysing their relationship to other pre-existing communication technologies, the phenomenon of so-called 'mediamorphosis' (1.1.4).

1.1.1 The diffusion of technological innovations

When a new technology becomes available on the market, the way by which it comes to be adopted within a social community usually does not follow a linear and continuous path (see Figure 1.1). The study of the impact of new technologies on social groups shows that the process of adoption (or refutation) of technologies can be very complex and manifold.

Two models can help us in explaining the diffusion of innovations: the model of linguistic change and that of ecological systems:

1   The model of linguistic change explains the phenomenon of innovations in human languages: that is, how a new element (a new word, a new syntactical construction, and so on) enters the language system and gets to be used by a given community. The introduction of a new element into the language follows three steps: the new element is created/invented by someone who first coins it and uses it or a new sense is given to an existing element (*innovation*): 'everything in which the speech goes far from the existing models of the language in which the speech is established is an innovation' (Coseriu 1981: 55). The new element is then adopted and used by the hearer (*adoption*): 'the acceptance of an innovation by the hearer as a model for further expressions is adoption' (Coseriu 1981: 55). Finally, the new element spreads in the system; for instance, a word becomes part of the lexicon of a language, is inserted in the language dictionaries, and so on (*change*): 'linguistic change is the

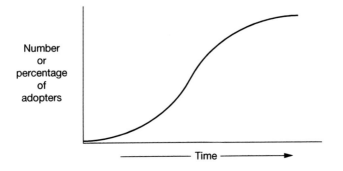

Figure 1.1 An S-curve represents the rate of adoption of an innovation over time
Source: Fidler 1997. With permission.

diffusion or the generalization of an innovation, that is, necessarily, a series of subsequent adoptions' (Coseriu 1981: 56; see also Cantoni and Di Blas 2002: 30).

Technological innovations follow similar steps in their diffusion: a new technology is first invented; it is then adopted by a small community; it finally spreads in a society, partly overlapping with other existing technologies, partly overcoming old ones.

2   The impact of a technological innovation on the context in which it is inserted (a society, a community, an organization) can be well explained through the comparison with an ecological system. Ecological systems have two basic features:

a)   They are *high-interdependence* systems, i.e. all the elements of the system are highly interdependent with one another. This means that a little change made in a part of a system, such as, for instance, the arrival of a new animal species in a part of the system – let us say a lake – has consequences on the whole system: all the other elements will be somehow affected by the change, some more directly, some less so. For instance, all the animal species that were already present in the system will have their space reduced, the food chain of the system will necessarily be modified, and so on.

b)   Ecological systems are also characterized by the *non-reversibility* of their processes: once a process takes place, it is impossible to return to the status of the system before the process. If, for instance, a pollutant is spilled into the lake, it will have such an impact on the lake's flora and fauna that it will be impossible to completely eliminate the pollutant and, as if nothing had happened, let the lake return to the way it was before.

High interdependence and non-reversibility are important features of communication systems as well. When a new communication technology is adopted, for example, by an organization, the adoption will affect the whole organization, since the new element necessarily gives rise to a reorganization of the whole system. If one introduces e-mail in an organization, the new element will necessarily be used for some tasks that were before carried out by means of fax, phone, mail or express carrier; each one of the 'old' technologies will thus have to re-negotiate its field of action (its territory) with e-mail; and if one then decides, for unpredictable reasons, to eliminate e-mail from the organization, one will never be able to restore the situation as it exactly was before the adoption of e-mail.

Since the second half of the last century, *diffusion theories* have analysed the diffusion of innovations in given social contexts. Everett M. Rogers defines an *innovation* as 'an idea, practice or object that is perceived as new by an individual or other unit of adoption' (Rogers 1995: 11), and *diffusion* as 'the process by which an innovation is communicated through certain channels over time among the members of a social system. It is a special type of communication, in that the messages are concerned with new ideas' (Rogers 1995: 5). We notice here that the novelty of an innovation is defined on the basis of the perception that a unit of adoption has of it, and not of its intrinsic qualities, i.e. of its 'real' novelty. Let's introduce the subject through two well-known examples, taken from Rogers' book *Diffusion of Innovations*:

1   The first example has nothing to do with communication technologies, actually it refers to something that can be considered a technology in a very broad sense: water boiling.

After the Second War World, the Peruvian public health service tried to introduce boiling of drinking water in a little Peruvian village, Los Molinas. During the two-year campaign, the service sent a health worker, Nelida, to the village whose task was to persuade the housewives of the village to add water boiling to their pattern of daily behaviour. In two years, Nelida was able to persuade only 5 per cent – 11 families! – of Los Molinas population to adopt the innovation.

Why did the adoption of this important and healthy innovation fail? First of all, because of the cultural beliefs of the villagers: in her campaign Nelida did not take into account the hot–cold belief system (see

Helman 2001), which is very common in most nations of Latin America, Asia and Africa. According to these beliefs, water is a 'cold' element, and boiling it would have made it 'hot', i.e. appropriate only for sick persons. Second, social reasons prevented the innovation from being adopted: Nelida worked with the wrong housewives of the village, because she ignored the importance of interpersonal relationships and social networks within that milieu; she did not work with the village opinion leaders, who could have activated local networks to spread the innovation; rather, she concentrated her efforts only on a few, socially excluded housewives. Furthermore, Nelida herself was perceived as an outsider by village housewives, in particular by lower-status ones (Rogers 1995: 1–5).

2   The second example deals more directly with ICTs: it is the case of the diffusion of the so-called 'QWERTY' typewriter (and computer) keyboard, named after the first six keys on the upper row of letters. The QWERTY keyboard is inefficient and awkward; it was invented in 1873 in order to slow down typists, since when they struck two adjoining keys too fast, often these jammed. The QWERTY keyboard, thus, allowed early typewriters to work satisfactorily by placing letters on the keyboard in such a way as to cut down on hasty jamming of two keys. In 1932, when the QWERTY design was no longer necessary, August Dvorak invented a much more efficient keyboard whose design was informed by the results of a series of time-and-motion studies. Nonetheless, the Dvorak keyboard did not spread at all: now – more than 70 years later – almost all typewriters and computers present a QWERTY design. It is not difficult to understand that vested interests prevented the Dvorak keyboard being adopted, even if it presented plain, obvious and proven advantages (Rogers 1995: 8–10).

Both examples clearly show that innovations do not always spread by virtue of themselves: as Fidler remarks, 'inventions and innovations are not widely adopted on the merits of a technology alone' (Fidler 1997: 19). A lot of concurrent factors contribute to the diffusion of innovations, such as social, cultural, economic and political factors, as well as technical ones (see, especially, Winston 1998).

Psycho-sociological factors play a very important role in determining the future of an innovation. In general, the appearance of a new technology tends to excite fear and uncertainty in future adopters, due to the fact that there is not yet a good knowledge and a well-established experience of the innovation.

Uncertainties can arise concerning different aspects of an innovation:

1   There are uncertainties concerning the technology itself: will the new technology have the same reliability, the same precision, the same capacity as the old ones? How long will the innovation remain new? When will it be displaced by a newer technology? The issue of the *potential obsolescence* of technologies is of particular relevance when speaking of digital technologies.
2   Uncertainties can arise about the financial investment required by the innovation: when will one have returns on his/her technology investment? Is it really worth spending so much?
3   Social uncertainties are relevant as well: the innovation spurs a re-organization of the roles within a society/organization, thus provoking the risk of internal conflicts. Well-established hierarchies can be subverted: is it worth running that risk?

Already, we can begin to see in this outline how much factors are pertinent to the development of the internet as well as other communication technologies. In order to facilitate potential adopters of a new technology to overcome their uncertainties, some key characteristics of the innovation must be perceived by them. Rogers calls these characteristics *perceived attributes*. Attributes 1–5 are reported by Rogers (1995: 15–17), attributes 6 and 7 are added by Fidler (1997: 13–17):

1   *Relative advantage*: the innovation must be perceived as better than the idea it supersedes. The advantage may be measured not only in economic terms, but also in terms of social prestige, convenience and satisfaction.
2   *Compatibility*: the innovation must be perceived as consistent with the values, norms, past experiences and needs of the adopters' community; the example of water boiling in Los Molinas clearly shows the importance of this feature.
3   *Complexity*: the innovation must be perceived as easy to understand and use. The more it is perceived as difficult, the less rapidly the innovation will spread. Obviously, this parameter cannot be univocally defined and measured, being relative to the contexts where technologies are introduced.
4   *Trialability*: the possibility of trying out and experimenting with the innovation before adopting it helps in reducing uncertainties.
5   *Observability*: the results of the innovation must be visible; this actually helps in exchanging information and stimulating discussions about it.

6   *Reliability*: the innovation must be perceived as reliable.
7   *Familiarity*: is the degree to which an innovation is perceived as familiarly linked to earlier or existing technologies, avoiding sudden breaks with the past. It is the case, for instance, of photography, which was initially perceived as a more efficient means of producing portraits and landscape art; mobile phones are strictly linked with wired telephones; and so on.

In addition to the innovation's attributes that need to be perceived, there must be other accelerators in order for an innovation to spread, such as an opportunity or other motivating social, political or economic reasons: Brian Winston calls them *supervening social necessities* (Winston 1995: 68 and 1998: 5–7). These necessities include social, economic, legal and political features, and derive from 1) needs of companies, 2) requirements of other technologies, 3) regulatory or legal actions, and 4) general social forces (Fidler 1997: 19).

The case of the diffusion of FM radio in the United States can help us in explaining the issue (Winston 1998: 78–83; Fidler 1997: 18–22). FM radio was invented in the early 1930s. From a technological point of view, it was decidedly superior to the existing AM radio; nonetheless it had almost no diffusion for three decades. Then it dethroned AM radio in less than 10 years. What happened during those 10 years? What were the accelerators? And what were the brakes for the preceding 30 years? The supervening social necessities that emerged in the 1960s cover the four above-mentioned categories:

1   The competition of television seriously threatened the future of AM stations. FM broadcasting, on the contrary, had much lower costs, thus making FM stations particularly appealing for manufacturers, media companies, entrepreneurs and investors (*needs of companies*).
2   High-quality broadcasting technology was required by the advancement of recording and playback technologies and the growing popularity of hi-fi and stereo recordings: FM provided it (*requirements of other technologies*).
3   In 1967 the Public Broadcasting Act was drawn up, which regulated the use of FM frequencies by reserving space on the FM dial for new public radio stations (*regulatory or legal actions*).
4   Rock 'n' roll music and teenagers declared the success of FM: while AM stations targeted broad and undifferentiated audiences and had to avoid niche music, such as rock 'n' roll, FM could spread rock 'n' roll music, thus reaching the niche audience of teenagers, which increased the demand for FM technology, thus attracting advertisers' investments (*general social forces*).

As is shown by all these examples, the diffusion of innovations involves more complex dynamics than a mere comparison between technical parameters: different factors contribute to the process that leads from the appearing of the innovation to the decision of adopting it by its users.

1.1.2 Approaches towards technologies

In general, two 'philosophies' can be outlined in approaching technology, i.e. two different attitudes towards technology in general, and consequently also towards communication technologies such as the internet. The first is a deterministic and the second is an instrumental approach. Both are crucial when considering a complex and promising technology such as the internet. *Deterministic* views of technology believe that technology develops by virtue of itself, by means of necessary internal dynamics. Deterministic approaches can be divided into *utopian* approaches, which regard technology as a means of salvation that will lead humanity to progress and redemption, and *dystopian* approaches, which consider technology as a disruptive, alienating, harmful and noxious agent for people.

The utopian approach has also been called *technophilia*: technophiles are, according to Graham, 'those who believe that technological innovation is a cornucopia which will remedy all ills' (Graham 1999: 9); the term was coined by Neil Postman, who defined technophiles as those who 'gaze on technology as a lover does on his beloved' (Postman 1993: 5).

A well-known example of a dystopian approach towards technologies is provided by the Luddites, the followers of the legendary Ned Ludd, who in early nineteenth-century England destroyed machinery in Yorkshire's and Nottinghamshire's factories, 'fearing that these new devices would destroy their jobs and livelihood' (Graham 1999: 6); they ended up being tried and hanged. As observed by Graham, their major contribution to history 'was to provide a name – Luddites – for all those who hopelessly and fruitlessly resist and oppose technological innovation' (Graham 1999: 6). Attributing this approach to the internet and the new digital ICTs, some authors speak of Neo-Luddism (see Graham 1999: 6–20). In fact, both utopian and dystopian perspectives are well represented when new media are taken into consideration: 'enthusiasts for cyberspace [. . .] credit the internet with creating a new culture, while conservative politicians speak as if the internet itself had called forth a new form of pornography' (Bolter and Grusin 1999: 76). The deterministic approach to new media is often associated with the name of Marshall McLuhan, the famous Canadian literary and media theorist who wrote his most influential works in the 1960s and 1970s. McLuhan's provocative claim is that 'the "message" of any medium or technology is the change of scale or pace or pattern that it introduces into human affairs' (McLuhan 2001: 8; see also McLuhan 1962). McLuhan insists very much on the irrelevance of content to understanding media needs 'in order to focus his readers upon: 1) the power of media technologies to structure social arrangements and relationships, and 2) the mediating aesthetic properties of a media technology' (Lister *et al.* 2003: 79). McLuhan has been strenuously criticized and discredited for his provocative pronouncements; however he has several influential followers, and his ideas were taken up and developed by a number of media theorists.

One thinker whose pronouncements may be seen to be in contrast to those of McLuhan is Raymond Williams, who 'sought to show that there is nothing in a particular technology which guarantees the cultural or social outcomes it will have' (Lister *et al.* 2003: 72; see also Williams 1974, 1983a). According to Williams, the technology must be seen 'as being looked for and developed with certain purposes and practices already in mind. [. . .] These purposes and practices would be seen as *direct*: as known social needs, purposes and practices to which the technology is not marginal but central' (Williams 1974: 293).

By contrast with technological determinism, the *instrumental* approach can be summed up succinctly. It regards technological development not as unavoidable internal dynamics, but as the convergence point where technological dynamics meet other kinds of factors, such as social, cultural, economic, politic and legal ones (Cantoni and Di Blas 2002: 126–7). As with other technologies, the internet has been primarily affected amidst these dynamics by the crucial process of adoption.

1.1.3 The adoption process

Again Rogers depicts five stages in the process that leads people to the decision of adopting an innovation (the *innovation-decision process*, depicted in Figure 1.2):

1   *knowledge* stage: the 'adoption unit' becomes aware of the existence and the working of a new technology;
2   *persuasion* stage: the individual forms a favourable attitude towards the innovation;
3   *decision* stage: the individual decides to adopt or reject the innovation;
4   *implementation* stage: the individual puts the innovation into use;
5   *confirmation* stage: the individual seeks reinforcement of the decision already made and seeks to avoid a state of dissonance or reduce it.

(Rogers 1995: 161–85)

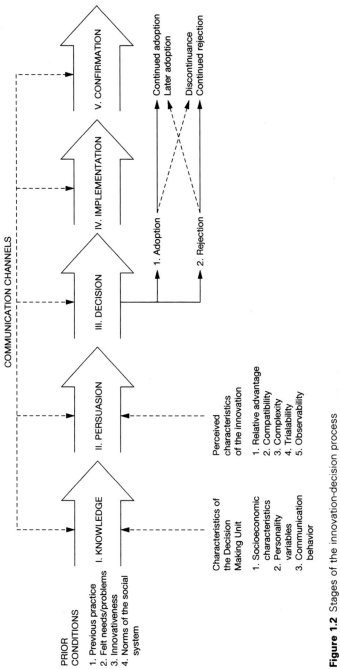

Figure 1.2 Stages of the innovation-decision process

Source: Rogers 1995. With permission.

As Rogers shows, the adoption process does not end with the decision of adopting an innovation; what is important in the stages that follow the decision is *communication*: in order for the innovation to be accepted in a community and for all the innovation-bound uncertainties to be overcome, communication, information and education activities play an essential role. In an organization, for instance, the innovation has to be welcomed through suitable information and education activities addressed to all those who will have to use it; through communication activities addressed to all the management; through a strong internal sponsoring; and so on (Cantoni and Di Blas 2002: 127). Adoption, of course, is strongly tied to mediamorphosis.

1.1.4 Mediamorphosis

Under the term 'mediamorphosis', Roger Fidler means 'the transformation of communication media, usually brought about by the complex interplay of perceived needs, competitive and political pressures, and social and technological innovations' (Fidler 1997: 22–3). The image of metamorphosis stresses the fact that new communication media do not arise from nothingness, as through spontaneous generation, but emerge step by step from the metamorphoses of earlier media. Furthermore, existing media are usually not completely displaced, but they go on evolving and adapting themselves to the new context, usually by carving out a niche for themselves.

The central concept in mediamorphosis is that of *change*: 'established forms of communication media must change in response to the emergence of a new medium – their only other option is to die' (Fidler 1997: 23).

The *metamorphosis principle* relies on three basic concepts: 1) coevolution, 2) convergence and 3) complexity.

1   *Coevolution* and coexistence mean that

> all forms of communication are [. . .] tightly woven into the fabric of human communication system and cannot exist independently from one another in our culture. As each new form emerges and develops, it influences, over time and to varying degrees, the development of every other existing form. Coevolution and coexistence, rather than sequential evolution and replacement, have been the norm since the first organisms made their debut on the planet.
>
> (Fidler 1997: 23–4)

Examples of this are numerous: the use of parchment paper as a support tool for writing has dramatically reduced since the coming of paper but has not completely disappeared; in the mass media field, radio did not spell the end of newspapers, nor did TV replace radio, and the same may be said of the internet in relation to other communication technologies. Even if a technology disappears and is replaced by another, very often some features hand down from the replaced technology to the next: it is the case in the metamorphoses that occurred from the gramophone to the 78 RPM record player up to the 33 RPM one, then to compact disc, mini disc and DVD; the support has changed, but a lot of features concerning functionalities, use and shape have been maintained.

2   *Convergence* is the idea that diverse technologies of communication and media are getting closer to one another and coming together. The digitizing of the signal in electronic media made this process particularly apparent, since it permitted the encoding and the unitary processing of communication acts that were earlier completely separate. However, convergence is not something characteristic only of the digital era, since it has always been essential to evolution and mediamorphic processes: as observed by Fidler, 'the forms of media that exist today are actually the result of innumerable small-scale convergences that have occurred frequently throughout time' (Fidler 1997: 27).

3   *Complexity*

> refers to the events that take place within certain apparently chaotic systems. [. . .] By recognizing that the human communication system is, in fact, a complex, adaptive system, we can see that all forms of media live in a dynamic, interdependent universe. When external pressures are applied and new innovations are introduced, each form of communication is affected by an intrinsic self-organizing process that spontaneously occurs within the system.
>
> (Fidler 1997: 28)

The model of the ecosystem (see section 1.1.1) can help in understanding this issue, since an ecosystem is always in *unstable equilibrium*, i.e. it is characterized by a chaos situation, where new ideas and new tools emerge, which are able to give a new stimulus to the system.

Starting from these hypotheses, Fidler states the *six fundamental principles of mediamorphosis*:

1   *Coevolution and coexistence.* [. . .]

2   *Metamorphosis*: New media do not arise spontaneously and independently – they emerge gradually from the metamorphosis of older media. When newer forms emerge, the older forms tend to adapt and continue to evolve rather than die.

3   *Propagation*: Emerging forms of communication media propagate dominant traits from earlier forms. [. . .]

4   *Survival*: All forms of communication media, as well as media enterprises, are compelled to adapt and evolve for survival in a changing environment. Their only other option is to die.

5   *Opportunity and need.* [. . .]

6   *Delayed adoption*: New media technologies always take longer than expected to become commercial successes. They tend to require *at least* one human generation (20–30 years) to progress from proof of concept to widespread adoption.

(Fidler 1997: 29)

We will see later how the internet relates to these six fundamental principles. First, however, we must consider the growth of ancestral communication technologies. The internet is clearly constituted by aspects of previous communication technologies and probably the most salient of these are the ones that have to do with the word.

1.2 STAGES IN THE DEVELOPMENT OF THE TECHNOLOGIES OF THE WORD

Diffusion theories and the concept of mediamorphosis clearly show that new communication technologies do not arise spontaneously from nothing, but emerge from the coevolution of older media. This holds true for the internet as well, the internet being one of the newest communication technologies. In this section we provide a historical sketch of the main stages in the development of communication technologies, starting from the most important and most used: writing. The section is divided into three parts, corresponding to three main periods of innovation that gave rise to as many cultural revolutions:

1   the invention of *writing* (IV millennium BCE);
2   the invention of *printing from movable type* (1456);
3   the *electric and electronic revolution* (from the nineteenth century onwards).

1.2.1 Orality and literacy

Orality precedes literacy not only chronologically, but also logically (Cavallo *et al.* 2003). Oral expressions, in fact, can exist without writing; by contrast, writing cannot exist without orality. Only about 80 languages out of *c*.3,500 currently existing have a written form; in the whole history of the world, only a few more than 100 languages have been able to develop a literature of their own (Ong 2002: 7). As a matter of fact, writing is a technology in the usual sense of the word, since it requires the use of a series of tools, such as pens, ink, paper, and is completely artificial: there is no way to write 'naturally' (Ong 2002: 81–3). Because of its close relationship with writing, Fidler regards spoken language as 'the first great mediamorphosis' (Fidler 1997: 56).

Writing was invented around 3500 BCE in Mesopotamia by the Sumerians (that is more than 40,000 years later than the appearance of *Homo sapiens*). The Sumerian writing system was called 'cuneiform', because of the peculiar appearance of their signs, which were made by means of a stylus on a clay tablet (see Figure 1.3).

Ong defines *writing* as 'a coded system of visible marks [. . .] whereby a writer could determine the exact words that the reader would generate from the text' (Ong 2002: 84). Writing was strengthened by the invention of the *alphabet*, i.e. of signs that do not refer directly to concepts, such as pictographs and ideographs, but to the sounds that compose

Figure 1.3 Example of cuneiform writing

Source: www.xtec.es/~jcanadil/nombres/actius/escriptiva_cuneiforme.jpg

words. The alphabet was invented around 1300 BCE in the Semitic area. Early alphabets were syllabic, i.e. each sign corresponded to a syllable; then signs got to refer to consonant phonemes; only in the eighth century BCE did the Greeks invent the vocalic alphabet. With the introduction of symbols representing vowels, the transformation of 'the evanescent world of sound to the quiescent, quasi-permanent world of space' was accomplished (Ong 2002: 91).

The invention of the phonetic alphabet had deep consequences in the ancient world. By means of writing, the protagonists of the communication event get separated from one another both spatially and temporally. The use of the alphabet marks the transition from the prevalence of auditory perception to that of the visual, from ear to eye, and creates a break between eye and ear, thus making visual values prior in the organization of thought and action (Havelock 1986; de Kerckhove and Lumsden 1988; McLuhan and de Kerckhove 1977; Ong 2002; McLuhan 2001: 83–96). According to Ong, writing is the most drastic of the technologies of the word, since it initiated 'the separation of the word from the living present, where alone spoken words can exist' (Ong 2002: 82).

The introduction of writing in ancient societies did not occur without disapproval and uncertainties, as is shown by Plato (427–347 BCE) in the *Phaedrus*, where the philosopher expresses all his perplexities about the new technology (see Plato, *Phaedrus*: 274b–5e). However, this cultural and social transition took place gradually. For a long while, writing was conceived and used for oral performances: texts were written in order to be spoken aloud, and reading itself remained during the Middle Ages in Europe a merely oral activity.

Cultures that do not know writing are called *primary orality cultures*, and have very different features from cultures that know writing:

- oral cultures have only a few thousand words (modern English has about one million and a half words);
- learning takes place through apprenticeship rather than through analytic studies;
- oral cultures encourage extroversion rather than introspection and self-reflection;
- they attach importance to tradition rather than to innovation;
- they favour listening rather than sight.

In considering the internet, it seems that this communication technology, then, belongs to and contributes to a culture much different from that of primary orality. Although its ultimate roots may be in orality, the internet is more directly related to writing and, especially, print.

1.2.2 Gutenberg and the alphabetic letterpress print

In 1456 the first printed book was produced: Johannes Gutenberg, a German goldsmith, printed in Mainz the Bible that goes by his name, the so-called *Gutenberg Bible*. However, Gutenberg did not invent print: images had been printed for thousands of years; Koreans, Chinese and Japanese had been printing texts from the eighth century. But the revolution associated with Gutenberg is the invention of movable alphabetic type: through this invention, type-letters pre-exist the words they are going to form. The alphabetic letterpress print

> embedded the word itself deeply in the manufacturing process and made it into a kind of commodity. The first assembly line, a technique of manufacture which in a series of set steps produces identical complex objects made up of replaceable parts, was not one which produced stoves or shoes or weaponry but one which produced a printed book.
>
> (Ong 2002: 118)

In other words, print gave rise to the first uniform and repeatable commodity (McLuhan 2001: 185–94). Along with this uniformity and repeatability, print also introduced another factor crucial to the later development of the internet: Gutenberg's invention sped up the process that writing started by instituting a technology of sight rather than hearing:

> [P]rint replaced the lingering hearing-dominance in the world of thought and expression with the sight-dominance which had its beginnings with writing but could not flourish with the support of writing alone. [. . .] Writing had reconstituted the originally oral, spoken word in visual space. Print embedded the word in space more definitively.
>
> (Ong 2002: 121–3)

The diffusion of print had very important social and cultural effects:

- it fostered the rise of national literatures, through the translation from Latin of classical texts and through the reproduction of vernacular texts;
- it favoured the broad diffusion of the cultural heritage;
- thanks to the possibility of exactly reproducing technical drawings and images, it promoted the birth of specialized knowledge, and, as a consequence, of modern science;
- it promoted the first steps towards universal alphabetization;

- it fostered personal and silent reading;
- it made books smaller than manuscripts, and, as a consequence, more transportable and accessible;
- it exerted a normalizing function on national languages.

(Cantoni and Di Blas 2002: 94–6)

All these effects of printing smoothed the way to mass communication: in the seventeenth century, the daily and periodical press, especially, took off. In 1665 the first magazine was born: the *London Gazette*, followed a few years later (1690) by the *Public Occurrences* in Boston. Print's impetus to mass communication also facilitated individual (rather than collective) consumption of written materials. As we will see, this combination of mass communication and individual consumption is absolutely central to understanding the internet.

1.2.3 The electric revolution and the emergence of mass communication

The diffusion of mass communication accelerated in the middle of the nineteenth century, thanks to all the inventions related to electricity and electronics. In this section we will present a brief sketch of the main technological inventions related to communications:

- In 1844 Samuel Morse opened the first telegraph line from Washington to Baltimore; the invention of the telegraph had two relevant consequences: for the first time information was emancipated from its physical support and distance was broken down. However, information still needed physical support, such as telegraph wires and poles, receivers and transmitters.
- A few years later, around 1850, Louis Daguerre invented photography: reality could be not only represented, but also 'reproduced'. The possibility of reproducing facts through photography has changed the way of presenting news, since less space is now required by the description of facts.

Two fundamental inventions in the last years of the nineteenth century are worthy of note: cinema and radio.

- The first movie projection was held in Paris on 28 December 1895, by the brothers Lumière. From the very beginning, cinema demonstrated two opposite trends: on the one hand, it attempted to eliminate the gap between image and reality; on the other, it did

not reproduce reality, but it tried to create, like a demiurge, a fictitious world.

* In 1898, Guglielmo Marconi broadcasted the first radio messages in
  Morse code: he performed the first wireless broadcasting through
  the water, from Ballycastle to Rathlin Island (Northern Ireland).
* In 1906, words and sounds could be broadcast via radio, thanks to
  Reginald Fessenden (for a detailed history of the radio, see Doglio
  and Richeri 1980).
* In the same year, the first television set was created, thanks to the
  association of the cathode tube with the photocell, both invented a
  few years before. In 1939, NBC was founded.
* In the 1960s, the first experiments in computer graphics were
  promoted, that is the production of images starting from a set of
  numeric values. In the 1980s. the digitalization of signals marked the
  birth of multimedia; at the end of the last century, informatics,
  telematics and virtual reality spread (for a detailed history of media
  technologies, see Winston 1998).

With regard to the new electronic communication media, Ong claims
that 'electronic technology has brought us into the age of "secondary
orality". [. . .] It is essentially a more deliberate and self-conscious
orality, based permanently on the use of writing and print' (Ong 2002:
136). New communication media, such as television and cinema, restore
the role of the ear, by requiring an integration of sight and hearing. That
this is the case in twentieth-century communication technologies is
clearly one reason why the internet, as an emerging technology, would
not remain wedded to a print ethic of sight alone.

1.3 A FOUR-LAYER TAXONOMY OF THE TECHNOLOGIES OF THE WORD

While considering the various 'technologies of the word' mankind has
developed during the centuries, we can organize them according to
different perspectives, taking into account their peculiarities as well as
their common features. We thus propose a taxonomy organized along
four relevant layers to be considered in relation to the internet.

1   The first layer considers which aspects of communication a technology is able to fix and to crystallize outside living thought and outside
the evanescent act of an oral communication. In fact, every technology
can represent only some aspects of living communication acts and of
the world they refer to and occur in – their verbal content, still images

(black and white or coloured), moving images, sounds, etc. – while omitting many others: intonation, physical setting, flavours, and so on. From this point of view electronic media allow for a great convergence of previous media, digitized texts can be combined with (digital) images, sounds, movies, graphics, etc. Separate worlds such as printed texts and cinema movies can now be brought together and be combined in the digital realm.

2   If the first layer takes into account what part of reality/communication a given technology of the word can fix and objectify in an artefact, the second layer considers the activities and processes required for this bjectification, the resources and costs needed. What are the processes required to produce, modify, replicate and preserve a communication object belonging to a given technology of the word? If we think of handwriting, we know that it requires a lot of time and labour to reproduce a book but we know also that manuscripts can last many centuries without being corrupted or damaged. With the printing press, reproducing a text has become much more efficient (both from the point of view of time and resources and from the point of view of accuracy). In handwriting, cancellations and modifications are easy to carry out, while in print they are not at all easy, and require the set-up of a new 'original' document. Electronic texts, on the other hand, partake of both modes: they can be modified and reproduced very easily, making it almost impossible to distinguish the original from its copies (see section 2.2.2). Yet, where presentation is concerned, the electronic world seems very fragile, and we do not know whether an electronic document will be preserved for centuries. What we do know is that physical supports are not strong, hardware and software standards change at a very fast pace, requiring a continuous upgrading of every digital collection. Once a technology of the word leaves specific elites and becomes accessible to large groups of a society, it raises the issue of alphabetization or literacy. This happened to handwriting – first an activity for a closed social group: the 'scribes' – to photography, to printing (after desktop publishing was born), to audio and video registration.

The relative ease through which an electronic document can be produced and its accessibility to large parts of society raises, nowadays, the issue of digital literacy (see Daley 2003). Unskilled people can take their digital pictures, shoot (digital) movies, write and print texts, or publish them over the internet.

3   Connected with the physical supports of communication is also the possibility of moving them in space, which constitutes the third layer of

our taxonomy. While in the period of orality, knowledge moved along with the knowing persons (of course, it was also somehow embedded in every human artefact), distribution of written and printed documents made this movement much more easy. If books are physical objects to be moved in space, the telegraph and the telephone required only a physical *connection* (the wire) and allowed for almost immediate trans-missions. Wireless telegraph, radio, television and mobile phones are all technologies that dispensed with the need for any physical link (besides the obvious hardware for sending and receiving signals). The internet, from this point of view, allows for almost instant bi-directional and multi-directional communications, at a global level, being able to convey elements belonging to all sorts of semiotic codes.

4   Communication artefacts are not only used to represent thought and reality, to be produced and reproduced, or to be preserved along time and moved along space, they need to be accessed and interpreted (without this, i.e. their being *communicated*, they are just purposeless). Every technology of the word imposes a number of conditions for its fruition: speaking requires the air (the simplest condition to be met: if air is absent, not only human communication, but also life is impossible); writing requires light, whether natural or artificial; while the telegraph, radio, and so on, require electricity and suitable apparatus. Electronic documents require hardware and software to be accessed. Today we can read cuneiform documents because they require just eyes and light to be accessed, but we are unable to access a CD-ROM or a file on a hard-disk or the internet without having suitable hardware and an appropriate piece of software. Obsolescence here is so fast that some supports used only a few years ago are no longer available (think, for example, of many data-cassette or floppy-disk formats), and files codified in 'old' operating systems and programmes cannot communicate anything any more. In the electronic world's recent history, changes are the only stable rule: let us see now the most immediate ones that accompanied and affected the birth and the development of the internet.

1.4 HISTORY OF THE INTERNET

So far, we have considered the history of communication technologies insofar as it has contributed to the modes associated with the internet. However, we stopped on the threshold of the digital revolution. In this section, we will focus on the birth, the development and the widespread diffusion of the internet.

1.4.1 ARPA and the origins of computer networks

The internet is the newest major communication technology, yet its history dates back more than 40 years. Almost all the authors dealing with the origins of the internet, start telling the story from 1957, to be precise from the 4 October 1957: on that date the Soviet Union launched *Sputnik I* into space. The fact marked the supposed technological superiority of the Soviets, and could not go unnoticed in the rest of the world. As a reaction to the Soviet launch, US President Dwight Eisenhower founded in 1958 a special agency under the Department of Defense, the Advanced Research Projects Agency (ARPA). The mission of the agency was to develop long-term highly innovative and hazardous research projects. The first financial plan of the agency was based on a funding platform of up to two billion dollars (Blasi 1999: 14). In 1962, the Information Processing Technology Office (IPTO) was instituted, a department of the ARPA devoted to computer science projects. The development of the first prototype of the internet is due to this office, which developed a computer network known, until 1983, as ARPANET.

There has been much speculation on the reasons for the institution of the ARPA and of the consequent supposed military origin of the internet; we will come back to this point later on. For now, however, it is worth noting that the history of the internet runs parallel with that of computers and informatics in general. In the 1960s, computers were quite different from how we conceive of them now. They were very expensive and cumbersome machines, a rare and little-known commodity; basically they were used as computing tools, in order to process lots of data and complex operations in a short time. In those years, two fundamental computer processes were developed: *time sharing* and *packet switching*. Thanks to them, more users were allowed to use the same computer being linked to it through different terminals, and many concurrent communications could be activated through the same circuit, thus allowing the sending of a message through different routes.

These technologies were developed quite simultaneously in the 1960s by three different research groups: at the Massachusetts Institute of Technology (MIT), at the RAND (Research and Development) Corporation, and at the National Physical Laboratory, in England (Hafner and Lyon 1998: 25–6, 59–67; Gillies and Cailliau 2000: 4–11).

In the same years, at the RAND Corporation, Paul Baran was working at the development of a telecommunication network that had to be able to survive in case of an attack to the US or, more specifically, of a nuclear war. His research was funded by the US Air Force (USAF). He developed the concept of *distributed network*, as opposed to centralized and decentralized ones. While centralized and decentralized networks are 'obviously vulnerable as destruction of a single central node destroys communication between the end stations' (Baran 1964), distributed networks have a mesh (or web) topology that makes them much more secure, since there is no hierarchy between nodes, they are strongly symmetrical, and there are no predetermined routes between nodes (see Figure 1.4).

As can be easily understood, the application of packet switching to the concept of distributed network is today at the basis of the internet. Baran's researches had strictly military aims; his work deeply affected the ARPA research group; so, if it is true that, according to some authors, the rumour 'that the ARPANET had been built to protect national security in the face of a nuclear attack' was 'a myth that had gone unchallenged long enough to become widely accepted as fact' (Hafner and Lyon 1998: 10), the indirect influence of the military nevertheless played an important role in the birth of the internet.

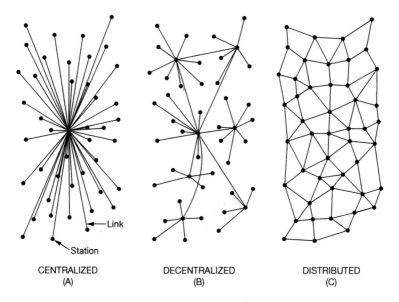

Figure 1.4 Centralized, decentralized and distributed networks
Source: Baran 1964.

1.4.2 The computer as a communication device: from ARPANET to internet

In the late 1960s, the revolutionary idea that computers could be used as a communication device – and not only as a processing machine – started to spread (see Licklider and Taylor 1968). In 1969, the first core of a computer network, ARPANET, was effective and four universities were connected: the University of California Los Angeles (UCLA), the Stanford Research Institute in Palo Alto, the University of California Santa Barbara (UCSB), and the University of Utah. This first network was used to share computers rather than to communicate. ARPANET, developed by Lawrence G. Roberts, could see the light thanks to the strict collaboration between the four universities, the ARPA agency, Bolt Beranek and Newman (BBN), a private organization, and the computer industry Honeywell. The collaboration between academic world, government agencies and private organizations is very important in order to understand the planning and funding system of technological innovations in the US during the 'cold war' (Blasi 1999: 28–9).

In 1971 ARPANET had 23 hosts, 11 years later (1982) 235, in 1990 313,000; as is evident, the growth of the network did not follow a linear path, but experienced a big acceleration in the second half of the 1980s. This acceleration was due mainly to the great changes that occurred in personal computers (PCs), which partially filled the gap between offline and online multimedia that existed up to the early 1980s. The invention that most directly affected the internet was that of the communication protocol TCP/IP. Protocols are needed in order to allow communications between computers and systems verydifferent from one another, and to link to one another many different networks with different architectures and features. In 1973, a workgroup composed by people from ARPA, Stanford University, BBN and UCLA developed the Transfer Control Protocol (TCP), which, together with the Internet Protocol (IP), defines the core of the internet still today. In 1983, TCP/IP was officially adopted by ARPANET; as Hafner and Lyon observe, 'the transition to TCP/IP was perhaps the most important event that would take place in the development of the internet for years to come. After TCP/IP was installed, the network could branch everywhere' (Hafner and Lyon 1998: 249).

In 1982 the experimental phase of ARPANET ended, and on 1 January 1983 ARPANET was split in two: a civilian network for the computer research community (ARPA internet) and a military one (MILNET). This can be seen as 'the day the internet as we know it came into existence' (Gillies and Cailliau 2000: 44). By the late 1980s, ARPANET was

no longer the centre of the internet: NSFNET (National Science Foundation Network), an academic network developed by the National Science
Foundation, was fast becoming the internet's spine (Hafner and Lyon
1998: 254).

1.4.3 The World Wide Web

Despite the real revolution that computers underwent in the late 1970s,
the world of computers and that of the internet remained completely
separated until the end of the 1980s, because the graphic level and the
multimedia richness of offline computers were still inaccessible to
network applications. The meeting of the two worlds occurred in 1993,
when the hypermedia model of the internet replaced the messenger
model, thanks to the invention of the World Wide Web (WWW). The
web was designed in the years 1989 and 1990 by Tim Berners-Lee at
CERN (Conseil Européen pour la Recherche Nucléaire – European
Organization for Nuclear Research) in Geneva (Switzerland). Basically,
Berners-Lee put together hypertext and computer networks. Thanks to
the invention of the web, the net was no more a place for fairly isolated
conversations between human beings, but became a tool for consulting
all kinds of documents (see Berners-Lee 2000: 37).

In the early 1990s, the NSFNET and the business network started to
change; in 1990 ARPANET was officially decommissioned, and one year
later commercial use of the internet was permitted. In the second half of
the 1990s the market was thriving in the US and began to spread in Europe
as well: internet users grew by 50 million in 1995. Until the second
half of the 1990s, the internet was just one of the many networking
systems existing in the world. The other systems were academic, organizations' networks (AT&T, IBM, DEC, etc.), consumer-oriented networks,
amateurs' networks (Usenet, America OnLine, CompuServe, Prodigy,
Delphi, Fidonet, Minitel, Videotel, etc.). By 1995, the internet was the
predominant networking system, which almost all other systems were
trying to comply with, in order to be compatible.

In the new millennium the trend seems to be toward the integration
of computers and the internet (web): computer operating systems and
applications integrate the browsers' functions more and more in order
to access the web; on the other hand, web browsers integrate computer
applications in order to be able to display as many document types as
possible. At the same time, a trend towards a separation of the internet
(web) from computers can be seen: this is the case, for instance, with
regard to webTV.

1.5 INTERNET AND ITS CONTEXTS

As seen earlier when presenting diffusion theories, new technologies do not diffuse only for the sake of their technological superiority: they need a favourable context in which they are tried and eventually adopted (see section 1.1). The same can be said about the internet. In the following section, some of these issues will be presented and discussed, namely: the close relationship between the internet and the telecommunication industry (1.5.1); the connected issues of internet accessibility and the digital divide (1.5.2); legal and political issues concerning ruling and governing of internet infrastructures and financing, and the issue of potential trusts (1.5.3); and the problem of internet terrorism and censorship (1.5.4). A brief discussion of ethics is then offered, highlighting the central issues (1.5.5).

1.5.1 Internet and telecommunications

It is very difficult to assess how many internet users there are worldwide: in 2004, they were estimated at about 934 million (www.clickz.com/stats/web_worldwide; for country-specific detailed data, see also the International Telecommunication Union (ITU) reports, www.itu.int). As we will see in more detail in the following chapter, the internet is a network in which computers are connected through every possible means (cables, radio, infrared, satellites, etc.) and share the same communication protocol (TCP/IP). Thus its diffusion depends – from a material point of view – on the availability of computers (or the like, e.g. palmtops) and telecommunication infrastructures, which, in turn, need a suitable technological context (again, just taking into account material elements), made of raw materials (hardware items and consumables) and electric power availability. The above-mentioned elements would also need to be diffused in a sustainable way, in a wider favourable economic, political, legal and social context, where they are produced, sold and bought, interpreted, used, integrated in meaningful (and sometimes profitable) ways.

The geography of the internet is thus closely mapped onto the geography of the telecommunication sector and, more generally, onto societies where ICTs are integrated in business and everyday life. In order to measure on a global scale the availability of new ICTs and the internet, the ITU has proposed the Digital Access Index (DAI),

> which measures the overall ability of individuals in a country to access and use new ICTs. The DAI overcomes limitations of earlier indices in terms of

its specific focus, wide country coverage and choice of variables. It is composed of a few considered variables in order to include the widest number of countries and enhance transparency.

The DAI is built around four fundamental factors that impact on a country's ability to access ICTs: infrastructure, affordability, knowledge and quality. A fifth factor, actual usage of ICTs, is important for matching the theory of the index with the reality in a country [. . .]. The inclusion of usage also captures other aspects not explicitly accounted for in the other four factors. Eight indicators are used to represent the five factors. Each indicator is divided by a 'goalpost' the maximum value established for that indicator. Each indicator is then summed to obtain an overall index score.

(ITU 2003a: 20)

Table 1.1 presents how the DAI is calculated, while Table 1.2 presents countries' ranking:

Table 1.1 ITU DAI definition 2003

DAI Goalposts: *DAI maximum values*

Indicator	Goalpost	Note
Fixed telephone subscribers per 100 inhabitants	60	Each has one half weight for infrastructure
Mobile subscribers per 100 inhabitants	100	
Adult literacy	100	Literacy has two-third weight and enrolment one-third weight for knowledge
Overall school enrolment (primary, secondary and tertiary)	100	
Internet access price (20 hours per month) as percentage of per capita income	100	The inverse of this indicator is used
Broadband subscribers per 100 inhabitants	30	Each has one-half weight for quality
International Internet bandwidth per capita	10,000	
Internet users per 100 inhabitants	85	

Source: ITU 2003a. With permission.

Note: The following steps are used to calculate the DAI: 1) Each indicator is divided by its goalpost. 2) The resulting values are multiplied by their weight and added to obtain a category index. For example, the infrastructure index is calculated as follows: [fixed telephone lines per 100 inhabitants / 60 × (1/2)] + [mobile subscribers per 100 inhabitants / 100 × (1/2)]. C) The overall DAI is obtained by multiplying each of the five category indices by 0.2 and adding them up.

Table 1.2 ITU DAI results 2003

DAI results: *DAI value, by access level, 2002*

High access		Upper access		Middle access		Low access	
Sweden	0.85	Ireland	0.69	Belarus	0.49	Zimbabwe	0.29
Denmark	0.83	Cyprus	0.68	Lebanon	0.48	Honduras	0.29
Iceland	0.82	Estonia	0.67	Thailand	0.48	Syria	0.28
Korea (Rep.)	0.82	Spain	0.67	Romania	0.48	Papua New Guinea	0.26
Norway	0.79	Malta	0.67	Turkey	0.48	Vanuatu	0.24
Netherlands	0.79	Czech Republic	0.66	TFYR Macedonia	0.48	Pakistan	0.24
Hong Kong, China	0.79	Greece	0.66	Panama	0.47	Azerbaijan	0.24
Finland	0.79	Portugal	0.65	Venezuela	0.47	S. Tomé and Principe	0.23
Taiwan, China	0.79	United Arab Emirates	0.64	Belize	0.47	Tajikistan	0.21
Canada	0.78	Macao, China	0.64	St Vincent	0.46	Equatorial Guinea	0.20
United States	0.78	Hungary	0.63	Bosnia	0.46	Kenya	0.19
United Kingdom	0.77	Bahamas	0.62	Suriname	0.46	Nicaragua	0.19
Switzerland	0.76	St Kitts and Nevis	0.60	South Africa	0.45	Lesotho	0.19
Singapore	0.75	Poland	0.59	Colombia	0.45	Nepal	0.19
Japan	0.75	Slovak Republic	0.59	Jordan	0.45	Bangladesh	0.18
Luxembourg	0.75	Croatia	0.59	Serbia and Montenegro	0.45	Yemen	0.18
Austria	0.75	Bahrain	0.58	Saudi Arabia	0.44	Togo	0.18
Germany	0.74	Chile	0.58	Peru	0.44	Solomon Islands	0.17
Australia	0.74	Antigua and Barbuda	0.57	China	0.43	Uganda	0.17
Belgium	0.74	Barbados	0.57	Fiji	0.43	Zambia	0.17
New Zealand	0.72	Malaysia	0.57	Botswana	0.43	Myanmar	0.17
Italy	0.72	Lithuania	0.56	Iran (I.R.)	0.43	Congo	0.17
France	0.72	Qatar	0.55	Ukraine	0.43	Cameroon	0.16
Slovenia	0.72	Brunei Darussalam	0.55	Guyana	0.43	Cambodia	0.16
Israel	0.70	Latvia	0.54	Philippines	0.43	Lao P.D.R	0.15

Uruguay	0.54	Oman	0.43	Ghana	0.15
Seychelles	0.54	Maldives	0.43	Malawi	0.15
Dominica	0.54	Libya	0.42	Tanzania	0.15
Argentina	0.53	Dominican Republic	0.42	Haiti	0.15
Trinidad and Tobago	0.53	Tunisia	0.41	Nigeria	0.15
Bulgaria	0.53	Ecuador	0.41	Djibouti	0.15
Jamaica	0.53	Kazakhstan	0.41	Rwanda	0.15
Costa Rica	0.52	Egypt	0.40	Madagascar	0.15
St Lucia	0.52	Cape Verde	0.39	Mauritania	0.14
Kuwait	0.51	Albania	0.39	Senegal	0.14
Grenada	0.51	Paraguay	0.39	Gambia	0.13
Mauritius	0.50	Namibia	0.39	Bhutan	0.13
Russia	0.50	Guatemala	0.38	Sudan	0.13
Mexico	0.50	El Salvador	0.38	Comoros	0.13
Brazil	0.50	Palestine	0.38	Côte d'Ivoire	0.13
		Sri Lanka	0.38	Eritrea	0.13
		Bolivia	0.38	D.R.Congo	0.12
		Cuba	0.38	Benin	0.12
		Samoa	0.37	Mozambique	0.12
		Algeria	0.37	Angola	0.11
		Turkmeni-stan	0.37	Burundi	0.10
		Georgia	0.37	Guinea	0.10
		Swaziland	0.37	Sierra Leone	0.10
		Moldova	0.37	Central African Rep.	0.10
		Mongolia	0.35	Ethiopia	0.10
		Indonesia	0.34	Guinea-Bissau	0.10
		Gabon	0.34	Chad	0.10
		Morocco	0.33	Mali	0.09
		India	0.32	Burkina Faso	0.08
		Kyrgyzstan	0.32	Niger	0.04
		Uzbekistan	0.31		
		Viet Nam	0.31		
		Armenia	0.30		

Source: ITU 2003a. With permission.
Note: On a scale of 0 to 1 where 1 = highest access, DAI values are shown to hundredths of a decimal point. Countries with the same DAI value are ranked by a thousandth of a decimal point.

Due to the fact that in telecommunication there is a tendency to a convergence between audio, data and video communication, telecom companies are interested in managing them all, providing access to many different (but technologically closely related) services.

In fact, basic internet access is usually offered at very low connection rates; this is mainly for two reasons: the telecom industry makes profit from telephone connections anyway, so many efforts are made to promote a wide internet diffusion, foreseeing that the main profits will come once people are accustomed to it (for a more extensive overview of internet business models, see Chapter 6). Actually, wherever possible – mainly through satellite connections and fibre optics – added value services are offered (and invoiced); in other cases, discounted audio communications are sold, which operate through internet connections, thus requiring less bandwidth than a normal audio connection (VoIP: Voice over IP).

Internet publication – mainly through the web or via mailing lists – is also usually less expensive than any other kind of paper-based publication. Actually, if writing and layout costs (which are about the same) are not considered, web publication dramatically reduces paper, stock, delivery and distribution costs, allowing at the same time much wider document accessibility. In fact, in many cases printing costs are just shifted to the end-user, who has to print out long or complex documents in order to read them (screen reading is still far behind the quality and comfort of paper reading).

1.5.2 The digital divide

As seen earlier, technological infrastructures are not equally distributed in different countries/areas of the world, and – even in the same country – internet access and literacy are related to physical ability, age, cultural, economic and other factors (Utsumi 2001).

The digital divide refers to 'the inequalities that exist in Internet access based on income, age, education, race/ethnicity, and [. . .] between rural and metropolitan areas, through such factors as pricing and infrastructure' (Hill 2004: 27).

On this issue Principle 17 of the Geneva Declaration makes the following recommendations:

> We recognize that building an inclusive Information Society requires new forms of solidarity, partnership and cooperation among governments and other stakeholders, i.e. the private sector, civil society and international organizations. Realizing that the ambitious goal of this Declaration – bridging

> the digital divide and ensuring harmonious, fair and equitable development
> for all – will require strong commitment by all stakeholders, we call for digital
> solidarity, both at national and international levels.
>
> (ITU 2003b: 3)

Computer literacy and familiarity with the net have a major impact on people's employability in many sectors and areas, and access to the internet means an increased access to information, education and economic opportunities as well as more opportunities for communication and political participation. Lack of access to it could mean fewer chances in the same areas; in fact, as long as countries enter the so-called information society – defined by the European Union as being 'a society in which low-cost information and ICT are in general use' – or knowledge society – where 'knowledge' stresses 'the fact that the most valuable asset is investment in intangible, human and social capital and that the key factors are knowledge and creativity' (www.europa.eu.int/comm/employment_social/knowledge_society/index_en.htm) – access to information and the use of it become the most important competitive factors at a national and regional level, as well as at a company and individual level (COM 2002).

Improving telecommunication infrastructure is, then, both an effect of economic development and a major driving force of it. For this reason, all the economically developed countries and many developing ones foster the diffusion of ICTs and computer literacy among their citizens, through political and economic incentives. The Lisbon European Council stated that 'the shift to a digital, knowledge-based economy, prompted by new goods and services, will be a powerful engine for growth, competitiveness and jobs. In addition, it will be capable of improving citizens' quality of life and the environment' (European Parliament 2000).

Many international organizations and private non-profit companies run programmes in developing countries to help their citizens reach a higher and better mastery of ICTs. For example, in 2001 the UNO established an ICT Task Force, which is

> helping to formulate strategies for the development of information and
> communication technologies and putting those technologies at the service
> of development and, on the basis of consultations with all stakeholders and
> Member States, forging a strategic partnership between the United Nations
> system, private industry and financing trusts and foundations, donors,
> programme countries and other relevant stakeholders in accordance with
> relevant United Nations resolutions.
>
> (UNICT Task Force 2004; see also Utsumi 2001)

1.5.3 Legal and political issues

As underlined before, diffusion and success of ICTs in their many application areas dramatically depend on a clear and favourable political and
legal framework, where efforts and investments can be safely made, and
potential conflicts resolved clearly and univocally (see the case of FM
radio in section 1.1.1). The internet, being in itself neither physical, nor
geographically defined, rather a worldwide continuous stream of information and transactions with an ever-changing configuration, has posed
new challenges to every effort of ruling it. For our purposes, we can
distinguish three different areas of interest, where legal and political
issues arise: 1) a first area concerned with the internet itself: how its
standards are ruled and evolve; 2) a second area of technical infrastructures: that of hardware, software, networks and the like; and 3) a third
area concerned with information and transactions that happen through
the internet.

1   The never-ending debate about 'who owns the internet' and all connected issues belong to the first area. In fact, as we have already mentioned, and shall see in more technical details in the next chapter, the
internet is just a network of computers, connected through very different means (cables, radio, fibre optics, etc.), sharing the same communication protocol. While computers and interconnecting networks belong
to their single owners, the protocol and other shared elements necessary
to the internet in order to work properly are not actually 'owned' by
anybody, nonetheless, they are ruled by specific bodies. We can see here
something similar to the stock market: options are the property of their
owners, while the market itself is not properly owned, although it needs
regulatory bodies, which indeed have and use different levels of power.

> The economics of technical standards on the Internet are a classic example
> of network externalities at work, in that a standard's utility corresponds
> directly to the number of consumers using it. For the Internet to be useful
> for informational and commercial purposes, producers need to agree on the
> technical protocols that permit users to successfully transmit and access
> data. Although common protocols create obvious public goods, such stand-
> ards can also reap disproportionate benefits for actors that either own the
> standards in a proprietary fashion or have first-mover advantages in
> exploiting those standards. Because of the huge network externalities that
> are evident in the Internet, however, we would expect a large bargaining
> core among states, leading to a harmonized standards outcome.
>
> (Drezner 2004: 490)

As concerns the internet, technical standards are ruled by many different bodies (see Chapter 2); but also other elements require regulation. In particular, in order to manage its interconnecting goal, every computer connected to the internet needs to be univocally identified by a number (IP number, for example 192.168.70.211), hence it needs an authority to assign IP numbers. Also a naming authority (or more) is needed, in order to decide what are the available extensions (e.g. .org; .net; .int; .ch; .uk; .it, etc.), and to resolve alphanumeric addresses, such as www.unisi.ch into its corresponding IP number (195.176.176.173).

In fact, after its first phase of being a research project, and a brief period – 1992–7 – in which a private company: Network Solutions, Inc., maintained the Top Level Domains, .com, .org and .net, the US Department of Commerce (which had taken over from the US National Science Foundation) promoted the establishment, in 1998, of the ICANN corporation (Internet Corporation for Assigned Names and Numbers, www.icann.org). ICANN is a private, non-profit organization that manages the Domain Name System (DNS) – see section 2.3.3); according to ICANN's statements and bylaws, in fact, its 'mission appears to be at best both technical and policymaking' (Fuller 2001).

2 A second layer of interest is concerned with technical infrastructures, as well as with hardware and software issues. As seen earlier, telecommunication industries are the most important driving force here; governments and private bodies bear a relevant interest in its diffusion, both for economical reasons (development, commerce) and for political reasons (military/strategic reasons, participation, eGovernment, see Chapter 6; see also Lazer 2001).

In this layer, a main area of concern is that of potential trusts: private companies owning (or getting a predominant market share of) infrastructures or software applications necessary to get access to the internet. The fact, for instance, that the vast majority of internet users access the web using a proprietary browser has raised a significant concern and legal trials arose (referred to as the 'browsers' war'). The same could be said every time a quasi-monopoly is established, although through fair market competition. There is not a single answer to this kind of concern: on the one hand, the internet itself calls for as much standardization as possible (necessary to foster interoperability), on the other hand, the less players there are in the internet market, the more power the existing ones get.

If governments and international organizations need to monitor this area carefully to avoid risks, a significant answer is coming from the open source movements. Open source software consists of applications whose source code is freely accessible: no one owns it, and everybody is allowed to use and modify it. Free communities of volunteers gather together in order to develop and improve open source applications collaboratively: in fact, the applications would be hardly possible without the internet and the communications it makes possible. The main short-coming of open source applications is that they are just based on an ever-changing group of volunteers, hence they cannot offer the same level of assistance as their for-profit counterparts do, nor the same mid-term assurance that they will be further developed, upgraded and maintained. In addition, if it is true that open source is free, it imposes additional hidden costs: in particular – due to the fact that is not supported by a company and does not offer any commercial/legal assur-ance – it needs dedicated expert human resources, able to manage it and carefully follow its evolving history; in many cases the costs of a commer-cial software licence could be less expensive than those required to manage in-house an open source application.

If open source software can be a solution only in some specific cases/areas, its existence has pushed ahead the debate about 'who owns the internet', and has greatly contributed to a deeper awareness on the side of public opinion and policy makers, and a more open attitude towards this issue by internet-related companies (for example, Microsoft has made available the source code of its operating systems to national governments that want to receive it; see www.microsoft.com/press pass/press/2003/jan03/01-14GSPrelease.mspx).

3   The third area is concerned with information and transactions that happen through the internet. The 'inner' nature of the internet – its being something evanescent as well as its disregard for political borders – has raised and is raising countless new legal issues, ranging from intel-lectual property rights to copyrights. These range from how to ascertain one's identity to digital signature validity, from ruling contracts made through the net (in particular that of buying/selling something) to protect companies and other bodies' names from being registered and used by unauthorized people as websites' domain names, to other examples of so-called cyber-squatting.

In fact, as affirmed by Spar (1999: 47), 'international organisations lack the power to police cyberspace; national governments lack the authority; and the slow pace of interstate agreement is no match for the rapid-fire rate of technological change'.

As already mentioned earlier, many different strategies and (partial) solutions have been implemented and in attempts to face internet regula-tion issues; Table 1.3, borrowed from Drezner (2004: 483), presents a taxonomy of them, generated from the distribution of state preferences.

Table 1.3 A typology of internet governance issues

Great power distribution of preferences	North/south distribution of preferences	
	High conflict	Low conflict
High conflict	Sham standards (Censorship)	Rival standards (Consumer privacy)
Low conflict	Club standards (Intellectual property)	Harmonized standards (Technical protocols)

Source: Drezner 2004. With permission.

Many countries have at first applied analogically to the internet's already existent laws and rules, but it is becoming clearer every day that new rules are required to cope with new and original cases (made possible only by the net), and a significant legislative corpus is growing day by day as a result of legal trials.

It is not possible to discuss the above-mentioned issues in detail; however, in the following section, two relevant issues will be further elaborated: those of internet terrorism and censorship, issues closely related to internet governance in a broad sense.

1.5.4 Internet terrorism and censorship

The concept of internet terrorism can be divided into a hierarchy of different levels of severity. Introvigne (2000) suggests that the internet can be the privileged source used to spread information politically aimed at damaging or destroying a particular organization or single individual. He argues that it is a way of circumventing possible censorship by the mainline media, and of making legal counter-attacks more difficult.

In order to combat internet misuses, possibly dangerous at various levels, many activities have been implemented both in families and companies, as well as at national levels; in general, they could consist in reducing access to the web or to e-mail, or in filtering it (Deibert and Villeneuve 2005). For example

> Internet filtering by governments is widespread. Almost every state – including countries with an ostensibly strong commitment to democratic principles and civil liberties – filters or censors access to Internet content in some way. However, the location, quantity, and manner of the filtering vary greatly. Filtering by state actors in the United States takes place primarily in schools and libraries, where the government can assert a 'compelling

interest' [. . .] China, Saudi Arabia, Iran, Singapore, Burma, and a series of countries in the CIS and Asia – where civil liberties are typically more restricted – filter more extensively. Such filtering may disallow access to certain Web sites, block or re-route e-mail traffic, or return search results different from those requested by the user.

(OpenNet Initiative 2004: 4)

The main reasons for filtering are those of upholding 'community standards' or 'morals' and of ensuring 'national security' (OpenNet Initiative 2004).

If filtering or other ruling activities are to a certain extent necessary – consider, for instance, the protection of children from illegal contents published by websites outside one's state jurisdiction – their scope and extension are far from being an agreed issue. Every nation (company/ family) interprets them in different ways, according to different political and cultural points of view, and does so in the absence of standards internationally shared or proposed by international organizations such as the United Nations.

One more point needs to be discussed here due to its connection with censorship on the one hand, and with the hierarchy of sources on the other (Gackenbach and Ellerman 1998); it is the case of a sort of indirect censorship, consisting in forgetting/ignoring information just because it is not available online. Every new technology of the word, in fact, can enact this sort of censorship as long as it becomes the common 'forum', where people go and look for available information; thus, absence from view could mean *not being at all*.

For instance, many studies have been conducted to ascertain the advantage of electronic publications from the point of view of visibility. Visibility here means that a publication is more known, and then accessed, and eventually cited, hence acquiring a higher impact on the scientific community. An analysis of 119,924 conference articles in computer science and related disciplines has shown that the mean number of citations to offline articles is 2.74, and the mean number of citations to online articles is 7.03, or 2.6 times greater than the number for offline articles (Lawrence 2001). In particular, new generations that are more accustomed to the web, are more prone to consider it as the ultimate information landscape, being in danger of ignoring what has not yet been translated into electronic form and made available through the internet, or – even worse – what, intrinsically, cannot be digitized at all.

This last point opens a wide subject: that of ethics of/in the internet.

1.5.5 Ethics of the internet

As is common with all other media, the internet has also raised a significant concern about possible damages, or risks for human beings: their psychological, cultural, religious, moral development; hence – and in connection with the previously discussed issues – a global debate is in progress that involves not only ethical experts and common citizens, but also politicians and religious leaders (see, for instance, Langford 2000 and Foley 2002). While a detailed discussion of all the issues and positions concerned is not possible in the scope of this section, the main points for consideration are offered in what follows.

The digital divide is among the direct areas of concern, due to the possible danger of keeping vast areas of human population away from the main information and communication flows (and consequently – in the knowledge society – from economical development). But global interconnection requires sensitivity in what concerns cultural relationships: globalization through the internet could mean a significant loss of local and less powerful cultures, allowing for a domination of single points of view (e.g. those considering and valuing only material and economical aspects of life, subject to economic transactions).

Freedom of expression is another area of debate, as we saw earlier when discussing the issue of internet terrorism and censorship. In fact, here, a delicate balance between freedom of speech and the common good is needed; authoritarian governments present, in this respect, the most significant imbalance, through the fear of free access to information and communication.

On the other hand, on a more personal level, it is not desirable for freedom of speech to become an *excuse* to publish false and/or offensive documents. In this respect, both educative institutions and professionals in the media (first of all, journalists) are required to make a great effort in order to equip their public to become better and more aware users of the internet itself (media education and media awareness).

> As with other media, the person and the community of persons are central to ethical evaluation of the Internet. In regard to the message communicated, the process of communicating, and structural and systemic issues in communication, 'the fundamental ethical principle is this: The human person and the human community are the end and measure of the use of the media of social communication [. . .]'
>
> (Foley 2002)

So, as we have seen in this chapter, the internet is not simply a communication technology defined by its use value. To be sure, it assists in the general process of communication and even global communication. However, as it does so, it recapitulates its own curious history of determinations. Use of the internet has come about as a result of a specific process of diffusion whose outcome is by no means inevitable. Furthermore, the tangled political economy of the internet – involving questions of its physical status as a technology, the aims of telecom companies and a complex set of ethical and regulatory issues – entails that the internet facilitates a very particular form of communication.

Dependence on computer hardware and software leads us to ask 'what kind of communication is facilitated by the internet?' The next chapter will be devoted to answering this question.

2

COMPUTER MEDIATED COMMUNICATION (CMC)

Features and technologies

Through the internet almost every kind of communication is allowed: it is possible to have spoken conversations as well as written interactions; one-to-one communications as well as one-to-many or even many-to-many ones; it is possible to publish written texts with images and audio and video as well; it is possible to communicate in real time or to send messages that will be read later; it is possible to send and share documents of all kinds; and so on. The features of the communications taking place over the internet are strongly dependent on the tools employed: different tools impose different constraints and offer different options to interlocutors. In this chapter we are going to present the main features of interpersonal communication via the internet, the so-called CMC.

CMC is usually intended as people-to-people interaction through a computer. The origin of CMC can be traced back to the origin of the internet itself, since technically CMC is nothing but a decentralized form of electronic communication (Weinberger and Mandl 2003: 82). Studies on CMC arose in the late 1980s as a branch of the wider field of human computer interaction (HCI); the growth and the worldwide diffusion of the internet have moved the attention of HCI studies to communications taking place between human beings by means of a computer. As a consequence of a networked use of computers, 'HCI studies became less concerned with the design of interfaces intended to enhance cognitive compatibility between isolated PCs and equally isolated individual users and began to worry about improving the connectivity among communities of humans and computers' (Mantovani 2001: 138). In this view, computers are no more seen only as a tool for individual work or as the final terminal of human operations, but also as a social tool for connecting people, as a real communication medium.

It is useful to draw a map of CMC and of its different tools/media (2.1) before presenting its features (2.2); in the last section of the chapter a brief overview of the main technical aspects of CMC will be presented (2.3).

2.1 MAPPING CMC

Since CMC relies basically on the technology of the internet, it inherits from the internet its potential as well as its limits. One important aspect concerning CMC is therefore its bandwidth, i.e. the capacity of transmitting data measured in bps (bits per second). This implies the social rule of saving bandwidth, i.e. of transmitting information using as little bandwidth as possible. Weinberger and Mandl (2003: 82–5) propose to classify CMC media according to their bandwidth: thus, they distinguish low-bandwidth from high-bandwidth CMC media. *Low-bandwidth* media are mainly text-based, while *high-bandwidth* media encode information through other, more cumbersome, channels such as pictures, videos, sounds, and so on. Low-bandwidth, text-based media include e-mail and mailing lists, newsgroups, chats, messengers and MUDs (Multi User Dungeons (sometimes Multi User Domains)); high-bandwidth, audio-visual CMC covers video-conferencing systems, 3D (visual) chats, shared applications.

However, CMC media can be classified according to other relevant parameters as well, which concern the use of CMC media rather than the media themselves. They are highly dependent on the contexts of use of computer-based media; nonetheless they are often ascribed to specific media, since specific cultural practices have emerged regarding distinct CMC media. The most important of these parameters concerns time: some computer-based media allow for *synchronous* communications, i.e. communications where interlocutors are supposed to take part simultaneously in the discussion, as in FTF interactions; other media allow only for *asynchronous* communications, exactly as in written communication exchanges.

CMC shares with written communications another relevant feature: *persistence*. Every CMC, in fact, leaves a physical track. The persistence of CMC is twofold: on one hand, text-based CMC messages remain – exactly as any other written text – at the interlocutors' disposal, so that they can more easily cognitively manage conversations and interactions (Herring 1999; see also section 2.2.2); on the other hand, the persistence of electronic interactions is of great importance for CMC researchers, since, thanks to log files (see section 5.1.2), they can easily get huge corpora of recorded conversations at very low costs (Paolillo 1999). In this view, online communications present typical features both of written texts (persistence) and of oral conversations (synchronicity).

The last relevant feature of CMC media is the degree of *anonymity* they allow: depending on the media used, participants may remain anonymous or assume different identities, by using nicknames or fake addresses; on the other hand, however, participants may also reveal some information unwillingly, for instance their server address by means of log files (see Weinberger and Mandl 2003: 83).

2.1.1 The tools of CMC

The most diffused and most used CMC tool is undoubtedly *e-mail*. Through e-mail it is possible to send a text message to one or more addressees simultaneously. E-mail is a low-bandwidth, text-based technology, even if it is possible to attach all kinds of files to an e-mail message, thus allowing the exchange of multimedia documents between interlocutors. E-mail is mostly used as an asynchronous tool, somehow like normal mail, since e-mail messages are mostly intended to be recorded, thus not requiring immediate reading and answer; however, e-mail might be used as a (quasi-)synchronous tool as well, for instance when the sender knows that the addressee is online or is intent on his/her e-mailbox when sending the message. Finally, e-mail is often regarded as lacking anonymity, since e-mail messages always provide some information about the sender, such as his/her address.

E-mail messages can be sent to a *mailing list* as well. In this case, they will be received by all the members who subscribed to the list. A mailing list is nothing but a list of e-mail addresses used for sending messages. Mailing lists can be one-to-many or many-to-many: in the former case, messages can be sent only by the manager of the list, whereas in many-to-many lists each member is allowed to send messages to the whole list. Mailing lists are a very powerful tool for web promotion (see section 5.1.1).

Newsgroups are discussion forums that rely on e-mail technology in order to build big archives of messages sent by users and hierarchically divided into topics. Newsgroups are a kind of electronic bulletin board related to specific topics, where everybody can leave messages that anybody else can read just by connecting to the server that hosts the newsgroup. In the server, messages are recorded on a database and archived in discussion threads: once a new discussion topic has been opened, all the messages related to that topic will be graphically displayed as replies to the first or the subsequent messages, thus building a cascading discussion thread. Newsgroups are asynchronous; they may be more or less anonymous according to users' choices: users, in fact, can decide to post messages with their own name or with a nickname.

The biggest difference between e-mail and mailing lists on one side and newsgroups on the other can be traced back to the difference between *push* and *pull technologies*: the former are technologies that deliver information automatically to the user, while the latter require that users find it; in short, with pull technologies you have to find the information you need, with push ones information finds you (Lepori *et al.* 2002). A technology that helps people receive new information items as soon as they are published (hence a sort of information push, or – better – automatic information pull) is provided by Rich Site Summary (RSS), an XML (Extensible Markup Language) format developed to syndicate web content. Users can subscribe to RSS content, and automatically receive new information, such as news feeds, updates, blog items and the like. Similar in nature is 'podcasting', the possibility of automatic download of audio files onto an iPod (or similar device) from web services one has subscribed to.

Chat systems are synchronous CMC tools where participants can exchange short text-based messages either in private, i.e. with specific interlocutors, or in public, i.e. with any other interlocutor connected to the system. In graphic chats, interlocutors may be represented by virtual figures (*avatars*) that users can move in the virtual environment in order to get closer to other interlocutors. Possible delays in chat communications are attributed to technical problems, such as lags, and typing speed, or to participants not attending to the conversation well. Chats are mostly intended as anonymous tools, unlike *messenger* systems, which allow for synchronous communications with other people who have previously been inserted in a contacts' list; thus, messengers allow communications with friends, colleagues, and in general with already known people.

Similar to chats are the so-called *MUDs*, which played a very important role in earlier studies about CMC. MUDs are text-based virtual environments created by the interactions among users; they allow participants not only to interact synchronously, like chat systems, but also to visit the text-based virtual space where they are situated and to interact with the objects available in that space, thanks to special commands that allow users to take specific actions. Two different kinds of MUD are to be distinguished: adventure MUDs, where playing interactions mostly occur, and social MUDs, which have experimental and didactic aims, such as the building of virtual cities by means of online textual interactions. In earlier MUDs multimedia were banned, and interaction took place only by means of textual exchanges; now graphical MUDs can be found as well, which are similar to online games. Interaction in MUDs is mostly anonymous.

Video and *audio conferencing* are high-bandwidth, audio-visual synchronous CMC tools. They require additional computer equipment, such as a video (web) camera and a microphone (and, if necessary, headphones). Video conferences resemble to a certain degree FTF interactions, depending on the quality of sound and image transmitted through the net (Weinberger and Mandl 2003: 85). Compared to text-based CMC tools, video conferences provide much more information about participants, such as prosodic, paraverbal, and non-verbal information; thus, video conferences are by no means anonymous. Moreover, video conferences are often held in known groups, such as virtual seminars, workgroup meetings, and so on. Audio conferences are just a little more anonymous, since they do not have visual connections; they also need a lower bandwidth than video conferences.

In distant groupworks, video conferences may be combined with *shared applications*, i.e. with a virtual space where interlocutors can collaborate by sharing and simultaneously manipulating programs, documents, and so on. Thus, 'shared applications' refers to communication scenarios rather than to proper CMC tools. Shared applications may include also 3D or graphic chats.

A particular kind of resource sharing that deserves some attention is so-called *file sharing*. Under this term, the possibility of sharing files of different types – mostly audio and video files – with other users is labelled; in other words, through appropriate software a user can decide to share his/her audio and video files with other users, allowing other users to access and download his/her own files, and being him/herself allowed to access and download other users' files. Software for file sharing basically relies on a *peer-to-peer (P2P) architecture*, i.e. 'a type of network in which each workstation has equivalent capabilities and responsibilities. This differs from client/server architectures, in which some computers are dedicated to serving the others' (www.web opedia.com/TERM/p/peer_to_peer_architecture.html). The issue of file sharing has raised – and is still raising – important legal issues concerning the copyrights of the documents (mainly music and movies) that are shared and exchanged: in 2001 Napster, which was the most famous and widespread application for free file sharing, was forced to close down because of a series of legal actions brought by the Recording Industry Association of America (RIAA); in October 2003 Napster could reopen as a payment service, but could not regain its old diffusion, due to the emergence of other applications for free file sharing.

We left until the end the CMC tool that, together with e-mail, is no doubt the most used and known: *websites*. The notion of website is as intuitive as it is difficult to define; we report here just the definition given by the Webopedia (www.webopedia.com), a very useful online encyclopedia dedicated to computer technology (see Chapter 4 for a more detailed analysis of websites):

> A site (location) on the WWW. Each Web site contains a home page, which is the first document users see when they enter the site. The site might also contain additional documents and files. Each site is owned and managed by an individual, company or organization.
>
> (www.webopedia.com/TERM/w/web_site.html)

Finally, we just mention two particular kinds of websites, which in the last years are spreading more and more: blogs and wikis.

Blogs (short for we*b logs*) are web pages that serve as a publicly accessible personal journal for an individual; usually they are updated daily. Blogs are web-based electronic diaries that reflect the personalities of their authors. Thus, web logs are very useful tools for micropublishing, since they 'enable the process of quickly and easily committing thoughts to the Web, offer limited discussion/talkbacks, and syndicate new items to make it easier to keep up without constant checking back' (Hall 2002).

Wikis (the name is taken from the Hawaiian word 'wiki wiki', which means 'quick') are collaborative websites

> comprised of the perpetual collective work of many authors. Similar to a blog in structure and logic, a wiki allows anyone to edit, delete or modify content that has been placed on the Web site using a browser interface, including the work of previous authors.
>
> (www.webopedia.com/TERM/w/wiki.html)

Thus, while blogs are mostly conceived as tools for a one-way communication to the reader, although they often allow readers to reply and give feedback in provided discussion areas, wikis are really collaborative spaces where any visitor can offer a contribution, since s/he is allowed to make any changes to the original material.

2.1.2 E-mail and netiquette

As long ago as 1972, during a showcase for ARPANET, one of the participants argued that 'the only use of computers' network that interests people is e-mail'; still now e-mail is seen as the 'No. 1 reason people use the Internet' (Middleberg 2001: 187). To illustrate the parameters of e-mail, the following protocols offer some sense of how it is an effective and powerful tool, particularly in professional settings.

Generally speaking, the rules people expect to be observed when communicating via the internet have been codified as 'internet etiquette', or *netiquette*. After Wood and Smith (2001: 118–19) five general guidelines can be identified, which apply to every CMC. They are:

1   Assume publicity. In CMC, every message can be stored and easily forwarded to other addressees; thus, every CMC message should be conceived as if it could be made public.
2   Avoid spamming (see sections 2.3.3 and 5.3.1.2).
3   Flame off. Flames are messages that are perceived as hostile and often give rise to proper flame wars, i.e. to exchanges of electronic messages that are real verbal wars; flames are considered to be a common feature of CMC.
4   Be brief. In CMC long messages and diatribes are viewed as bothersome.
5   Observe good form. Due to the ease of writing electronic messages and to the need of sending them quickly, often standards of grammar, spelling, style, and document form are abandoned (see section 4.2.1).

Of course, these guidelines are very general, and their effectiveness and validity depend on the context where single communications occur.

When dealing with e-mail in particular, many professional organizations advise caution. First of all, it is to be noticed that an e-mail message is, like a letter, asynchronous, not pervasive, persistent, and, like a phone call, immediate and direct. However, despite these clear benefits, professional communication involves some questions when using e-mail:

*   Is it really useful/necessary to send this message? Will I cause a waste of time?
*   Is e-mail the right channel for sending this message? Are there other channels that are more suited to this message? E-mail lowers the threshold of communication, because it has very low costs in terms of time required, difficulty of sending, and so on; but the fact that it is often the handiest communication tool does not always mean that it is also the most appropriate.

- What is my mood when writing this message? What will be the mood of the addressee? As a matter of fact, one of the main features of e-mail communications is the lack of the immediate feedback that in FTF conversations is granted by the mutual visibility and/or audibility of interlocutors. Thus, moods are not so easily modified.

Usually, only a few e-mail messages require an immediate answer; however, a policy for answering messages is often observed, and, if necessary, explicitly stated, by organizations. For instance, the time(s) in the day when the mailbox is checked and the messages are answered.

The structure of an e-mail message can be roughly divided into two sections: 'a preformatted upper area (the *header* or *heading*) and a lower area for the main text (the *body* or *message*)' (Crystal 2001: 95).

The header is composed of different fields:

- The *From* field contains the name of the sender: this is the first information that drives the addressee's expectations; thus, the name through which one wants to be represented is usually chosen carefully.
- The *To*, carbon copy (Cc) and blind carbon copy (Bcc) fields contain the receivers of the message: in the field *To* only the addressees of the message are usually inserted; other possible interested people are usually inserted in the *Cc* field. The *Bcc* field contains receivers who can read the message without being seen by other receivers; this function is useful, for instance, when one single message must be sent to a long list of e-mail addresses: this way, the list is not made public.
- The *Subject* field summarizes the importance of the message for the receiver: in a few words the kind of message (e.g. request, invitation, reply, information, etc.) and its content are usually stated.

The *body* of the e-mail contains the message itself. Text paragraphs are frequently brief and separate from one another; the message itself is often brief. When it is present, the *electronic signature* gives information about the sender's authority: his/her affiliation (name and website of the organization), his/her role in the organization, his/her contacts (phone and fax number, physical address).

When replying to a message, it is commonly the practice that the single points of the original message are clearly referred to, allowing the possibility of the whole history of the e-mail exchanges being easily recoverable. E-mail allows this by reproducing (if chosen) the entire text of the original message.

2.2 THE FEATURES OF CMC

CMC has peculiar features that differentiate it both from oral FTF and written communication; at the same time, CMC shares many features with both oral and written communication. Some authors coined, in alternative to CMC, the word Netspeak (Crystal 2001: 17), which emphasizes the double face of CMC: ' "speak" here involves writing as well as talking, and [. . .] any "speak" suffix also has a receptive element, including "listening and reading". [. . .] The heart of the matter seems to be its relationship to spoken and written language' (Crystal 2001: 17–18, 24). Other authors define internet language as 'written speech' (see Crystal 2001). In this section, we will present the main features of CMC, from the perspectives of the settings in which it occurs (2.2.1), of the messages it produces (2.2.2), and of the language it uses (2.2.3).

2.2.1 CMC settings

FTF conversation is the basic setting for language use; it is the primary communication setting (Clark 1996: 4–11). FTF conversation is a spoken setting, thus being universal to human societies; it does not require special skills, unlike reading and writing, which require years and years of schooling; it is the basic setting for language acquisition, since in the first two or three years of their life, children learn their first language almost solely in conversational settings: 'face-to-face conversation is the cradle of language use' (Clark 1996: 9).

FTF conversation is the only *immediate* setting of communication, since it is the only process where 'messages are transmitted more or less directly, without the aid of exterior technology'; all other settings are *mediated*, since communicators are separated 'through some technology – from the simplest types like paper to the most sophisticated kind of computer device like a wireless Web unit' (Wood and Smith 2001: 6).

Herbert Clark has singled out some features that make FTF conversations the basic setting for language use; as long as a medium intervenes and communication gets mediated, one or more of these features may be missed. These features can also be seen as constraints imposed by a medium to interpersonal communications (Clark and Brennan 1991: 140–2) or, on the contrary, as the oppositions offered by a medium (Brennan 2002: 9). The features are:

1 copresence: the participants share the same physical environment;
2 visibility: the participants can see each other;
3 audibility: the participants can hear each other;

4   instantaneity: the participants perceive each other's actions at no
     perceptible delay;

5   evanescence: the medium is evanescent, it fades quickly;

6   recordlessness: the participants' actions leave no record or artefact;

7   simultaneity: the participants can produce and receive at once and
     simultaneously;

8   extemporaneity: the participants formulate and execute their actions
     extemporaneously, in real time;

9   self-determination: the participants determine for themselves what
     actions to take when;

10   self-expression: the participants take actions as themselves.

(Clark 1996: 9–10)

Features 1 through 4 have to do with the immediacy of FTF conversations and regard the mutual relation of participants; features 5 through 7 reflect the medium; features 8 to 10 have to do with control over what is done and how. We notice here that 'recordlessness' implies that communication exchanges cannot be reviewed by participants, and extemporaneity implies that messages cannot be revised by their authors, thus making it more complicated to produce self-repairs of mistakes.

Compared to FTF conversations, telephone communications, for instance, lack copresence and visibility, whereas a written letter lacks also all other features except 9 and 10.

In Table 2.1, adapted from Clark and Brennan (1991), Clark (1996) and Brennan (2002), the features of different communication settings are presented; the last five rows concern settings mediated by CMC tools:

Table 2.1 clearly shows that it is not possible to establish a general setting for CMC, since different CMC tools provide different communication settings. Some tools provide settings similar to written communications, such as e-mails and websites, other tools provide spoken conversation-like settings; some tools, such as chats, MUDs and messengers, provide hybrid settings.

Let us make just some remarks about the Table 2.1:

- E-mail's degree of instantaneity, as it has already been shown, depends on the communication context: if interlocutors mutually know that the other interlocutor(s) are online, communication can occur quasi-instantaneously; otherwise, it resembles all other written communications.
- Video conferences have a lower degree of visibility, if compared with FTF conversations, since usually participants can see only the faces of other participants.

Table 2.1 Features of different communication settings

Feature / Setting	Spoken/written	Copresence	Visibility	Audibility	Instantaneity	Evanescence	Reviewability	Revisability
FTF conversation	S	++	++	++	++	++	—	—
Telephone conversation	S	—	—	++	++	++	—	—
Letters	W	—	—	—	—	—	++	++
E-mail	W	—	—	—	??	—	++	++
Chat, messengers	W	—	—	—	++	+	+	++
Video conference	S	—	+	++	++	++	—	—
Websites/blogs	W	—	—	—	—	—	++	++
Wikis	W	—	—	—	—	—	+	+

Key: ++ means that the feature is present in the communicative setting; + means present to a limited degree; ?? means that the setting may have or may not have that feature; — means that the feature is not present in the setting.

- Chat and messenger systems have a lower degree of reviewability, when compared to other written media, since chat messages can be reviewed only as long as the chat window is open; once the communication is over and the user closes the chat's window, messages fade and the interaction cannot be reviewed any more.

As can be seen, in CMC copresence, intended as the sharing of the same physical environment, is always lacking: computer mediated interaction is not bound up with interlocutors' physical copresence, but rather with *telepresence*, i.e. with 'the experience of presence in an environment by means of a communication medium' (Steuer 1993: 6).

Telepresence is a feature typical of all synchronous CMC: in chats, messengers, MUDs, video conferences, application sharing, interlocutors share the same communication environment, i.e. they can interact and see – at different degrees in different tools – the same things on their computer screens or computer windows as other interlocutors. In some cases, as in video conferences, they can also directly see other interlocutors; in other cases, as in some chat systems or in messengers, they can partially see what interlocutors are doing, for instance if they are typing a message. In interactions mediated by computers, as well as in some other mediated interactions, participants perceive not only the physical environment where they are, but also the environment presented by the medium: 'telepresence is the extent to which one feels present in the mediated environment, rather than in the immediate physical environment. [. . .] "Presence" refers to the *natural* perception of an environment, and "telepresence" refers to the mediated perception of an environment' (Steuer 1993: 6).

In this sense, telepresence is not an exclusive feature of CMC, since any other medium, in different ways and at different degrees, conveys the experience of telepresence: let us think, for instance, of television, which has the power of representing real or fictitious spaces and presenting them to viewers with a relatively high degree of vividness; also by means of the telephone, interlocutors may be said to be 'electronically present in the same virtual reality created by the telephone system' (Steuer 1993: 9); even books can describe real or fictitious places, thus giving the reader the impression of 'being there' and sharing that virtual space with the author or with the text's characters. Nevertheless, digital media have strongly enhanced the experience of telepresence, thanks to their capacity to reproduce virtual spaces and to allow users to interact in them.

2.2.2 The electronic text

So far, we have dealt with the settings in which electronic communications take place. In this section, we are going to present the features of CMC messages, i.e. the features of the texts that are the result of communication exchanges mediated by electronic/digital tools.

The digitalization of the technologies of the word has brought into the foreground the complex reality of electronic writing. In this chapter we will use interchangeably the terms 'electronic writing' and 'digital writing', even if, according to Bolter, some authors 'prefer the term "digital writing" to "electronic writing", on the grounds that the essence of these new forms is their digital method of representation. Electronic devices are used currently to embody the digital computer' (Bolter 2001: xiii). Thus, electronic text is the product resulting from the process of digital writing.

Electronic texts have some peculiar features, which depend both on their support and on the communication setting in which they are produced; we are now going to present them after Cantoni and Di Blas (2002: 137–9), see also Manovich (2001):

- Electronic texts are directly *inaccessible to human senses*: whereas books or any other text written on paper or on other supports can be directly accessed by human senses (sight in particular), texts coded in computer files need the mediation of other tools (hardware and software) in order to be seen and read. In other words, a book needs just to be opened in order to have its text accessed by readers; opening a text file requires, besides the physical support where it is stored – such as a CD-ROM; a floppy disk; a server; a PC; etc. – other mediation tools, such as software for text editing or reading; computer and monitor; if necessary, modem; internet connection; CD-ROM or floppy disk drivers; etc. Electronic text shares this feature with other supports for information, such as for instance vinyl records, or audio and video cassettes.

Furthermore, electronic texts are inaccessible as a whole, since it is possible to access only a part of an electronic text at a time, namely the part that appears on the monitor (or that is read by the audio interface for visually impaired people). While when taking a book, one can immediately realize its length, weight and consistency, when dealing with electronic texts, one can access bit by bit only the part presented by the monitor interface.

This feature of electronic text is strictly connected with the *frailty* and the *potential obsolescence* of its support (see section 1.3).

• Electronic texts are *immaterial*, since they are physically just a sequence of bits. Immateriality is one of the basic features of cyberspace as a whole; Anna Cicognani explains cyberspace's immateriality exactly in terms of its linguistic nature:

> Scholars are ready to agree that cyberspace is not a place for molecular manifestations. [. . .] Any phenomenon which takes place is, in fact, a result of electronic transformations of linguistic events. Which is the 'matter' of cyberspace, then? [. . .] The matter of cyberspace is language: it is written by it, and it is navigable by it; the navigation tools are nothing else but pieces of software, id est: language.
>
> (Cicognani 1998: 20)

The immateriality of digital documents makes them very easy to transport, reproduce and access.

• Electronic texts are perfectly *reproducible*. As already shown in the first chapter, thanks to the invention of letterpress print the word became the first uniform and repeatable commodity. Furthermore, as observed by Walter Benjamin, every artefact made by humans has always been reproducible by humans (Benjamin 1973). Thus, technical reproduction is not a novelty of electronic texts:

> Around 1900 technical reproduction had reached a standard that not only permitted it to reproduce all transmitted works of art and thus to cause

> the most profound change in their impact upon the public; it also had
> captured a place of its own among the artistic processes.
>
> (Benjamin 1973: 213–14)

However, digitization brought the process to an end: in electronic texts, in fact, not only it is not possible to distinguish the master from the copies, as, for instance, in printed books and in cinematographic films, but often it is not even possible to locate them in the space, due to their immateriality. In this perspective what Benjamin said of the work of art in the age of its technical reproduction can be applied to electronic text:

> Even the most perfect reproduction of a work of art is lacking in one
> element: its presence in time and space, its unique existence at the place
> where it happens to be. [. . .] The presence of the original is the pre-
> requisite to the concept of authenticity. [. . .] One might subsume the
> eliminated element in the term 'aura' and go on to say: that which withers
> in the age of mechanical reproduction is the aura of the work of art.
>
> (Benjamin 1973: 214–15)

Furthermore, it is much easier to duplicate and reproduce parts of electronic texts, and to paste electronic texts or parts of them into parts of other electronic texts.

• If it is true that electronic texts are directly inaccessible to human senses, yet they may be – thanks to computer networking – always *accessible without any limit of space*. A document available on the internet is always 'close' to its readers, wherever they are, provided that they have internet access. If a student needs a book that is in a university's library, s/he needs to go to the library and borrow it; but if the book has already been borrowed by another student, s/he cannot do anything but wait for the copy to be brought back to the library. An electronic document available online, on the contrary, could be 'borrowed' at any time and from any place, provided there is internet access.

• An electronic text can be *modified* as much as one wants. In digital documents, parts of a text can be added, deleted or edited at a user's will. Unlike printed texts, which cannot be modified anymore once they have been concluded and printed, electronic texts remain always at the author's (and reader's) disposal and can be altered whenever required; in this sense, electronic texts may be said to be 'never over'. With regard to this feature, digital writing is similar to handwriting, which allows as many text modifications as one wants; however, in handwritten texts modifications leave tracks and remain visible always, while electronic ones can be altered without leaving any trace.

- Electronic texts are *potentially multimedia* documents. As a matter of fact, thanks to their digital nature, in electronic documents elements belonging to different semiotic codes can be integrated, such as pictures, images, audio, video and animations.

- Electronic texts are *persistent*: as already observed, persistency is a basic feature of CMC. We have to distinguish here three different meanings of 'persistent', when talking of electronic conversations: 1) conversation can be persistent due to the medium used: it leaves a persistent trace in the electronic world, which can be recorded and read many times; 2) the conversation can last more than a few occasional exchanges: we meet here the persistency of the same conversation. For instance, we can encounter not only long exchanges, but also references to other conversations, held in previous days; 3) conversational exchanges are situated along a continuum, from little to more deep personal engagement: and this helps in devising a third meaning of 'persistency'. In this case, communication is rooted in the persons who communicate, helping them change in some ways. It is their personal 'persistency' (their being the same in different times and spaces), and their being somehow affected by the meanings they exchange, that may constitute the deepest definition of a 'persistent conversation' (on the issue of persistent conversations, see Erickson 1999).

- Electronic texts are often the result of *interactive communications*: as a matter of fact, CMC is always interactive, since it makes it easy and fast for senders and receivers to interact. This way, internet communication is really (potentially) dialogic and interactive (see also section 3.1.3); it does not belong to the mass-media model, where the message is unilaterally broadcasted, but rather to a model where communication, though being open to an indefinite number of receivers, offers them more interaction possibilities, at least from a technical point of view.

- Finally, internet communication allows a higher degree of *customization* than mass-media communication: electronic messages may be designed in order to meet more closely the needs of single users or of specific groups.

2.2.3 Linguistic features of CMC

The particular setting of CMC and of its support affects also the linguistic characteristics of electronic texts, i.e. the way people write via the computer, the language they use, and so on. Of course, linguistic features of electronic texts depend on many other factors as well, such as the kind of text (for instance narrative texts, scientific papers, commercial websites, messages in a newsgroup, e-mails to colleagues, etc.), and all the variables that affect texts of every kind; however, some particular linguistic features of communication exchanges through the internet can be singled out. In this section, we are going to present them.

As observed earlier, CMCs mix features of spoken communications with features of written texts: for instance, chat conversations mix up synchronicity (typical of spoken conversations), with lack of visibility and audibility between participants (typical of written exchanges). According to David Crystal, this is the interesting aspect of CMC:

> [W]hat makes Netspeak so interesting, as a form of communication, is the way it relies on characteristics belonging to both sides of the speech/writing divide. At one extreme is the Web, which in many of its functions (e.g. databasing, reference publishing, archiving, advertising) is no different from traditional situations which use writing. [. . .] In contrast to the Web, the situations of e-mail, chatgroups, and virtual worlds, though expressed through the medium of writing, display several of the core properties of speech.
>
> (Crystal 2001: 28–9)

This means that in CMC, as in any other kinds of written communication, one of the basic elements of verbal communication is lacking: *ostension*, i.e. the silent intervention of some aspects of the context within communication. Ostension is a mute moment of communication, since it has no explicit verbal expression; it must be considered in any case as a part of communication, because FTF discourse would not make sense if it was left aside (Rigotti and Cigada 2004: 45–7; see also Sperber and Wilson 1995). In conversations, ostension plays a fundamental role, since often facial expressions, hand gestures, and other paraverbal signals take the place of verbal expressions, acting as proper textual moves within the conversation; also intonation (apart from the limited device of emphasis in *italics*, by CAPS, etc.) is lacking in written as well as in CMCs. The lack of ostension, intonation and of all kinds of paraverbal signals involves the lack of simultaneous feedback signals as well, such as the tone of voice, the pauses, the silences, and so on. In FTF conversations, all these elements are often used to manage the exchange of conversational turns, since they contribute to guaranteeing an adequate sequence of speaking turns and to maintain interaction between interlocutors. Their lack in CMC messages has important consequences for participants' interaction, since it makes it more difficult to manage turn sequences and to guarantee their coherence, as observed by Susan Herring:

> [S]imultaneous feedback plays an important role in signalling listenership, timing turn-taking effectively, and maintaining continuous interaction. [. . .] Conversely, the absence of simultaneous feedback may result in discontinuity and/or overlap within turn sequences, as well as generally making it more difficult for message producers to tailor their messages to respond to recipients' interests and needs.
>
> (Herring 1999)

In other words, in CMCs the lack of ostension, joined with the synchronicity of turns, often causes incoherent sequences of conversational turns, where a message can be displayed many lines below the message to which it is an answer.

Another basic component of verbal communication challenged in electronic conversations is *deixis*. Deictics are those linguistic elements we use to anchor our discourse to the context (i.e. to the interlocutors, to time and to space) we experience: for instance, personal pronouns ('I', 'you'), spatial and temporal adverbs ('here', 'there', 'now', 'yesterday') and demonstrative adjectives or pronouns ('this', 'that') are deictic expressions, since we use them to refer to a specific element in the context; for instance, 'I' refers to the person who is speaking, 'here' to the place where conversation is taking place, 'today' to the day when conversation is taking place, and so on (Rigotti and Cigada 2004: 43–7; Benveniste 1973). In online interactions, such as in visual chat conversations, a new syntax of space can be outlined: for instance, the deictic element 'here' can alternatively mean very different rooms, while remaining a deictic element: 1) the place where people are sitting and typing: their real space; 2) the virtual room where they are chatting; 3) the space-without-space of chatting 'in private' with someone; 4) that Middle Earth constituted by one's screen: where to click, and without which the virtual realm cannot be accessed. Deixis is concerned not only with space, but also with time: in the case of electronic conversations, temporal deictics are strongly related with communication persistency (see section 2.2.2).

Another important feature of CMC is bound up with *politeness*: electronic exchanges often seem less polite than spoken conversations, due to the costs of producing 'polite' electronic utterances. As a matter of fact, whereas such politeness markers as 'hedges' (or qualifications) take almost no effort at all when speaking, they require much more effort when typing because additional words are required (Brennan and Ohaeri 1999; see also Brown and Levinson 1978).

Much attention has been paid to *lexical features* of CMC messages as well. As a consequence of the lack of simultaneous feedback and of the need of writing fast in order not to lose the synchronicity of conversations, CMC presents some peculiar lexical features; we mention here just the most common cases: emoticons, emphatic conventions and acronyms.

- *Emoticons* (from 'emotion' and 'icons', i.e. icons that represent the communicator's emotions and moods) are graphic symbols that feature a stylized face in order to simulate facial expressions. They act as a verbalization of the elements of facial expressions, gestures, body posture and distance (the so-called kinesics and proxemics), which in FTF conversations are part of the ostension. Emoticons are created by means of punctuation marks: colon or semi-colon represent the eyes, dash represents the nose, and round brackets represent the mouth. The face must be read from the left to the right:

  - :-)   is the smiling face ☺;
  - ;-)   is the winking face;
  - :-(is the sad face ☹;
  - :-o   is the surprised face; and so on.

  Some text editing programs automatically replace punctuation marks with the corresponding emoticon. Emoticons can be considered as a reaction of CMC users to the lack of other ostension means.

- Other communication systems, such as some chat systems and MUDs, provide particular commands that act as proper meta-comments on the verbal messages exchanged. CMC users have developed other strategies in order to supply to the lack of prosody and paralanguage. Some of them are taken from traditional writing, such as repeating letters ('aaaaaahhhhh', 'sooooooo', etc.) and repeating punctuation marks ('no more!!!!', 'who he????', etc.); others are peculiar to CMC, such as writing capitals for 'shouting' ('I SAID NO'), letter spacing for 'loud and clear' ('W H Y N O T ?/ w h y n o t ?'), and asterisks for emphasizing ('the *real* answer') (see Crystal 2001: 34–5).

- *Acronyms* and *abbreviations* are often used in CMC because of the need to shorten the typing time of a message; of course, this trend is stronger in informal and unofficial conversations, such as chat conversations. Some of these acronyms and abbreviations have crystallized and are nowadays widely used: the most common for the English language are CUL8R ('see you later'), HowRU ('How are you?'), 2B ('to be'), IMHO ('in my humble opinion'), ROFL ('rolling on the floor laughing'), LOL ('laughs out loud'). As it can be easily noticed from these few examples, CMC tends often to be close to oral language and to write words as they are pronounced, at least in informal exchanges. Also, these features have most likely proliferated in recent years as a result of the popularity of Short Message Service (SMS) text messaging particularly among (young) mobile phone users.

Thus, the peculiar features of the medium and the possibility of having written synchronous conversations make CMC a rather specific kind of communication, which has its own communicative and linguistic characteristics. Of course, all these features vary very much depending on the CMC tool used. Generally speaking, CMC has more properties that link it to written language than to speech. However, as observed by David Crystal: 'Netspeak is more than an aggregate of spoken and written features. [. . .] It does things that neither of these other mediums do, and must accordingly be seen as a new species of communication' (Crystal 2001: 47–8). What, then, are the main guiding features that dictate different kinds of CMC?

2.3 TECHNICAL ASPECTS: A BRIEF OVERVIEW

This section is intended to enable readers to better understand what is behind internet functionalities and not to get lost when reading such terms as 'HTML' (HyperText Markup Language), 'SGML' (Standard Generalized Markup Language), 'hit' and the like. Due to the nature of this work, the presentation will remain at a quite high level of granularity, leaving aside many details (for an extensive overview, see, among others, Panwar *et al.* 2004). The first concept to be presented will be that of digital, as opposed to analogical (2.3.1); afterwards the concepts of codification and codes will be introduced (2.3.2). A general overview of how a computer network – and the internet itself – works will follow, explaining what are TCP/IP, browsers and related elements (2.3.3).

2.3.1 On analogical and digital

To represent and/or communicate something one can use an analogical strategy or a digital one. An analogical system bears a similarity with what it represents, having a sort of isomorphism with it; for example, in a picture, or in a microphone, there is a similarity (or a quasi-identity) between certain aspects of the represented thing and of its representation, namely colours and shapes in the picture, volume of the speech and membrane movements of the microphone in the second example, movements which will be analogically reproduced by the loudspeakers themselves.

Non-analogical systems do not have any kind of isomorphism between represented things and their representations: for example in natural languages there is not any kind of isomorphic relation between a thing and its word (except for very specific areas, like that of onomatopoeia). As is well known, natural languages present a 'double articulation' structure (Martinet 1970; Mahmoudian 1993): a string can be divided into meaningful substrings (first articulation), and these substrings can be further divided into atomic elements, without any connection with meaning (this being one of the most important differences between human languages and animal communication; see Benveniste 1973; Cantoni 1999).

In the digital field, representations consist of strings simply composed by 0/1 values: digits (binary structure). A single digit is called a *bit* – whose value can be only 1 or 0 – while a string of eight digits, able to represent 256 different states, is a *byte*. A binary structure presents many advantages from a computational point of view: it can be easily computed/processed and it can be reproduced as many times as needed without losing information (let us think, on the other hand, of what happens if one photocopies a page (analogical reproduction), and then photocopies the photocopy itself, and so on, losing representation quality every time). In fact, in the digital field, it is impossible to distinguish between original and copy, both being just the same string of digits.

2.3.2 On codification and codes

In order to represent/communicate a reality, one needs a set of rules to build up its representation in a given semiotic domain (encoding) and to interpret/understand the representation back again (decoding), one needs a code/language (Eco 1979; Rigotti and Cigada 2004). In digital systems many codification/decodification standards are available: to encode characters (hence being able to digitally represent natural languages' texts as well as other text-based representations); to encode formatted texts, mathematical formulas, instructions (as they are by programming languages), colours, sounds, still and moving images, links, and so on, translating everything in a so-called machine readable format (MRF).

While computer networks – and namely the internet – make use of all available MRF used by stand-alone computers, they have pushed ahead the search for new codes, in order to support wider and better representations/communications. As is the case with natural languages, they are not important only because they are able to assist the double way between meaning and text and vice-versa (Mel'čuk 1970; Gatti 1992), but also for their being used by a community (Cantoni 2002), for being shared by a group of people who use them. The same happens in the digital domain: many codification standards are being proposed and available, but their strength does not rely solely on their representation capacity, but also on their actual use by a community of people. The global interconnectivity offered by the internet puts a strong emphasis on standardization, a condition of real interoperability.

If the main effort in codification is that towards 1) *standardization* – to provide codes/languages that are shared by as many platforms/users as possible – other relevant efforts are intended; 2) *to expand the spectrum of what can be digitized*; 3) *to enhance its quality*; and 4) *to reduce the required bandwidth*. Let us briefly present them in order.

1   The need for standardization has already been presented earlier; it is worth adding that the standardization process is a quite long one, and presents intermediate steps.

In the internet world, standards are mainly set by general purposes as well as by dedicated bodies: IEEE, the Institute of Electrical and Electronics Engineers (www.ieee.org); ISO, the International Organization for Standardization (www.iso.org); GBDe, the Global Business Dialogue on electronic commerce (www.gbde.org); IETF, the Internet Engineering Task Force (www.ietf.org); ISOC, the Internet Society (www.isoc.org); ICANN, the Internet Consortium for Assigned Names and Numbers (www.icann.org) and the W3C, the WWW Consortium; the latter 'develops interoperable technologies (specifications, guidelines, software, and tools) to lead the Web to its full potential. W3C is a forum for information, commerce, communication, and collective understanding' (www.w3.org); its long term goals are:

1.   *Universal Access*: To make the Web accessible to all by promoting technologies that take into account the vast differences in culture, languages, education, ability, material resources, access devices, and physical limitations of users on all continents;
2.   *Semantic Web*: To develop a software environment that permits each user to make the best use of the resources available on the Web;

3.   *Web of Trust:* To guide the Web's development with careful consideration for the novel legal, commercial, and social issues raised by this technology.

(www.w3.org/Consortium/)

In fact, a distinction is to be made among different steps in the standardization process, ranging from just research and development concepts to technical specifications, to reference models, up to accredited or de facto standards (Masie Center 2003).

2   Efforts are made to digitally encode new semiotic domains – such as, for instance, that of tastes and smells.

3   The issue of quality concerns different activities: one is that of encoding more nuances. While in the analogical field what is a continuum in reality (e.g. colours, shapes, sound volumes, and so on) is represented on a continuum, the digital world knows only discrete values, thus requiring representing a continuum through a non-continuum. The only way to capture nuances in the digital is by adding intermediate discrete values. If, for instance, one wants to digitally represent a colour, one can use a scale with 8 elements – the basic colours of the rainbow – or one with 256 (as it is used for some web encoding), or one with millions of items. Each colour, if one chooses the first code, must fit one of the eight possibilities, while in the second more nuances can be represented, and in the third one almost every visible difference can be captured. The same can be said for sounds and all other semiotic domains.

The quest for quality concerns also the development of ways to better capture/represent specific domains, not directly connected with our senses. To represent a reality, in fact, one has to choose the level of granularity to be used; if we take the example of a poem, one can move from a very high-level presentation to a fine-grained description: the simple representation of its characters, to adding paragraph information, the title, the name of its author, the book title, the year of publication, etc. In this quality field, many activities are in progress, both to develop shared codification standards for given domains, and to develop a general framework to build domain specific codes. This issue will be further discussed at the end of this section, while presenting HTML, XML and SGML.

4   As it is quite intuitive, the more precision/quality is reached, the more digits are required for the representation. If the colour continuum is divided into only 8 states, a string of 3 bits is needed, while 8 bits (one

byte) are required if the same continuum is divided into 256 colours, and 24 bits are needed to encode millions of colours. File dimensions (a file being a string of bytes characterized by being a unity and having a single file name) need different requirements for what concerns computation power, recording space, and transmission bandwidth, all of which having an impact on access time. Hence, the need for more quality is counterbalanced by the need for more speed, one pushing towards bigger files and more demands on the technical infrastructure, while the second pushes towards more speed, thus requiring – *ceteris paribus* – more small files. In fact, the point of balance is ever-changing, due to technical improvements and cost reductions, as well as to different quality needs (which depends also on social perceptions) and to compression algorithms (zipping), which allow for lesser file dimensions without reducing representation quality.

Three languages: 1) HTML; 2) XML; and 3) SGML are to be briefly presented here, due to their close connection with the development and success of the internet.

1   HTML – HyperText Markup Language – is the language mostly used on the WWW; its main features consist in its being able to represent hypertextual connections, and in its use of marking elements (tagging).

An HTML file consists of elements all included between the tags <HTML> . . . </HTML>, and marked at their own turn by specific tags. HTML tags fulfil two very different goals: to qualify elements as belonging to a type (e.g. title, head, alternate, etc.): *descriptive markup*; and to give instructions to the browser on how to represent them (e.g. bold, italic, H1, etc.): *procedural/prescriptive markup*.

An HTML file can contain instructions written in specific languages (script languages), or reference to pieces of software, such as, for instance, Java applets.

Websites are usually made of HTML files, which share a common root address (e.g. www.newmine.org), and with a common homepage, accessible through the root address.

Depending on the actual content of HTML files being already present in them, or being built up on the flow, depending on certain variables, getting data from one or more database(s), a website can be named 'static' or 'dynamic'. In fact, as we will see in detail in Chapter 3, in many cases the website author/editor cannot at all foresee what a page's content will be, because the page will get its actual content from a database, getting different data depending on different changing parameters. A very simple case can be that of a products' catalogue: every product can be represented in a website through a dedicated page, or there can be just a single page for a product's representation, which gets its content from the database of products depending on the queries made by the user; the same could happen, for example, in a website of a museum, where a single web page serves to represent all the pictures in the exposition, whose data are recorded in a dedicated database (the web page could serve to represent only pictures of the running exhibit, thus getting contents from the database depending on the date the website is accessed).

Moreover, data presented on a dynamic website could depend on customization choices carried out in advance by the user (e.g. to see only elements available in a given language, to see only a certiain number of items on each page, etc.), on access rights (given items being displayed only to paying subscribers), to previous user interactions (as is the case for buying procedures, where the content of the shopping cart/basket depends on user's selections), etc. The expression 'invisible web' makes reference to this phenomenon, stressing the fact that just numbering web pages does not give a good account of available web contents: a single web page could – in fact – have countless values.

2   XML – Extensible Markup Language – is a paired-down version of SGML, intended to enhance data interchange especially in web documents (it is a specification of W3C). It enables the definition of dedicated sets of tags, through which mapping a given semantic domain, or different device-dependent peculiarities (e.g. contents to be displayed differently according to their presentation on a computer screen, on a palmtop, on a mobile phone, etc.).

In fact, XML can be considered as being a specific instance of SGML.

3   SGML – Standard Generalized Markup Language – developed and standardized by ISO,

> is an international standard for the description of marked-up electronic text. More exactly, SGML is a *metalanguage*, that is, a means of formally describing a language, in this case, a *markup language* [. . .].
>
> By markup language we mean a set of markup conventions used together for encoding texts. A markup language must specify what markup is allowed, what markup is required, how markup is to be distinguished from text, and what the markup means. SGML provides the means for doing the first three.
>
> (Sperberg-McQueen and Burnard 2002: 2, 3)

An SGML document consists of an SGML prolog, which contains an SGML declaration about the dialect being used and a Document Type

Definition (DTD), which defines which types are allowed to be present in the document, and a document instance (the document itself, in naive terms).

2.3.3 On networks, protocols, browsers, cookies and other dangerous things . . .

Computers can be connected to each other to form a network, in order to share applications, data and hardware; connections can be physical (telephone wires, dedicated cables, fibre optics), or wireless (infrared, microwaves, radio, etc.).

In order to be connected, computers need to share a suitable communication protocol, i.e. a set of shared communication rules, which enable networked computers to manage every transaction: identification, rooting, controls, and so on. The internet is, in itself, a network; better still it is a meta-network, being able to interconnect many networks through a common protocol: the TCP/IP (hence the name: Mother of all the networks; for a brief history of the TCP/IP protocol, see Chapter 1).

Every computer connected to the internet uses the same protocol as all the others to manage file exchanges; in particular, every connected computer is given a unique IP number (such as, for instance, 192.168.70. 211), so that data can move along the network reaching their intended end. Data are divided into different packets (packet switching) that can follow different paths to reach their ends, in order to optimize the network use, and not to be hindered by possible failures in single nodes; once they have reached the target computer, they are re-assembled and used. This kind of structure is very efficient, and yields to a very flexible, while at the same time stable, structure. Built on the low-level TCP/IP protocol, many specific IPs can run, to manage e-mail, the WWW, newsgroups, file transfer, etc.

Every application for the internet requires a suitable piece of software to be run: in particular, to access the web a browser is needed. Browsers are applications that enable users to surf the web, interpreting HTML files and scripting languages, managing requests to web servers, links and the like. While the first browser was NCSA-Mosaic (National Center for Supercomputing Applications), today the most used is Microsoft Internet Explorer, followed by Netscape, Firefox and Opera. While browsers are software applications, their extensive use in very different contexts – from web browsing to accessing an intranet, to running a remote application – tends to make them transparent to their users, who perceive them as being just a common computer inter-face (maybe the commonest one, together with the operating system interface); in fact, the integration of Internet Explorer in the Windows Operating Systems has worked towards this direction.

Also application developers have started to implement, whenever possible, a web-like interface for very different applications, in order to maximize the usability of their applications by end-users, and to reduce the need of a dedicated software (or at least the perception of needing it); a sort of software convergence can be seen here, where the browser is not any longer a mere web browsing tool, but a sort of universal application, hence the frequent use of the web to mean all of the internet. To interpret some web pages, the browser needs dedicated software applications, which have to be installed in the browser itself (plug-ins). Let us follow step by step what happens when a web address is typed in the browser, to get an idea of what the browser does, and of how the web is structured.

When the URL is inputted, for example, www.unisi.ch (the URL of the University of Lugano, in Switzerland), the browser requires it to be 'resolved' by a DNS: the DNS translates the alphanumeric string (www.unisi.ch) into a unique IP number (195.176.176.173), as we have seen. A request is then sent to the computer with this IP number, where a dedicated software application – a web server – manages it. The web server responds to the browser (which acts as a client in a client–server interaction), sending the requested file(s) or an error code (for a specific analysis of this interaction from the point of view of web communication analysis, see Chapter 5). Once the file(s) has reached the client's browser, or while it is being loaded, the browser represents it on the screen, following the tags' instructions (and – if necessary – correcting/supplementing them, in order to be as error-tolerant as possible).

Clicking on an active link makes the browser follow a similar procedure. A web server can – provided the browser is not set to block them – set a 'cookie' in the client's computer; cookies are little text-only files, which can store information on client–server transactions, allowing the server to recognize the client when it connects again. Although cookies can help to improve the user experience (e.g. for customization zpurposes, or to avoid the repetition of annoying procedures), relevant privacy issues arise.

While web communication is managed through HTTP (HyperText Transfer Protocol), transactions can be secured by encrypting them via SSL (Secure Sockets Layer), or using a secure HTTP connection (HTTPS); these are used whenever secure transactions are needed, for instance, for e-banking, to get access to extranets, etc. Attempts to breach internet security are quite frequent: being a public access network, every online service is exposed to attacks from many sources and locations. Direct attacks are performed by so-called 'hackers', people who try to violate security measures (usually in place through firewalls) to get money or just to prove their ability and the weaknesses of technology (Yourdon 2002); indirect attacks are usually performed through viruses, pieces of software intended to damage systems through a number of different strategies (ranging from Trojans to Spyware).

E-mail spam messages are very often used to distribute viruses, some of them, in turn, replicate themselves on the attacked computer, and use its e-mail client to propagate further, thus spam and viruses are referred to as being 'the deadly duo', and are considered among the major threats to internet security and professional use. While the internet is in general a worldwide public access network, intranets and extranets grant access only to authorized people, usually identified through a user-id/username and a password. In general, intranets and extranets are organized like websites, through HTML pages, and provide access to data and applications via the single browser application.

Another relevant distinction is to be made between portals and vortals: portals are websites that provide access to a large range of other resources, organizing and indexing them according to given strategies, while vortals are vertical portals, devoted to specific thematic domains. In the early days of the internet – when the advertising business model (see Chapter 6) seemed to be easily implemented: the more clicks you receive, the more banner you display, the more money you get – portals began to sprout up like mushrooms in a wood after the rain. Put another way, many low-quality websites and websites with limited use value started to call themselves 'portals', without providing any actual added value. Today this term is better used to name just a few really wide-scope applications, such as internet directories.

As we have seen, then, the kind of communication facilitated by the internet is possible as the result of manifold technical developments. Much of the technology has been geared to enabling CMC in respect of print textuality, especially e-mail. However, the growth of the internet after 1995, advances in technology and the demands of users, have dictated that multimodality has developed in internet communication. Written interfaces are now increasingly supplemented – and sometimes supplanted – by communication based on pictures and sounds. Nevertheless, one of the most important features of the internet, particularly from the inception of websites to the present, has been a technology of communication that is thoroughly grounded in writing: hypertext. Because of the importance of this integral feature of the internet, the whole of Chapter 3 is devoted to discussion of it.

3

HYPERTEXT

In the last chapter, the features of electronic text have been presented both from the point of view of its support and of its communicative and linguistic peculiarity. In this chapter, we will focus in particular on one kind of text produced by computers: hypertext. Hypertext deserves particular attention not only for historical reasons, since it *gave rise to* the web and the consequent diffusion of the internet, but also for theoretical ones, since the success of electronic hypertext put under discussion the very concept of 'text'.

In the first section (3.1), a general definition of hypertexts and hypermedia is provided, and their basic elements and general features are presented. Then, hypertexts are approached from the point of view of ancient rhetoric, by applying to them the five-step process for the building of a rhetorical speech (3.2): we will see that hypertext encourages processes of reading that are not necessarily new and unique. In the last section (3.3), a brief history of hypertext is sketched out, from the pioneers who first conceived hypertextual systems to the rise of the first hypertext theories. This will also demonstrate that hypertext did not come from nowhere – it has its own history and development, which have been crucial for the evolution of the internet.

3.1 HYPERTEXTS AND HYPERMEDIA

Hypertexts are textual structures that have the peculiarity of allowing different paths to fruition. A 'hypertext' therefore consists of 'itself' but, more importantly, leads elsewhere, to other texts. Typically, it allows words to be highlighted in HTML within CD-ROM or WWW documents, thus indicating that specific issues to do with that topic in the text can be accessed separately by an instant transfer to another place in cyberspace. A hypertext on the topic of communication, for example, may contain underlined words such as sign, verbal, non-verbal, gesture, kinesics, proxemics, language and technologies, indicating that other pages may be accessed that address these topics more closely.

Although the term 'hypertext' was coined in the computer science field, a hypertext is not necessarily a digital document: paper hypertexts exist as well. However, if not otherwise specified, we will refer in this book to 'hypertext' as a particular kind of electronic text whose textual elements are connected to one another by means of links. If hypertexts present, besides textual elements, also iconic elements, sounds, animations or videos, they are said to be multimedia hypertexts or hypermedia. In the following sections we will use the term 'hypertext' with reference to hypermedia as well, using the two terms interchangeably.

In the field of electronic writing, hypertext plays a very important role for different reasons:

- As shown in Chapter 1, hypertext is at the basis of the invention of the WWW and of the consequent worldwide diffusion of the internet. Indeed, the application of hypertext to computer networks led Tim Berners-Lee to create the system for the distribution of hypertextual documents known as the WWW; nowadays, the WWW certainly represents the area of widest application and use of hypertext.
- Hypertext plays an important role in different fields from a theoretical point of view as well: in the field of literary studies, for instance, reflection on hypertext has given rise to several discussions about the re-definition of the notion of 'text' itself, about the roles of writers/authors and readers/users; in the field of HCI studies the notion of interactivity has been central; in cognitive and education sciences new learning models have been conceived based on hypertextual structures; and so on.

Many authors have proposed different partitions of the architecture of a hypertext. According to Nielsen, hypertextual structures can be divided into three levels: 1) the Database level; 2) the Hypertext Abstract Machine (HAM) level; and 3) the Presentation level. Let us consider Nielsen's levels:

1   Database level: it is the deepest layer, where information is stored; really, it has nothing specifically to do with hypertext, since

> as far as the database level is concerned, the hypertext nodes and links are just data objects with no particular meaning. Each of them forms a unit that only one user can modify at the same time and that takes up so many bits of storage space.
>
> (Nielsen 1995: 132)

2   HAM level: this is the intermediate layer, where 'the hypertext system determines the basic nature of its nodes and links and where it maintains the relation among them' (Nielsen 1995: 132).
3   Presentation level: this is the level of the user interface, which 'deals with the presentation of the information in the HAM, including such issues as what commands should be made available to the user, how to show nodes and links, and whether to include overview diagrams or not' (Nielsen 1995: 133).

As shown also by Nielsen, hypertexts are basically composed of two elements: content units, or 'nodes', and links. Hypertext 'is a variable structure, composed of blocks of text (or what Roland Barthes terms *lexia*) and the electronic links that join them' (Landow and Delany 1994: 3; their reference is to Barthes 1974). We prefer to speak of 'content units' rather than 'blocks of texts', since, as already mentioned, nowadays 'content can be made not only of text, but also of images, video, graphic, audio streams etc.' (Cantoni and Paolini 2001: 36). So, let us provisionally define hypertext, after Cantoni and Paolini (2001: 36), as 'things and links in-between', and go a little deeper into what are nodes and links.

3.1.1 Nodes

Nodes are the content units of hypertexts, i.e. they are the elements ultimately accessed by hypertext's readers, either available on the same monitor page or on the same web page. Nodes can be defined as the minimal fruition units perceived by readers; they are something that readers have to receive at once, in total, without having the possibility of choosing to receive only parts. Thus, nodes are outside the range of choice readers can make when accessing a hypertext. This does not mean that they are designed and produced as such by hypertext's designer(s). On the contrary, in most existing hypertexts authors and designers have a rather particular control on their work: they usually do not define the content of each and every node, but rather they 'just' set the rules for their arrangement (Cantoni and Vittadini 2003: 329–30; Cantoni and Paolini 2001: 39–41).

For instance, the designer of the website of a newspaper does not decide which content is to be put on one page, which news is to be visualized in the homepage, and so on; s/he just decides that in the homepage the central slot will host one picture and not more than three text lines regarding the most important recent news, the next right slot will contain two text lines for each of the other five most important recent news items, the underlying slot will contain other news divided into the newspaper main sections (e.g. politics, news, opinions, culture, business, sports, arts and living), the upper slot will contain an advertisment banner, and so on. Very often, hypertext designers have control over the rules for presenting contents in the hypermedia's nodes, but not over the nodes as they will be accessed and seen by users. These kinds of hypertexts are called *dynamic* hypertexts, since they automatically produce nodes and links starting from a database, whose contents may change all the time; dynamic hypertexts are very commonly used in website applications that are very big and need to be updated very frequently, such as web portals, news websites, eCommerce websites, and so on.

Other kinds of hypertexts worth mentioning here are *adaptive* hypertexts: they create different nodes each time in response to a recorded reader's profile, to his/her previous moves within the hypertext, to other users' behaviours within the hypertext, to other external conditions such as the device used (PC, palmtop, mobile phone, etc.); in other words, adaptive hypertexts try to adapt the content presented to the users' needs. As observed by Peter Brusilovsky, adaptive hypermedia systems 'can be useful in any situation when the system is expected to be used by people with different goals and knowledge and where the hyperspace is reasonably big' (Brusilovsky 1997: 12). In adaptive hypermedia adaptations can be made both at the level of content presentation ('adaptive presentation') and at that of links ('adaptive navigation support') (Brusilovsky 1997: 13–16). Adaptive hypertexts could be very useful in applications where keeping a track of users' behaviour is important in order to have as many customized communications as possible, as for instance in educational hypertexts and eCommerce websites.

The diffusion of dynamic and adaptive hypertexts shows the importance of defining a node in terms of perception on the side of the reader rather than in terms of precise design on the side of the author: as shown earlier, often

the page that the reader sees was not designed or produced as an 'atom', but it is the result of several concurrent actions, performed when the node itself was requested. It is possible that, if sophisticated strategies based on user profiles are used, nobody else in the world has seen or will see that page.

(Cantoni and Paolini 2001: 40)

Moreover, in the WWW it is impossible to know exactly what a reader will see on his/her screen, due to different factors, such as the kind of monitor, the operating system, the browser s/he is using, and so on.

Situating the notion of 'node' in the realm of users' perceptions has some relevant consequences in the field of designers' activity:

1 designers do not produce nodes, as already shown, but sets of syntactic and semantic rules that control the construction of nodes;
2 the connective/syntactic structure of hypertexts does not concern only links, but the whole hypertext as well, nodes included;
3 the unity of a hypertext must be granted by an accurate planning of the internal structure of nodes, and not only by links and graphics.

(Cantoni and Paolini 2001: 41)

3.1.2 Links

Links are connections between nodes. Berners-Lee defines a link as 'a reference from one document to another (external link) or from one location in the same document to another (internal link), that can be followed efficiently using a computer. The unity of connection in hypertext' (Berners-Lee 2000: 235). Links have an activation point (an *anchor*), i.e. a part of a node that acts as the starting point of the link, and a destination point, i.e. a node or a part of it accessible via the link. Generally speaking, every kind of medium (text, image, audio, video, animation) can be the destination point of a link; activation points, on the contrary, are mostly texts or images. As exemplified by Berners-Lee's definition, links can be internal, when they connect two parts of the same node, or external when they refer to a part of another node. In hypermedia, anchors are usually recognizable, because the cursor changes its appearance when going over them; furthermore, when the activation point is a piece of text, it is very often made distinguishable from normal text, for instance because it is underlined, coloured in a different way, boldfaced, and so on.

Actually, links do not only allow access to other nodes, or to part of them, but they show a possibility of interaction allowed by hypertext; in other words, by means of a link it is not only possible to ask for another piece of content, but, more generally, also to perform one action (or more actions) associated to the link. In this sense, links can be regarded as actions one can perform when reading a hypertext. By means of links, hypertext readers can perform very basic actions, such as passing to another hypertext's node, as well as much more complicated and significant activities, such as buying and selling products, sending messages, subscribing to services, voting in online polls, and so on (Cantoni and Paolini 2001: 42). For instance, when clicking on the 'I agree' button of an electronic contract, the reader not only gets access to a new node, but enters also into an agreement, a purchase, a selling contract, etc. (Cantoni and Vittadini 2003: 330–1).

In cases like this, clicking on a link can be seen as similar to uttering a performative sentence. According to the British philosopher of language, John L. Austin, the word 'performative' 'indicates that the issuing of the utterance is the performing of an action'; in performatives 'to *say* something is to *do* something; [. . .] *by* saying or *in* saying something we are doing something' (Austin 1962: 6, 12; see also Benveniste 1973 and Cantoni 1999). Austin provides some examples of performative utterances: 'I bet you sixpence it will rain tomorrow'; '"I name this ship the *Queen Elizabeth*", as uttered when smashing the bottle against the stem [of a ship]' (Austin 1962: 4). By saying 'I promise . . .', 'I bet . . .', 'I baptize . . .', 'I condemn . . .', etc., people say what they *do*, and at the same time they do it. The utterance itself is the performing of the action uttered, provided the contexts are suitable. In fact, these sentences depend on the persons who utter them and on the contexts where they are uttered: if a chairperson, for instance, states 'The session is opened', s/he produces the state s/he has uttered, while if a journalist utters the same words, s/he only describes the same state, without producing it.

As mentioned earlier, in hypertexts there is room for performative utterances:

> when someone clicks onto the 'I agree' button, s/he both agrees on the terms of the contract and 'says it', or choosing the 'I buy it' declares his or her intention and realizes the economical transaction. And calls for another node.
>
> (Cantoni and Paolini 2001: 42)

3.1.3 Hypertexts as dialogues

In the perspective presented in the previous section, links are the basic elements that provide hypertexts with *interactivity*. Interactivity is the quality of systems whose behaviour can be influenced by users: interactive systems 'are dynamic systems where some aspects of the way in which the system evolves through time can be influenced by a person using the system' (Barfield 1993: 31). Analogously, Schulmeister defines interaction in a website as 'controlling the object, subject or contents of a page' (Schulmeister 2003: 65); he then proposes a scale of six levels of interactivity offered by the system to the user, ranging from the basic level of 'viewing objects and receiving' to the highest interactivity level of 'constructing the object or contents of the representation and receiving intelligent feedback from the system through manipulative action' (Schulmeister 2003: 65–71).

In the case of hypertexts, interactivity can be seen as a particular kind of *dialogue*: by means of links, hypertext readers engage in a continuous dialogue with the hypertext system. The peculiarity of hypertextual dialogues is that in them the system/hypertext poses the question, the user/reader answers, and the system/hypertext in its turn *re*-acts to the answer posing another question: 'readers are continuously requested to answer hypertext's questions: "what do you want afterwards?" From this point of view, a hypertext can be seen as a (partially foreseen) dialogue, being actualized by (partially foreseen) dialogical exchanges' (Cantoni and Paolini 2001: 43).

If it is not surprising – and even quite obvious – that interactive systems such as hypertexts are a kind of dialogue, it could perhaps seem a little strange that in these dialogues questions are posed by the hyper-text. In fact, in interactions with hypertexts, as well as with any other interactive system, the first move is actually always taken by the reader, who decides to access and use/read the hypertext in order to achieve a goal or to fulfil a need, a desire or an expectation s/he has. Thus, it could be said that, in a very broad and general sense, it is the reader who poses the first question, since s/he accesses the hypermedia having in mind the question corresponding to his/her goal, desire or need. At this level, users can have very vague as well as very definite questions; for instance, a user can ask the hypertext s/he is accessing generic questions such as 'I want to have some fun. What do you offer?', more detailed ones, such as 'What is the latest news from the Olympic Games?' or 'How can I get some information about the Italian painter Caravaggio?', or even very precise questions, such as 'How much does it cost to fly from London to Madrid?' or 'When was the Chartres cathedral built?', and so on. So, if we intend questions in a very broad sense as the equivalent of goals, needs and desires, the first question in the hypertext–reader dialogue is no doubt asked by the reader.

Anyway, once the reader has posed his/her main question, the hyper-text takes command of the interaction by providing the reader with a set of links, i.e. with a set of possible actions the reader can take. In other words, the hypertext presents to the reader some options, from which s/he has to choose: 'Do you want to have information about Caravaggio's biography, about his paintings, about his critics or about other painters related to him?' This way, users' interactions with hypertexts can be translated into dialogic moves, where the hypertext asks questions by providing different options in the shape of links, and the user answers each time by selecting the chosen link (Di Blas and Paolini 2003: 222–6; see also Bolchini *et al.* 2002). A clear example of the dialogic nature of hypertexts is provided, for instance, by screen-readers or voice browsers, i.e. by systems that allow navigation of the screen presented by the operating system or by the web browser using speech (or Braille) output, thus allowing also visually impaired people to access web contents (for a list of resources for alternative web browsing, see the W3C – Web Accessibility Initiative (WAI) website, www.w3c.org/WAI).

3.1.4 Hypertexts as languages

As it was shown earlier, hypertext authors do not design actual texts or dialogues, but only sets of syntactic rules and basic elements, i.e. they produce a sort of grammar. In this sense, hypertexts can be considered as new languages. In other words, hypertext authors design potential dialogues, which will become an actual communication, i.e. a complete exchange of meaning, only when one reader navigates through the hypertext's structure:

> [the author] produces a sort of new language, which allows only discourses on specific realities (e.g.: a CD-ROM on geography), and excludes some stands about them (e.g.: Milan is in Switzerland). Of course, only some specific stands on the concerned subject are allowed (Milan is in Italy), but they are taken only under the condition that some links are activated and specific nodes are got.
>
> (Cantoni and Paolini 2001: 45)

To a certain extent, the same could be said of any written text: only once someone reads them can they be considered real communications; if a text has never been read, it remains a virtual/potential communication. However, in the case of hypertexts, this is much more evident: in fact, written text authors can define and, to a certain extent, foresee the reading experience and its path. In contrast, hypertext designers can only define sets of rules and constraints, while the reading path can only be moulded by readers, by means of the pieces of content made available.

Thus, hypertexts can be considered as languages, as possible grammars that need adopters in order to become actual communications.

In this particular kind of grammar two syntactic layers are to be distinguished, namely a nodes' syntax and a links' one. Nodes being 'consumption units', they must be stand-alone units, they have to be perceived as autonomous and self-supporting. At the same time, nodes are complex units of different elements that stay together and have reciprocal relations. From this point of view, nodes can be compared to phrases where all the morpho-syntactic structures are saturated, i.e. to phrases that can be uttered by themselves. When producing the node-layer syntax, hypertext designers determine the elements that are to be accessed at one time: they have to define the elements constituting a node and their reciprocal distribution within the node. Thus, the lexical units designers have to handle when dealing with this syntactic layer are the minimal semantic hypertext elements, such as text's pieces, images, audios, videos, animations.

Link-layer syntax, in contrast, operates between nodes, and determines the accessibility rules of nodes to each other, excluding at the same time the connections that are not allowed. The lexical elements of this second syntax are nodes themselves. While elements of node-syntax stay together, the elements of link-syntax cannot stay together, since they have to be accessed one after the other. In the tradition of structural linguistics, a tendency that is usually traced back to the Swiss linguist Ferdinand de Saussure (1857–1913; see de Saussure 1983 and Cobley 2001: 270–1), two kinds of relationships among signs have been detected: *paradigmatic* relations, i.e. 'a set of signs linked by partial resemblances, either in form or in meaning' (Harris 2001a: 233); and *syntagmatic* relations, i.e. 'those into which a linguistic unit enters in virtue of its linear concatenation in a speech chain' (Harris 2001b: 273). The elements linked by paradigmatic relations cannot be combined to one another (hence they are also called *in absentia* relations), because they have the same functions; on the contrary, syntagmatic relations hold *in praesentia*, because the elements of a phrase have complementary functions. Borrowing this terminology, we can affirm that elements of node-layer syntax have *in praesentia* relations, elements of link-layer syntax have *in absentia* relations. In other words, at this syntactic level, designers have to decide the options' sets – in structural terminology: the *paradigm* – that in each node are to be provided to readers; then it will be the readers' task to activate one option/link and access a new node. In this way, the grammar provided by designers will materialize as an actual communication thanks to the reader's choices.

Continuing with the linguistic model, we can say that in adaptive hypertexts a morphologic layer can be detected as well: as in some human languages, some kinds of words change their form depending on the context (e.g. in English, the third person of verbs in the present tense has the suffix *-s*: I think, she thinks), in adaptive hypertexts the nodes' elements are modified depending on the user's choices, the user's profile, and so on.

Finally, the grammar of hypertexts is much concerned with the semantic layer as well: while natural languages are not very concerned with semantics and allow speakers to talk about everything – and even to utter meaningless inconsistent sentences – hypertexts tend to allow the creation of texts only about definite topics (e.g. a CD-ROM about Italian literature will not talk about the coral reef; a website that sells books will not sell railway tickets) and with definite stances on that topic (e.g. Dante Alighieri is an Italian poet), as already shown earlier (Cantoni and Di Blas 2002: 139–40; Cantoni and Paolini 2001: 43–5).

3.2 SOME INSIGHTS FROM ANCIENT RHETORIC

In order to better understand the structure and the peculiar features of hypermedia communications, a comparison with ancient rhetoric is very useful. The parallel between rhetoric and hypertext is very common in hypertext studies, as observed already by Gunnar Liestøl before widespread use of the internet (Liestøl 1994: 99). In particular, the five-step process developed by ancient rhetoric for the creation of an oral speech can enhance our understanding of different aspects of hypertextual communication; actually, Liestøl himself recognizes that these five components had been given little attention in hypertext studies, and sets out on this path as well (Liestøl 1994: 98–103). Ancient rhetoric singled out five steps in the creation of a speech, i.e. five activities the orator had to embark on in order to perform a good public communication; the five steps were called: *inventio, dispositio, elocutio, memoria, actio*. We are going to analyse in more detail each one in the rest of the section.

3.2.1 *Inventio*

Inventio (from the Latin verb *in-venire*, 'to chance upon something') is the activity of discovering, selecting and collecting the ideas the orator wants to communicate. The very first moment of the process of creating a speech is a creative one: the orator has to gather the meanings s/he wants to present to his/her listeners and the arguments s/he wants to use in order to support his/her point of view. Thus, the phase of *inventio* has much more to do with 'artistic' inspiration rather than with logical reasoning. *Inventio* can be compared with brainstorming and brain-mapping activities. Brainstorming is the activity of collecting all the possible ideas about a specific topic; it is often used in companies as a method for creative thinking: meetings of people are arranged, who have to say 'everything crossing their mind' on a specific subject, in order, for instance, to think up the new slogan for a product. All the ideas emerged during the brainstorming are then mapped, i.e. they are gathered together according to their type.

Dealing with hypermedia, *inventio* could entail different activities: to find out the idea about the content of the hypertext, the idea about the navigational structure, the overall idea of the hypertext, the narrative idea, and so on. However, none of these possibilities is completely satisfactory: in hypermedia design, *inventio* is to be regarded as the activity of finding out the idea behind what a hypermedia work/title actually is. Within the Interactive Dialogue Model (IDM), which will be sketched in the next chapter (4.4.1), *inventio* corresponds to shaping the hyperbase, i.e. deciding 'what the application is about in terms of content structure and basic semantic properties' (Cantoni and Paolini 2001: 47). For instance, in the first moment of the design process the designer(s) of a hypermedia application about the history of Italian literature could decide that the basic elements of the application will be the authors, the literary works, the literary movements, and an historical chronology; and that each work will be linked to its author(s) and to the historical period when it was written, each author to his/her works, to the possible literary movement s/he belonged to, to the period when s/he lived, and so on.

3.2.2 *Dispositio*

Dispositio is the activity of ordering the ideas and the arguments selected during the *inventio*. In this phase, the orator has to decide what to say in which moment of his/her speech: the map of all the ideas collected is given a linear chronological order. There are no general rules for establishing which is the best order for the arguments: in some cases it could be better to present the strongest arguments at the beginning in order to immediately gain the listeners' confidence; in other cases it is better to keep the best arguments for the end of the speech, in order to deal the final blow to the antagonist.

The issue of *dispositio* gives rise to very interesting considerations in the field of hypermedia analysis: as a matter of fact, one of the main features that is commonly ascribed to hypertexts is their *nonlinearity* (or *non-sequentiality*) or *multilinearity* (or *multicursality*) (see, for instance,

Aarseth 1994, 1997; Liestøl 1994; Slatin 1994; Landow 1997; Bolter 2001; Fagerjord 2003). At the beginning of the second section we provisionally defined hypertext as a textual structure that allows different fruition paths: this is precisely what is meant by multilinearity. As Blasi (1999: 70) observes, to say that hypertexts are non-sequential is ambiguous, since it is not clear whether this feature refers to the *dispositio* or to the reading process. Thus, it is worth making some remarks about nonlinearity.

From the point of view of the hypertext reader, the fruition of a hypertext is no doubt in some respects linear; since the reader gets a linear sequence of nodes, s/he activates one node after the other. On the one hand, the reading session is always linear, since nodes follow one another in the reader's fruition. In this respect, the *dispositio* performed by the reader is the same *dispositio*, as it was intended in ancient rhetoric: 'in the act of selecting nodes and following links, of consuming the nonlinearly stored documents, the hypermedia reader performs dispositio' (Liestøl 1994: 100). On the other hand, it is not to be forgotten that the linear session the hypertext reader experiences is the result of a set of choices the reader has made by activating the options/links the designer offered him/her.

This seems to greatly differentiate hypertexts from written/printed texts; yet the difference must not be overestimated. On the one side, in fact, a hypertext can be much more linear than a printed text: it is the case, for instance, of some hypertextual CD-ROMS, which, in order to let the reader access their contents, force him/her to read (or look at or away from, sometimes even for many seconds) the opening credits; no printed book can oblige a reader to read its cover for a fixed time every time the reader opens it. Furthermore, some hypertexts can show only parts of their content depending on some conditions: for instance, in educational hypertexts the designer could decide that a node (e.g. a test in a lesson) will be displayed only after some other nodes (e.g. the contents of the lesson) have been read; again, with printed books it is not possible to make some pages invisible (Cantoni and Vittadini 2003: 331–2). Thus, while hypertexts can potentially force readers to a reading session that – in extreme cases – could even be absolutely linear, written texts can never do this. As Aarseth notes:

> hypertext can be a much stronger linear medium than the codex, should its author decide so. [. . .] A hypertext path with only one (unidirectional) link between text chunks is much more authoritarian and limiting than (say) a detective novel, in which the reader is free to read the ending at any time.
> (Aarseth 1997: 46–7)

So, if on the one hand, hypertexts can be absolutely linear, on the other, reading written/printed texts is not always a linear activity: for instance the footnotes, the index or the bibliography of a printed book are elements that can tempt a non-linear reading of a text. Moreover, such texts as journals, newspapers, encyclopedias and others, where flitting back and forth is the norm, can hardly be classified as linear: talking of the website of the largest Norwegian newspaper, Fagerjord observes that

> much of it [i.e. multicursality] does not operate in a radically different way
> from a similar property inherent in the print version of the newspaper, where
> stories also continue from the first page and several stories are placed next
> to each other on a page, leaving the reader to decide which to read first.
>
> (Fagerjord 2003: 319)

In such cases it is very difficult to say what a linear reading is, and even whether it is possible.

Nevertheless, it certainly seems to be the case that hypertexts can offer much higher multilinearity capabilities than written and printed texts do (Cantoni and Vittadini 2003: 333). Going back to the *dispositio*, it is clear that the degree of multilinearity in hypertexts depends on the designer's choices: hypertext designers can decide the amount of paths allowed to readers and, in this way, the degree of freedom to be given to readers. As a matter of fact, hypertext designers do not specify the *dispositio* of nodes, since they do not determine the exact sequence in which they will be accessed; designers specify the rules upon which nodes' sequences could be built: they 'must create a machinery for creating possible *dispositiones*, rather than explicitly defining one or more of them' (Cantoni and Paolini 2001: 47). This makes the task of designers very important and difficult, since they have to guarantee that all good *dispositiones* are generated, and at the same time that all bad ones are avoided.

The fact that hypertext readers are often free to choose the *dispositio* they prefer has in some cases been interpreted as a weakness on the side of the author/designer and as a higher power on the side of readers, who become, to a certain extent, co-authors of the hypertexts they are reading. This is only partially true: as it has already been shown, the author of a hypertext has much greater control over linearity than the author of a printed text has, since s/he can decide which *dispositiones* are to be allowed and which are not. This suggests that the power of hypertext readers depends on the author's will: if the author decides to permit a large navigational freedom within the hypertext, the reader will be more powerful; otherwise, his/her freedom and power will be very limited (Cantoni and Di Blas 2002: 140–1). In other words, if it is often true that hypertext readers have more power than printed text readers, this happens because hypertext authors have much more control over their texts than book authors have:

> [N]o longer an intimidating figure, an electronic author assumes the role of a craftsperson, working with prescribed materials and goals. She works within the limitations of a computer system, and she imposes further limitations upon her readers. Within those limits, however, her reader is free to move.
>
> (Bolter 2001: 168)

Thus, in hypertexts the mutual relationship between authors and readers is to be rethought, since in electronic hypertexts

> the reader participates in the making of the text as a sequence of words. This participation is true of hyperfiction and even of conventional pages on the WWW. In both cases, if the author has written all the words and chosen all the images, the reader must still call them up and determine the order of presentation by the choices made and links followed. The author writes a set of potential texts, from which the reader chooses, and there is no single univocal text apart from the reader. The role of the reader in electronic fiction therefore lies halfway between the customary roles of author and reader in the medium of print.
>
> (Bolter 2001: 173)

An important feature of hypertexts related to their particular *dispositio* is that of *maps*: 'maps are a special form of visual communication, a representation of the three-dimensional world in a coded two-dimensional form. They are found in one form or another in every culture' (Kahn and Lenk 2001: 17). Maps are a common feature of websites: they are a visualization tool, which proves very useful in supporting their websites' planning, analysis and navigation. Thus, maps basically have the functions of representing the structure of the knowledge of a hypertext/website, of acting as an access layer to its content, and to aid the reader's orientation within the hypertextual structure.

Hypertexts' or websites' maps can be very different from the points of view of their graphic appearance, of the objects they represent, of the level of abstraction, and so on: 'There is no common definition of a site map. It may be an index, a table of contents, an overview, or a diagram' (Kahn and Lenk 2001: 72). In a certain sense, maps play the same role in hypertexts as tables of contents (TOCs) and indexes play in printed texts. In fact, in printed books TOCs and indexes give directions to the readers about the kind of content of the book, about how to access it (through a reference to a page number), and about the suggested reading path. TOCs seem to fit well in the way information is structured in printed books, since they are mostly linear, while they cannot always represent the real structure of the contents of a hypertext or website: in such cases other forms of maps may be used. Generally speaking, a pair of basic features common to all maps can be singled out:

1   'The map is not the territory': a map never reproduces the whole website, since it would be as a geographical map representing the whole territory in a 1:1 scale. This means that . . .
2   . . . a map is always an abstraction of the territory: it selects the relevant features of the object it wants to represent, and it represents only these features. This is true for geographical maps as well as for websites' maps. For instance, a geographical map can represent the physical appearance of the territory (physical map), the borders and the main cities of a nation (political map), the streets of a portion of territory (road map), the location of the points of interest in a given territory (tourist map), and so on; equally, the map of a website can represent the main nodes of the website, the main links among nodes, the most important reading paths, and so on (for a detailed catalogue of maps and website maps, see Kahn and Lenk 2001).

When acting as an orientation tool, 'a site map is a navigation aid for the visitor to a web site' (Kahn and Lenk 2001: 72). Instead, because of the multilinear nature of hypertexts and websites, it is not always easy to browse a complex network of documents or web pages without getting lost. This phenomenon is commonly known as the Lost In Hyperspace (LIH) problem. Theng and colleagues single out the main conditions that the LIH problem refers to:

> In general, the 'lost in hyperspace' phenomenon refers to any of the following conditions: users cannot identify where they are; users cannot return to previously visited information; users cannot go to information believed to exist; users cannot remember what they have covered; and users cannot remember the key points covered.
>
> (Theng *et al.* 1996: 387)

In these cases, maps may be a solution to this cognitive problem, since they can help readers to find their way within the hypertext by providing them with a quick view of the whole hypertextual network. The usefulness of maps is well expressed by Armani and Rocci, who make particular reference to the use of them in educational hypertexts:

> With respect to a hierarchic table of contents (TOC) this type of representation has the advantage of being able not only to present the content in units and subunits, but also to make explicit to a certain extent the logical – argumentative, temporal or causal – relations that hold between the contents of these sections and subsections. These relations, which tend to be abstract, are expressed graphically through the use of metaphors.
>
> (Armani and Rocci 2003: 178)

3.2.3 *Elocutio*

The third step in the creation of a speech in ancient rhetoric is the *elocutio*, i.e. the activity of 'dressing' all the concepts and the arguments that have been arranged in a sequence with words; in this phase, the ideas are shaped with a linguistic form.

As observed by Liestøl, in computer discourse *elocutio*

> concerns not only linguistic ornaments but also the graphic layout on the screen and the way signs and icons trigger action and interaction. In hypertext, interface design, layout, the information value of link icons, and so on all belong to elocutio.
>
> (Liestøl 1994: 100)

In particular, three different activities in hypermedia design can be traced back to *elocutio*:

1　The choice of the elements to put in each node: at this stage, the hypermedia designer has to decide how many elements (or slots) are to be put in the nodes and what kind of elements (text, audio, image, video, animation). All kinds of elements must be planned at this stage, both elements related to nodes' content and elements related to the general application's structure, such as the navigation buttons, the background, and so on.
2　The architectural planning of the reciprocal disposition of the elements in the space of the node; if nodes present animations and/or audio and video, their theatrical disposition in time must be planned at this stage as well.
3　The internal semiotic structure and the appearance of each single element: how the text is organized, what the pictures look like, and so on.

Generally speaking, in the *elocutio* phase, the designer has to choose the media to be used in each single node to convey the intended meanings, and specify the nature of each single information item.

Let us demonstrate this point using the homepage of the website of the National Gallery of Art (www.nga.gov) as an example. Once the designers have established the basic elements of the whole application and all their possible *dispositiones*, they have to design the details of the interface and the layout of the nodes: so, they will first decide that the homepage will show a textual title, two different menus containing a series of textual links each, the logo of the Gallery, an image of a painting (which will vary periodically) and information about the copyright. Then designers will establish how all these elements will be disposed in the homepage: the title on the top, the image under the title, slightly on the right, the two menus under the title on the left, separated by a vertical line that reaches the top of the page, and so on. Finally, they will give full details of each element: the font of the texts, their alignment, the appearance of the image, its effects, the color(s) of the background, and so on.

3.2.4 *Memoria*

In ancient rhetoric, *memoria* (memory) played a very important role; ancient orators could not use print or paper to take notes and to type-write their speeches; thus why a very strong memory was crucial to them. In order to strengthen memory and to facilitate the memorization of speeches, a proper art was invented and different techniques and strategies were developed; many of them relied on the spatial localization and retrieval of ideas and arguments to be expressed.

According to Cicero (106–43 BCE), the inventor of the art of memory was Simonides of Ceos (*c.*556–469 BCE), a Greek lyric poet, who during a banquet was reproached by his patron Scopas for having devoted too much space to the celebration of the gods Castor and Polydeuces (the Dioscuri) in an ode in honour of him; Scopas paid only half of Simonides' fee and told him to apply to the Dioscuri for the remainder. After a while, Simonides was told that two young men were waiting for him outside the palace; he left the banquetting room, but did not find anybody; as soon as he was out of the room, the roof fell down and crushed Scopas and all his guests, mangling them so that their relatives could not identify the corpses. Simonides remembered the places where the guests were sitting and could show their corpses to the relatives. Thanks to this incident, the poet realized that an orderly disposition is crucial for a good memory (Cicero, *De oratore*, II, 86, 351–4).

The ancient art of memory (or 'mnemotechnique') relied on places (*loci*) and images (*imagines*): the first step of the technique was to fix in the memory a series of places (*loci*), which were mainly architectural places, such as a building with an atrium, lounge, bedrooms, halls, statues, other ornaments and so on. The images, whose aim was to call to mind the speech, were then located by means of imagination in the building's places that had already been fixed in the memory. When the orator had to call to mind the facts, he just needed to visit, in the right order, all the rooms of the building and recall all the images he left in each room (Quintilian, *Institutio oratoria*, XI, 2, 17–20). The images were divided into images for things and images for words: the former were useful to remember a subject, an idea, a 'thing', while the latter were for remembering every single word (Cicero, *Rhetorica ad Herennium*, III, 20, 33); obviously the memory of words (*memoria verborum*) is much more difficult than that of things (*memoria rerum*), and requires much more practice. This method guaranteed the recollection of all the points of the speech in the right order, because the order was fixed by the sequence of the places in the building.

It is interesting to note here that in ancient rhetoric the art of memory was compared to writing, which nowadays has in many respects displaced the role of memory: the *loci* were seen as similar to wax or paper (the writing supports), the images to the letters of the alphabet, the images' disposition to the writing, and the uttering to the reading (Cicero, *Rhetorica ad Herennium*, III, 17, 30). The art of memory had been highly thought of until the widespread diffusion of print; for instance, at the end of the sixteenth century Matteo Ricci (1552–1610), the first missionary allowed to enter the Celestial Empire, could astound the Chinese thanks to his mnemotechnique: after reading a lot of ideographs only once, he could repeat them by heart in the exact order in which they were written, then he repeated them again backwards (Spence 1994; for a detailed description of the development of the art of memory, see Yates 1966).

Memoria is strictly connected to orality; since the renaissance of rhetoric studies occurred in a context of written culture, this phase, as well as the *actio* phase, has often been regarded in recent rhetorical studies as a residue of oral cultures, thus being labelled as superfluous in written and printed contexts. But, as observed by Liestøl, the fact that *memoria* and *actio* 'gain new relevance from hypermedia supports Walter J. Ong's key argument that electronic culture, including computer technology, forms a secondary orality, an orality one step beyond literacy but dependent upon it' (Liestøl 1994: 102).

This concept of *memoria* clearly has interesting connections with hypermedia design and this is why we have dwelt upon it at length. It is particularly relevant to hypermedia's navigational aspects and the orientation of hypertext readers during one or different navigation sessions in the same hypermedia. In these cases, *memoria* comes into play in different ways:

1   The hypermedia can remember the nodes the reader has already visited. For instance, the back button of hypertextual applications or of the web browsers can lead the reader back to the node preceding the one s/he is currently in; hypermedia applications (and web browsers as well) record the navigational history of a user in the application, so that s/he is able to recall all the nodes already visited in a given time; usually, anchors that have already been activated by readers are marked with a different colour than other anchors; and so on.

2   In some applications, users may be allowed to create their own collections of nodes/objects, links and entry points (bookmarks), which are remembered by the system; it is the case, for instance, with the shopping carts or baskets of most eCommerce websites, where clients can store the products they want to buy, which will be remembered until the completion of the purchase (or the deletion of them by the clients).

3   In adaptive hypermedia the system is able to change its behaviour according to the context or the user, because it memorizes and 'learns' the user preferences and his/her navigation styles.

(Cantoni and Paolini 2001: 49–50; Brusilovsky 1997)

3.2.5 *Actio*

The last phase in the production of a speech is the *actio*, i.e. the phase concerning the performance of the speech. In this phase, the speaker has to plan the way s/he is going to perform her/his discourse, paying particular attention to diction and gestures. In one sense, then, the *actio* is a matter of 'style'. As regards hypertexts and hypermedia, the closest analogy is with their dynamic behaviour: the web counterparts of rhetoric's *actio*, then, are navigation style and rules, interactions, multimedia playing, and so on. Thus, in hypertexts *actio* can be seen, generally speaking, as the specific kinds of interaction of the reader with the hypertext, or as the interaction of the user with other users, i.e. as the acting of the user in interactive contexts such as role-playing games, MUDs, chats, and so on (Liestøl 1994: 101). In the first sense, however, a conceptual problem arises: in short, the interaction of the reader with the hypertext generates different *dispositiones*, as it was observed earlier. So, we have to conclude that in hypertexts the *actio* coincides with the *dispositio*: since the readers actualize, by means of their choices, one of the potential *dispositiones* offered by the designer, they perform the *actio* at the same time. In other words, the interaction of the reader with the system creates the actual (or 'acted') *dispositio*, i.e. the *actio*: this convergence is an important novelty introduced by hypermedia (Cantoni and Paolini 2001: 50). It is, once more, a merging of the role of 'author' and 'reader'. Despite the use of the terms 'author' and 'reader', though, which are both literary and print-based concepts, the roles enacted by the 'rhetoric' of hypertext also have a basis in the history of computer design.

3.3 THE HISTORY OF HYPERTEXT

The term 'hypertext' was coined in 1965 by Theodor Holm Nelson, during the twentieth national conference of the Association for Computing Machinery (ACM); on the same occasion he also coined the term 'hypermedia'. However, the concept of hypertext is commonly dated back to 1945, when Vannevar Bush published in the *Atlantic Monthly* and in *Life* his well-known article 'As we may think'. Bush was a very eclectic person: among other things, he was the science advisor to President Roosevelt during the Second World War, and the Director of the Office of Scientific Research and Development. In his article (see also Figure 3.1), Bush describes a device that acts as the user's memory expander (hence the name memex) as a

> device for individual use, which is a sort of mechanized private file and library. [. . .] A memex is a device in which an individual stores all his books, records, and communications, and which is mechanized so that it may be consulted with exceeding speed and flexibility. It is an enlarged intimate supplement to his memory. It consists of a desk, and while it can presumably be operated from a distance, it is primarily the piece of furniture at which he [i.e. an individual] works. On the top are slanting translucent screens, on which material can be projected for convenient reading. There is a keyboard, and sets of buttons and levers. Otherwise it looks like an ordinary desk.
>
> (Bush 1945: 45)

The main characteristic of the memex is its indexing and consultation method: the memex provides the user with the possibility of consulting the records not only by the usual scheme of indexing, but also by 'asso-

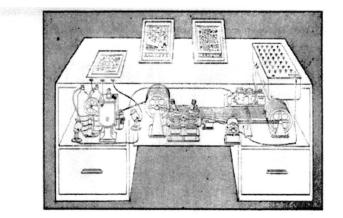

Figure 3.1 The memex as it was imagined and described by Bush
Source: Bush 1945.

ciative indexing, the basic idea of which is a provision whereby any item may be caused at will to select immediately and automatically another. This is the essential feature of the memex' (Bush 1945: 45). Clearly, the associative indexing as conceived by Bush is very similar to hypertextual links.

From a technical perspective, the memex has never been realized because of the success of digital technologies over analogical ones; yet it is worth considering in the history of hypertext for the above-mentioned reasons. (For an in-depth presentation of the evolution of Bush's thought, see Bush 1933, 1959 and 1967; Nyce and Kahn 1991).

If Vannevar Bush is to be considered the main precursor of the hypertext, the first conceptual development of the problem of hypertext is to be ascribed to Ted Nelson, as well as the invention of the name 'hypertext' itself. This is the passage where Nelson introduces for the first time the term 'hypertext': 'Let me introduce the word "hypertext" to mean a body of written or pictorial material interconnected in such a complex way that it could not conveniently be presented or represented on paper' (Nelson 1965: 144).

From 1960 Nelson had been working on a project for the development of a hypertextual software framework, which in 1967 he named Xanadu (www.xanadu.com). Xanadu aims at developing a huge library available to a computer network, which takes into account, by means of links, the different relationships existing among its texts/nodes. At the same time, Xanadu is a space of non-sequential writing that aims to publish documents that enlarge the library by means of their connections to other documents (Cantoni and Vittadini 2003: 325). Nelson's Xanadu has wider purposes than Bush's memex: not only information storage, but also information distribution; not only individual users, but rather a potentially universal target (Bettetini *et al.* 1999: 22–3). Xanadu did not materialize either: a prototype of it was released only in 1987, and after that date no final release was published. Nonetheless, Nelson's idea exerted enormous influence on the evolution of hypertext systems.

As observed by Jay David Bolter, 'Bush and Nelson had identified the key characteristic of hypertext long before practical systems were built' (Bolter 2001: 35). However, in 1968, only three years after Ted Nelson coined the term 'hypertext', Douglas Engelbart – a researcher at the Stanford Research Institute in Menlo Park, California, who invented, among other things, the mouse (see Figure 3.2), screen windowing, and the word processor – realized the first prototype of a hypertextual system: NLS (oNLine System).

The scope of Engelbart's research was to augment human intellect, i.e. to increase 'the capability of a man to approach a complex problem situation, to gain comprehension to suit his particular needs, and to derive solutions to problems' (Engelbart 1962: 1). For this reason he developed the Augmentation System, a hierarchical organization of information, structured through indexes and directories, where users are allowed to create links among documents (see Engelbart and English

Figure 3.2 Underside of Engelbart's mouse

Source: www.ul.ie/~idc/hci/lecture07/lecture07.html

1968: 235–6). The result of Engelbart's researches and of his Augmentation Research Center (ARC) was NLS, an innovative computer collaboration system based on the use of hypertextual links and on other of Engelbart's inventions. NLS was more or less completed in 1968, and it was demonstrated on 8 December 1968 to a small crowd of technology specialists participating in the Fall Joint Computer Conference in San Francisco. This event was soon dubbed 'the mother of all demos', as it is documented in Engelbart and English (1968).

3.4 EARLIER HYPERTEXT THEORIES

If the first hypertext system was presented in 1968, hypertexts began getting over academic experimentation starting only from the late 1980s, thanks to the release of some hypertext systems. An understanding of a large part of the internet's character as a form of communication can be grasped if we consider how hypertext has been theorized.

Theoretical reflections about hypertext took place in different disciplines, which, from different perspectives, gave rise to different concepts of hypertext. After Bettetini *et al.* (1999: 28–33) three main concepts of hypertext, corresponding to three research fields, can be singled out: 1) hypertext as a technology of writing, arising in the fields of history of writing and of cognitive psychology; 2) hypertext as a support for the diffusion and circulation of knowledge, from literary theories, philosophy and sociology; 3) hypertext as a textual construction, from literary theories and semiotics. What is common to all disciplines is the acknowledgment of the pivotal role played by the cooperation of the reader in the fruition of hypertext, and of the peculiarity of the reticular and associative structure of hypertext. Each discipline, however, faces these issues from its own perspective.

1   The view of hypertext as a technology of writing stresses the relationship between ways of writing and the development of knowledge modalities and thought processes. In this perspective, the main feature of hypertext is seen in its reticular and associative structure, which is intended as the reification of human knowledge and thought processes; the influence of Bush's and Nelson's ideas on these concepts is clear enough. In this view, hypertext is modelled on the example of an encyclopedia, conceived as a system of references and of display of possible links among its entries. According to Bolter,

> as it now moves into electronic media forms, the encyclopedic impulse is
> being directed in two channels. The first is the explicit remediation of the

> printed encyclopedia or handbook. [. . .] The other channel for the encyclo-
> pedic impulse lies in fact in the organization of cyberspace itself – in the
> many so-called portal Web sites that provide access for the millions of pages
> on the WWW.
>
> (Bolter 2001: 88–9)

The relationship between the structure of the hypertext and that of
the human mind is brought on also by recalling the theories about the
influence of the technologies of writing on human society and culture:

> [J]ust as we claim to write our minds, we can also claim to write the culture
> in which we live. And just as we have used print technology in the past, so
> we are now turning to electronic technologies of writing to define our
> cultural relationships both metaphorically and operationally.
>
> (Bolter 2001: 203)

2   In literary studies, hypertext, conceived as a support for the diffusion of knowledge, is thought of after the model of a book and/or of
literature itself. This perspective also derives from Nelson's concepts: 'A
literature is *a system of interconnected writings*. [. . .] And almost all writing
is part of some literature' (Nelson 1981: 445). This perspective, the
theory of literature, in particular in the reflection of George P. Landow
and of other authors at the Brown University and featured in Landow's
books (see, for instance, Delany and Landow 1994; Landow 1994a,
1997; Aarseth 1997), revisits some modern hypotheses proposed in the
studies about literary text, stressing some problematic points about the
common concept of text:

> [H]ypertext [. . .] has much in common with recent literary and critical theory.
> For example, like much recent work by poststructuralists, such as Roland
> Barthes and Jacques Derrida, hypertext reconceives conventional, long-held
> assumptions about authors and readers and the texts they write and read.
> Electronic linking [. . .] also embodies Julia Kristeva's notions of intertextu-
> ality, Mikhail Bakhtin's emphasis upon multivocality, Michel Foucault's
> conceptions of network of power, and Gilles Deleuze and Félix Guattari's
> ideas of rhizomatic, 'nomad thought'.
>
> (Landow 1994b: 1)

These authors challenge in particular the idea of the text as an authority
(*auctoritas*), i.e. as a complete work, with a beginning and an end, which
can be easily kept separate from other texts and cannot be modified
through time; the concept of the author as the ultimate responsibility for

the creation of a literary work is challenged as well: 'in hypertext the function of reader merges with that of author and the division between the two is blurred' (Landow 1994b: 14; see also Landow 1997). Hypertext's capability of connecting more texts into a meta-text renders it more similar to *a literature* than to a single work.

3   In the semiotic field, the possibility of enacting every connection among textual elements in hypertexts seemed to offer a validation of semiotic and literary theories that tend to solve the connection of meaning between words and reality in an infinite, recursive and self-referential semiotic process. This is the idea of 'unlimited semiosis' central to Charles S. Peirce's conception of the sign (1931–58) and expounded upon by Umberto Eco. Let us consider, for instance, the model Q, proposed by semiotician Ross M. Quillian, as it is presented by Eco:

> Quillian's model [. . .] is based on a mass of nodes interconnected by various types of associative links. [. . .] The model, in all its complexity, is based on a process of *unlimited semiosis*. [. . .] We can imagine all the cultural units as an enormous number of marbles contained in a box; by shaking the box we can form different connections and affinities among the marbles. This box would constitute an informational source provided with high entropy, and it would constitute the abstract model of semantic association in a free state. According to his disposition, his previous knowledge, his own idiosyncrasies, each person when faced with the sign-vehicle /centaur/ could arrive at the unit 'atomic bomb' or 'Mickey Mouse'. [. . .] A system is a rule which magnetizes the marbles according to a combination of mutual attractions and repulsions on the same plane.
>
> (Eco 1979: 122–6)

Hypertext – and the internet – can be seen as the materialization of such theories: elements can be arbitrarily connected to each other; by means of links every object can be made the sign of any other object. In this way, the hypertextual structure can proceed endlessly. But if it is true that hypertext allows us to magnetize and re-magnetize marbles as easily and rapidly as it has never been possible before, it is much more true that such practices cannot go beyond some interesting but short-ranging experiments with a very limited audience. Such processes are not really able to create real and stable communications: these theories promote playful and experimental hypertextual practice rather than communicative ones. In order to create a hypertext, it is not sufficient to pile up different semiotic objects by means of all manner of links: it is, rather, necessary to plan what one wants to say, to whom, and how, taking full responsibility for what is communicated, as in every real communication. The evolution of hypertextual communication, and in particular of the internet, clearly shows that playful, theoretically experimental practices are to be regarded as a childhood disease of hypertext technology rather than as its maturity (Cantoni and Vittadini 2003: 349–50). In the next chapter, then, the internet will be presented as a tool with the potential to produce real and effective communications, and a model for planning and analysing websites will be introduced in order to demonstrate the possibilities as well as the cul-de-sacs of internet communication.

4

WEBSITES AS COMMUNICATION

In this chapter one of the most used and best known 'objects' of the internet will be presented and analysed in detail: the website, which we introduced in Chapter 2, defined by Webopedia as:

> A site (location) on the WWW. Each Web site contains a home page, which is the first document users see when they enter the site. The site might also contain additional documents and files. Each site is owned and managed by an individual, company or organization.
>
> (www.webopedia.com/TERM/w/web_site.html)

Websites will be approached not as being just technological artefacts – which they also are, indeed – but from the point of view of communication, which is (one of) their structural purpose(s). To do so, the WCM will be presented (section 4.1).

WCM helps to distinguish five main areas of interest: those of *contents and services* offered through a website, which raise the issues of content quality and localization (4.2); *accessibility tools* (4.3); *publishers*, with the issues of website projecting, planning, running and maintaining (4.4). The fourth and fifth elements of WCM: *users*, with the issues of usability, web promotion and access analysis, and the *ecological context* of a website (i.e. its relationships with the web as a whole) are presented in Chapter 5.

A general caveat is required here: website communications cover almost all human communication practices, so the suggestions and strategies that will be proposed in the chapter are not intended as being always definitively valid (on the contrary, there are for sure some cases where they are not applicable). Instead, they must be considered as ideas that apply quite frequently and which are useful to be considered for the broad range of website communication.

4.1 THE WEBSITE COMMUNICATION MODEL

The importance of adopting a sound communicative point of view in approaching websites is well presented by van der Geest:

> Organizations are becoming aware that they have to give their visitors good reasons to visit their site and good reasons to return to it. The medium alone no longer is enough of a message. Increasingly, organizations find that the creation of web sites is not merely a hobby of their Information Systems people, but an essential part of their internal and external communication. Thus the website and the communication policy it embodies becomes the responsibility of managers and communication people, as well as the creation and maintenance of the organization's flyers, catalogues, commercials, annual reports or helpdesk service. Those people will approach planning and producing a web site as a communication design process, rather than a technical design process.
>
> (van der Geest 2001: 1)

That is why, borrowing and adapting the title of one of the most influential books in the field of language teaching theory, by George Widdowson (1978): *Teaching Language as Communication*, this chapter is titled 'Websites as communication'.

A first quite narrow approach to websites can be easily understood (and forgiven): as they appeared in the internet world, people interpreted websites as being either 1) a new technical object, hence to be produced and controlled by engineers; or 2) a sort of manifesto, an advertising tool like flyers and placards, hence to be left in the hands of visual communication experts. Indeed, both 1) and 2) are partially true: a website is also a technological artefact as well as a visual one, the same way as, for instance, one can say that a newspaper is something you can see, and needs many technical competencies in order to be printed (paper, ink and printers require biologists, chemists and engineers to be produced). Or one can say that a shop needs visual communication experts in order for it to be adequately painted and furnished, as well as architects, engineers, carpenters and bricklayers to build the premises.

But no one would say that in order to publish a good newspaper or to run a successful shop you can rely on visual and technical expertise alone. In addition, these competencies cannot work in isolation, or take the leading role in the project/activity. They are, rather, to be integrated and directed by more core competencies, directly linked to the specific 'business' of a newspaper or of a given shop. Moreover, reductions of this sort lead to an underestimation of the processes required to run a website, suggesting that they are static objects that you can produce and leave alone in the web; but just try to figure out a newspaper or a shop without a continuous stock, which is as important as (or even more than) the production of the first issue or of the simple physical structure.

To depict a comprehensive map of what a website is, we thus need a more complex model that could account both for the various dimensions in a synchronic perspective and for the processes required to project, build-up, run, maintain, promote and evaluate a website (diachronic perspective).

A metaphor can help (Cantoni and Piccini 2003; Bolchini et al. 2004). Let us think of a coffee shop: what is it? It is an ensemble of:

1 eatable or usable objects such as food, beverages or games; and
2 plates, glasses, tables and chairs, the kitchen and its tools, the premises, a game table, a TV set, etc. All these objects allow the previously listed objects to be made or enjoyed.

However, the coffee shop is not real, 'alive,' without:

3 a community of people who manage it, cook the food, serve the tables, etc.; and
4 a community of people who frequent it to eat, drink, play, stay with friends, etc.

These four dimensions, two of them (1 and 2) related to things and two (3 and 4) related to people, are also present in website communication.

A website, moving from this metaphor, can be conceived as being a cluster of:

1 *contents and services*, like voting, buying, selling, reserving, polling, interacting, chatting, customizing, etc.;
2 *accessibility tools*, i.e. technical tools that make available those contents and services;
3 *people who manage*; and
4 *users/clients*.

One more aspect is to be taken into consideration to complete the framework. Let us come back for a moment to our coffee shop: every element cannot be considered only in itself and by itself, but gets its meaning and its value only in a given context, in its 'semiosphere' (Lotman 2001). Every sign has to be defined not only for what it is, but also for what it is not, acquiring a specific value only in a given ecological context; the fact that a coffee shop is *the first one selling Italian food* (or *in the city centre, the most visited, the only one with live music*, etc.) does depend both on its nature and on the world it belongs to, where other competitors are working as well. As it happens for stock quotes, the exact value of each single item is due also to a complex market/social negotiation.

Figure 4.1 outlines the depicted framework of understanding. Let us now consider every element in detail, discussing some of its more relevant aspects.

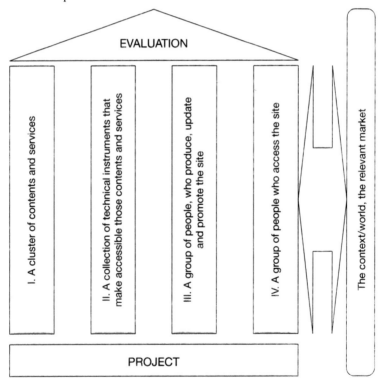

Figure 4.1 The Website Communication Model. Pillars 1 and 2 are things, while pillars 3 and 4 are persons. Project and evaluation activities are cross-pillar, while the relevant context/market affects all the elements

4.2 CONTENTS AND SERVICES (AND THEIR LOCALIZATION)

As mentioned earlier, a website is (also) a structured ensemble of contents/messages and services, such as interacting, voting, gambling, buying, and so on. Although contents can be interpreted as being sort of services: 'the possibility of accessing a message', it seems quite intuitive to keep them distinct (while, at the same time, closely connected). In any case, services could be strictly related to performative messages, since these declare services, describe them, and assist along all the service delivery. For example, the e-mail address one can find on a website is at the same time a content/message: 'our e-mail is: . . .' and an implicit declaration of a service 'if you send an e-mail to this address, we will read it (and most probably reply)'.

The following two sections will therefore deal with the issues of how to assess the character of such information (4.2.1) and the service (4.2.2) in mainly corporate and institutions websites. These kinds of websites provide a good preliminary example since their *raisons d'être* are usually (or should be) quite clear. An issue of some importance when it comes to contents and services, is that of website localization, which will be presented in 4.2.3.

4.2.1 Information quality

Information quality is one of the main concerns in the knowledge society. Two factors are to be considered as fundamental: availability and quantity.

- Data digitization has made available information as never before in history, while at the same time expanding the issues of assessing its quality and use (information overload).
- Internet web communication has dramatically lowered the publication threshold: to print a book or to issue a periodical in the real world one needs much time and many resources; to 'publish' on the internet, to make *technically* accessible to all internet users, requires much less (this is not to be naively interpreted as meaning the publication is accessed by millions of people). This very different balance between the possible information/communication impact and its cost has ended up in a 'publication bomb', which requires a constant awareness and a critical analysis.

Two main directions have been followed to define information quality: one is focused on fitting users/receivers' requirements, and the other stresses its compliance with some criteria; these – non alternative – paths move mainly from the related areas of total quality management and of marketing (Kahn and Strong 1998: 103–5; see also Eppler 2003; Eppler *et al.* 2004).

Among the many definitions, we mention here the model proposed by Kahn and Strong, who put together the two above-mentioned directions:

> The Product and Service Performance Model for Information Quality (PSP/IQ Model) integrates definitions from the Total Quality Management literature, specifically quality as conformance to specifications and quality as meeting or exceeding customer expectations, with the product and service characteristics of information.
>
> (Kahn and Strong 1998: 102)

Thus, information quality can be defined as the characteristic of information to meet or exceed customer expectations; and quality information is information that meets specifications or requirements.

A number of criteria have been proposed to assess website information; most of which derive from previous areas of assessment: the issue is dealt with in detail, for instance, by librarians, used to deciding what to buy/to subscribe to in a market where available books and journals exceed by far the library budget. A very interesting proposal was made by Alexander and Tate (1999), who distinguish five main evaluation criteria, which parallel almost completely the famous wh-questions used by journalists to structure an article: 1) accuracy (*what?* and *how?*); 2) authority (*who?*); 3) objectivity (*why?*); 4) currency (*when?*); and 5) coverage (*what?* and *for whom?*).

1   Accuracy can be divided into two main issues: formal accuracy (textual correctness) and substantial accuracy (correspondence between what is meant and the world). While the second one is by far the most important, the first suggests – also to people who are not subject matter experts – whether the message can be trusted or not. If I read a text full of grammatical mistakes, and with clearly erroneous figures, I will suspect that it does not deserve my trust. Actually, I could conclude also that it does not even deserve my time: if the sender did not devote enough time to proofread a text, what kind of communicative commitment is behind it?

> This fact [the page is free of spelling and typographical errors] does not assure the accuracy of the contents, but pages free of errors in spelling, punctuation, and grammar do indicate that care has been taken in producing

the page. Most important, [an accurate site enables] readers to verify the factual information contained [. . .]. Not only are the sources of the factual information named, but links are also provided to many of the original sources.

(Alexander and Tate 1999: 42)

Violations of accuracy occur quite often if websites are managed by people with technical expertise, but not trained in communication. An example can help make this clear.

When materials previously available only in printed form are digitized to be published on a website, a special software is used, called Optical Character Recognition (OCR), or Intelligent Character Recognition (ICR), which transforms the image acquired by the scanner into a text file. OCR has reached very high levels of accuracy in transforming texts, up to 99.xx per cent, meaning that it – under certain conditions – can correctly interpret almost every character on the original page. If you look at this procedure from a technological point of view, you can just go through it and publish the result on the web (as often happens, by the way). But if you look at it from a communicative point of view, you know quite clearly that 99 per cent of the characters do not mean 99 per cent of the meaning. Suppose, for example, that you acquire a medicine article on how to cure HIV positive people, and the OCR gets every-thing perfect, except for a figure, which said that 11 per cent of the people cured that way had a significant health improvement, interpreting it as being 71 per cent; the OCR error could be less than 0.002 per cent (and its correctness, conversely, more than 99.998 per cent), but the overall meaning is completely different. Unfortunately, as mentioned before, strict and sound publishing procedures for the web are still to come for many companies/institutions, and they will never arrive as long as they consider website communication as being a 'second choice' communication, hence underestimating its impact.

There could be three more reasons for lack of accuracy: one is the personal excuse the publisher allows him/herself: s/he can always correct the document without much effort, a fact that may encourage an elastic concept of 'tomorrow'. The second is that, quite often, without being aware of it, the publisher does not expect anybody to actually read the website, but just to browse it. The third – which will be discussed later in section 4.4.2 – happens when the use of the internet is just a secondary use: users already know the contents, and just browse the website to see how already known contents are represented there. This last reason was quite likely during the first years of the web, however, the more it is diffused, the more likely it is that people use the internet not just for leisure or confirmation, but to get pieces of information they do not have yet.

Last, but not least, an even greater attention is needed in one particular sphere: the possibility of copying website contents, and of reproducing them (e.g. by a journalist who is writing an article about a given company/institution, see Chapter 6) requires that all the texts, figures and data in the website be carefully checked and validated.

2   The authority of information on the web cannot be taken for granted. In fact, being a mediated communication, web communication puts a distance between sender and receiver: who is the sender? What is his/her expertise? Whom does s/he represent? Although it does not always happen, ultimately from the user's point of view it is important to offer clear and verifiable answers to these questions, to help illustrate better the ways in which the messages/services offered can be interpreted. Let us pretend to access a website devoted to insomnia: who is the author of its texts, who gives suggestions and proposes remedies? A university professor who leads a research team in the field? Or a journalist? Or a group of people who cannot sleep? Or is it just a spoof website?

A very important aspect of authority is representativeness: due to the above-mentioned mistake of leaving internet communication in the hands of technology and visual communication experts, one might quite often doubt whether a company/institution's website is really representative or not. Authority requires that the same quality processes, usually in place in the real world, used to assess and validate publications (e.g. press releases, brochures, books) are in use also when publishing something on the net. The more people use the internet to get information about companies and institutions, the more important this criterion will become, and the more people who are experts in internet communication will be needed, who can act on the web to represent their companies/institutions well.

Furthermore, to reduce distance and to ensure stable and deep roots in the real world, where real people live, competent institutional websites often publish not only e-mail addresses, but also physical addresses, where their managers responsible can be reached. In some cases, and with the same purpose, authors' pictures are also made available (e.g. in www.about.com).

3   Objectivity is one of the most debated issues in mass communication. Here, it stands for two main aspects: the possibility on the user's side to understand the website goals and the level of commitment of the sender in relation to every website element.

If we go back to the website devoted to insomnia, further relevant questions to be answered will be: why is it published? What are the interests involved? Who pays for it? Is it significantly different if it is published by a university, a governmental body, a pharmaceutical company or by a single person who cannot sleep? This does not necessarily imply that one is 'worse' than another, but just that users need this information to correctly interpret the website. If I find a list of drugs to cure insomnia, I need to know if they are suggested by an expert doctor, an insurance company, a producer, a fellow insomniac or a quack. A special case here is that of advertising. While the 'commitment' and reliability of a website is putatively at a maximum when presenting its own contents/services, it is usually considered to be lower when publishing advertisements. This means that advertisements are to be clearly distinguished by the rest of contents/services, and that the website commitment towards every element is to be clearly understood.

Many intermediate cases can be distinguished here: from full commitment, to embodying a testimonial, to publishing advertisements that are negotiated, to publishing advertisements without having any control on them (e.g. websites hosted by free services that add commercials). However, there is not any zero-case: no one could elude responsibility if, for instance, immoral, racist or violent contents were to be published in their website.

4   The criterion of currency acquires a new meaning on the web. While in preceding technologies the fruition time is clearly controlled by either the sender or the receiver, here a new time perception occurs. Let us introduce this aspect through the comparison presented in Table 4.1.

When people browse through a website, provided special time marks are not present, they tend to perceive a synchronicity between their act of use and the act of production: this means that what is offered by the website is (perceived as being) intended by its publisher at that same time.

From the point of view of the user, websites act more like radio and TV than like written books or manifestoes: in fact, the sender has complete control of the availability of the message. S/he can 'produce' and 'destroy' it every time.

From the point of view of the producer, websites are more flexible than other media. In a previous epoch, St Augustine of Hippo (354–430), for instance, had to write a book, the *Retractationes* ('Reconsiderations') to correct some of his writings: once one has written and published an article or a book, it acquires a sort of autonomous life; the web, on the other hand, has given much more power to publishers, who have a

Table 4.1 Controlling the fruition time in different media

Examples of communications	Fruition time controlled by:	Production and fruition time are:
Oral in presence or synchronous communication (dialogue, telephone call, audio conference) and chat	Sender	Production and fruition time are the same
Audio recorded message	Receiver	Production time was antecedent to fruition time (interesting in the case of telephone answering machine: whoever listens to the message could perceive a sort of synchronicity)
Written communication	Receiver	Production time was antecedent to fruition time
Radio and TV	Sender	Production and fruition time are the same (a 'replay' or 'from the archive' mark is needed, to mean that it is not the case)
The above, but recorded and cinema	Receiver	Production time was antecedent to fruition time
E-mail, SMS, Multimedia Massage Service (MMS)	Receiver	Usually production time was antecedent to fruition time, but some practices can push them towards synchronicity (such as in chats)
Web	Receiver	Production and fruition time are *perceived* as being the same (as it happens sometimes when listening to a telephone answering machine)

centralized control on their publications (and can thus correct or update them without new users necessarily knowing the website's history).

Bearing this in mind, currency is of the utmost importance on the web and its presence or lack becomes at the same time one of the easiest ways to assess website communication quality. If a company publishes the name of its president or CEO, or an item in the product list, and these items are out of date, the website user has a sure way to judge the website quality. This criterion is closely linked to that of accuracy – what I read is not true – and that of authority – we could say 'no living person exists behind the website'.

In order to meet this criterion, and depending on the resources a website manager has, some websites reduce deictic elements: adjective and adverbs such as 'tomorrow', 'this year', 'recently', or the future verb time, replacing them with forms that are not changing their truth value after a certain moment in time, e.g. '15 August 2005', 'in 2005', 'in the first semester of 2005', etc. The alternative is a more intensive activity of maintenance. Another alternative still is that of adding a clear time reference mark on each web page, although this also works to reveal how old (or lacking in currency) a website might be.

5   The coverage criterion requires that users can clearly understand what is the website's subject, what it is about; knowing a website's scope, it is easier to understand for whom it is published and intended, and to answer the most important question a user asks him/herself: chiefly, 'is this for me?'.

Here, a side effect of the ease of web publication can be noted: many publishers add items to their websites not because they are required to reach the intended communicative goal (if any. . .), but just because those items are available in electronic form, and there is no added cost in publishing them. In other words, they ask themselves the wrong question: 'why not?', instead of the right one: 'why?'. Examples are easy to find where the unplanned growth of a website, driven by extrinsic technological and economical reasons instead of intrinsic communicative and operative ones, ends up in a communication that is neither clear nor focused, and that will neither reach its target public nor its goals.

Websites, of course, are often adapted to different contexts and needs. One of the most interesting examples, online healthcare communication, is worth noting. Health communication is one of the most critical areas where information and communication quality are strictly regulated and many studies have been carried out in order to propose a coherent and subject-specific set of quality criteria. Among the many proposals, one of the most interesting and fortunate is that by the Health On the Net (HON) Code. Health On the Net Foundation (www.hon.ch) is one of the most respected not-for-profit efforts to improve medical information on the internet; it lists the following eight principles to assess healthcare communication quality:

1   *authority*: when a piece of advice offered is from a non-medically qualified individual or organization a clear statement is made;
2   *complementarity*: the information provided is designed to support, not replace, the relationship between a patient/site visitor and his/her existing physician;

3   *confidentiality*: confidentiality of data relating to individual patients and visitors is respected;

4   *attribution*: where appropriate, information contained on this site will be supported by clear references to source data and, where possible, have specific HTML links to that;

5   *justifiability*: any claims relating to the benefits/performance of a specific treatment, commercial product or service will be supported by appropriate, balanced evidence;

6   *transparency of authorship*: information is presented in the clearest possible manner and contact addresses for further information or support are provided;

7   *transparency of sponsorship*: commercial and non-commercial contributors are clearly identified;

8   *honesty in advertising and editorial policy*: if advertising is a source of funding it will be clearly stated. A brief description of the advertising policy will be displayed. Advertising and other promotional material will be easily recognizable.

If a website complies with the above-mentioned quality parameters it is allowed to display the HON Code of Conduct logo. Examples of other quality logos, in further domains are: Britannica Internet Guide Award (www.britannica.com) and ISI Current Web Contents (www.isinet.com). There can be little doubt that healthcare communication requires clarity of information. It requires regulation and all the above commitments. However, for present purposes, the quality decisions and guidelines connected with them in healthcare communication reveal a great deal about the character of websites in general.

4.2.2 Service quality

Where services are concerned, it is usually the case that a website has to clearly and truthfully state all the conditions of service, namely what kind of service it is, who can use it, at what cost (if any), and so on, without omitting legal and privacy issues. Some websites do not. Often, the issue is feedback. Let us consider a quick example: if a client enters our aforementioned coffee shop and asks a waiter for a coffee, s/he can check what the waiter does, thus knowing quite clearly at which step s/he is in the service process: is the waiter selecting a suitable cup? Is it being filled with coffee? Is the sugar bag being prepared together with a spoon and a little plate? When interacting via a phone, this kind of constant overview on the overall process is not equally available: that is why one could feel oneself getting lost if the speaker on the other end does not provide timely information on what is happening (e.g. 'the required extension is engaged', 'the person is not in the office but is coming soon: would you like to wait?', 'I am trying his/her mobile phone number', etc.). On the web, this kind of distance between the user and the service process is even bigger, and is sometimes bridged by information about: steps fully completed, steps still to be undertaken, what data are received by the system (to be checked by the user), what kind of commitment on each party is entailed by each step, if and how the process can be cancelled or not (e.g. 'clicking here, the order is placed', 'clicking here, the airline reserves a seat . . .', etc.). These are measures geared to enhance quality.

4.2.3 Localization

In presenting the accuracy aspect, an important element was left aside: the adequacy of contents to their readers/users from a cultural point of view.

As with every effective communication act, as well as with the web, it has to be adequate 1) to the reality it represents (truthful), and 2) to the receivers. In order to fulfil the second requirement, it has to be relevant (Sperber and Wilson 1995), i.e. to meet the receivers' needs and expectations, and to be understandable by them. In other words, it has to use appropriate linguistic elements that make reference to objects and experiences the receivers are able to interpret. When it comes to web communication, a careful analysis of this last aspect is often undertaken by corporate website producers to ensure that the intended audiences are correctly addressed, promoting solid communication.

The technical possibility of being accessed by people everywhere on the planet has pushed many website publishers towards translating their websites into numerous languages, hence trying to get in touch with as many people as they can. However, it is frequently the case that a wider cultural translation is needed, so-called *localization* (Esselink 2000), an area where cross-cultural communication experts are of the utmost importance.

The localization process has to consider all the elements that are represented in a different way in different cultures; among them:

- Dates and figures: 11.09.2001 vs. 09.11.2001; 2004 BCE (Gregorian calendar) vs. 1425 a.H. (Islamic – or Hijri – calendar); 25,234 vs. 25.234.
- Currencies: if one wants to sell something in Japan, it could be worthless (although true) to express costs only in euros.

- Measures and sizes: metres vs. yards, centimetres vs. inches, kilometres vs. miles, litres vs. gallons, Celsius vs. Fahrenheit, kilograms vs. pounds, US vs. Europe shoe sizes . . ..
- Rules and laws: to write that somebody was driving at a speed of 60 km/h, somewhere means that s/he is breaking a rule; elsewhere, however, it does not have this same meaning; to say that a selling/buying process is ruled by a given law is valid only where that law applies, but a different law has to be mentioned while localizing the text for another country.
- Historical, cultural, religious elements that are usually common sense or widely known in a given culture – 'common ground' (Clark 1996) – could be unknown in another. For instance, if I write that 'Hotel X is near Assisi, and it takes just ten minutes walking to reach St Francis's Basilica; unfortunately, many frescos are hosted in another area of the city', it is fully understandable by people who know where Assisi is, who St Francis was, what it means to be a saint in the Catholic Church, what a basilica is, that there were many frescos by Giotto, that the basilica was damaged by an earthquake, and so on. For the others, the message would sound like a strange list of words.
- Many other aspects are to be taken into consideration when localizing a website, for instance pictures, colours, word length (for designing menus), etc.

Many corporate websites are aware of the problem of localization. With this list of considerations, it should be easy to identify those that are not.

4.3 ACCESSIBILITY TOOLS

The second pillar in WCM represents accessibility tools. In particular, they are hardware, software, net connections and visual interface. It is not possible to present these elements in detail, which deserve an extended discussion in consideration of CMC generally. However, general rules have to be stated here: these are – as their name makes clear – *accessibility* tools. As long as website communication remains in the hands of technical or visual communication experts alone, it is in danger of being used for experimental purposes for its own sake, without a clear connection (a rationale) underlying its communicative/operative goals. Two issues are taken as examples: the issues of accessibility by disabled people, and by technically ill-equipped people.

The first one requires a careful consideration of the target public, and a website design to make it accessible by people who use a vocal browser (see, for instance, the WAI, by the W3C: www.w3.org/WAI): in this case, every message carried out only by visual cues is lost; hence being spectacular or visually rich is not always an added value.

The second issue suggests that the more technological equipment and competence are required on the users' side, the fewer users there will be. Every additional requirement could act as a sort of censorship against people who do not have the required (hardware or software) technology, or technological competence. Depending on how this issue is dealt with, the digital divide (see Chapter 1) will grow or diminish. A sense of the present state of website communication is offered, then, by a consideration of the extent to which these matters are currently addressed on the internet. Such a consideration also creates some dilemmas for website producers/publishers.

4.4 PUBLISHERS

As has been made clear with the coffee shop analogy, a website is a living entity, a communicative/operative *activity*, and not a sort of crystallized *action*, taken once and for all. The activities of projecting, producing, maintaining, promoting, evaluating and improving the website, as well as that of interacting with its users, belong to the third WCM pillar. While a detailed discussion of some of the aforementioned activities is out of this text's scope, we will focus in the next section on some issues arising for website producers/publishers.

4.4.1 Projecting a user-centred website

Hypertext's structure has been discussed in Chapter 3, distinguishing its different layers. What remain to be discussed here, though, are

1 the process by which that structure gets its form: eliciting user requirements and translating them into system specifics; and
2 the strategy designers can use to represent that structure to producers/publishers.

Translating it into our coffee shop analogy:

1 how the architect can understand and interpret his/her clients' needs; and
2 how s/he can present a model of the coffee shop before actually building it: usually through verbalization – just describing it – and,

more frequently and effectively, through visualization: a map, a scale model, pictures of similar structures (which are very often used to discuss furniture), computer simulation, and visiting with clients similar coffee shops.

To discuss 1) the Analysis of Web Application REquirements (AWARE) model (Bolchini and Paolini 2004a) will be introduced, while to discuss 2) the IDM (Bolchini and Paolini 2004b) will be presented.

1   The AWARE model recognizes the central role of all the relevant project stakeholders and their goals for eliciting, analysing and specifying requirements for internet applications, following an established practice in the field of requirements management. In particular, goal-oriented requirements engineering assumes that the 'why' of the stakeholders' needs and wants has to be sought and documented in order to highlight and keep trace of the reasons behind the design features to be stated.

Goals represent high-level target of achievements that may be owned by a variety of stakeholders, whose 'desiderata' have to be taken into account and carefully considered by the analysts to devise possible strategies and solutions to satisfy them by means of the application. To support the requirements, analysis activity of analysts and designers of internet applications, the AWARE model offers a set of simple principles enabling document requirements specification, as well as keeping traces of the requirements and design rationale. The main constructs offered by AWARE are described in the following sections.

Stakeholders
This construct models every type of user to be considered when the application builds and all the relevant clients and main persons to be involved (the company representatives, marketing managers, sponsors, decision makers and opinion makers). Stakeholders have goals with respect to the site-to-be and have a direct or indirect interest in its success.

Goal
A goal is a high-level objective of one or more stakeholders. Goals may represent both users' goals and main stakeholders' goals. As to user goals, they usually consist of plausible motivations for visiting the application, or – in other words – the objectives of their interaction. Users' goals may vary in granularity from low-level, specific and punctual information-seeking ('find opening hours of the park on day X'), also called 'functional goals', to higher-level, open-ended, ill-defined needs

or expectations ('decide if the city is worth visiting'), also called 'soft-goals'. As to the goals of the main stakeholders, they express what the main stakeholders want to achieve by means of the application, what the return is on investment (in terms of brand awareness, image, new contacts, new clients, revenues). The goals and the vision of the main stakeholders may be dictated or strongly influenced by the business model underlying the application.

Refinement process

AWARE adopts a refinement process to pass from high-level goals of the stakeholders to subgoals and eventually to application requirements.

The raw material gathered during elicitation may consist of an unstructured mix of very high-level goals, scenarios, pieces of design, examples of other sites, design ideas and sketches, design decisions, and detailed requirements. This first set of raw materials emerges during elicitation and is usually organized in order to be usable by the analysts, and fed into design. The refinement process will be guided by the following lines of inquiry:

- What does a given high-level goal mean? How can it be specified? Often, user goals and main stakeholder goals are too vague, abstract or generic, posing obstacles to devising operative indicators to the designers. For example, if a goal of a main stakeholder in a tourism website is 'attract new tourists', analysts might enquire as follows: What does it mean specifically to make a tourist remain longer in the relevant territory? Or to attract people who have never been in this territory? From which countries? And so on.
- What are the possible strategies to satisfy a high-level goal? Analysts will elicit possible subgoals that may contribute to accomplish the long-term goal. For example, 'How can we convince people to remain longer in this territory?' A possible subgoal may be: 'Highlight a variety of tours and attractions lasting one week or more', and so on.

Refinement involves a decision-making process for the communication strategy that will be implemented in the application. This is the activity in which analysts make the most important strategic decisions about the project. Note that the refinement process needs to be realistic, that is properly balanced with the constraints of the project, the priorities, the time and the budget available.

Finally, the refinement process is an iterative process of identifying a sufficient (not necessary) strategy to satisfy the upper goals. In fact, the refinement of a goal into a subgoal is not an absolute (or necessary) relationship, but it is relative to the specific needs of the project and to the visions of the stakeholders involved.

The refinement process also applies to user's goals. Goal refinement for users will involve such questions as: 'How may this user profile accomplish his/her goal?' For example, the user goal 'planning a visit to the city X' may be divided into a number of subgoals, such as 'know which are the "must see" parts of the city', 'decide a suitable hotel in which to stay', 'see interesting hotspots close to the hotel', and so on.

Task
While a goal is a wished state of affairs, a user task is a high-level user activity on the site, such as 'doing a keyword search for the hotels'.

Requirement
Goals are refined, elaborated into subgoals, tasks and eventually into requirements. Requirements in fact represent the end point of the analysis process.

Requirements are usually informally expressed in natural language and their level of detail is negotiated between analysts and the design team. Requirements are not aimed at capturing all the functionality of the application but only those crucial features needed by designers to shape the user experience and by stakeholders to agree on initial specifications. Note that the 'requirement construct' models both functional requirements and non-functional requirements.

As partially exemplified in Figure 4.2, requirements can be of different kinds: Content (marked with C), Structure of content (S), Access Paths to Content (A), Navigation (N), Presentation (P), User Operation (U), System Operation (O), and Interaction (I).

Scenarios
In order to facilitate the elicitation and refinement process, user scenarios may complement goal analysis. These will emerge within the requirements negotiation between the stakeholders and the designers, since they are task-oriented vivid descriptions of envisioned use of the application. These can assist analysts in discovering new requirements, exemplifying goals, revealing new goals and better defining stakeholders. Scenarios may take the form of narrative descriptions (also defined as 'stories about use') as well as of more structured examples of circumstances of use of the application by a specific user profile. Scenarios, then, are usually expressed in narrative form, as stories of typical users using the site, with their motivations, goals and experience.

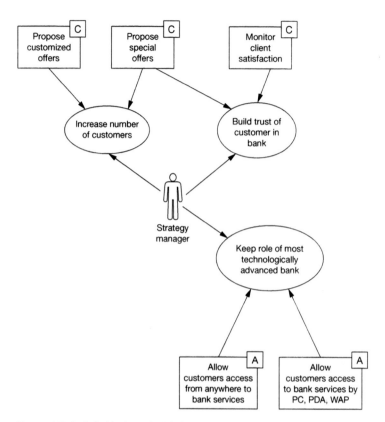

Figure 4.2 Stakeholder's goals (circles) and examples of corresponding requirements for the website

Scenarios may describe the user interaction, vividly representing a user performing a specific sequence of tasks with the application, or they can focus also on the context of use, describing examples of user motivations and goals within the environment (intentional, physical or social context).

Scenarios are partial descriptions of the wide spectrum of the potential interaction capabilities of the application to be developed. Therefore, they are used either to exemplify and make more concrete elements of the goal analysis or to anticipate design details and interaction paradigms already existent during requirements.

2   Requirements analysis provides the input for the design activity. Design entails producing a high-level description of the application-to-be independently from implementation details. Among the many existing

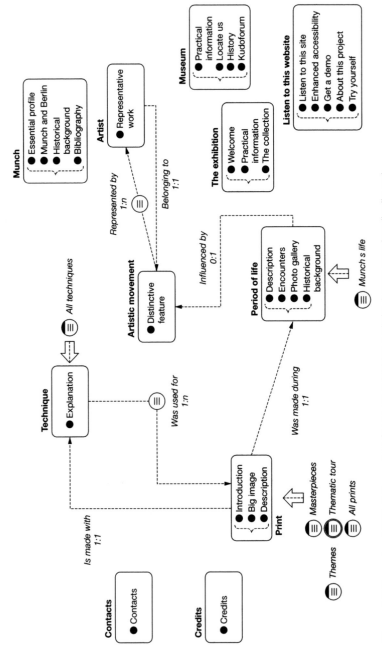

Figure 4.3 Example of IDM dialogue map for an art exhibition website (www.munchundberlin.org)

web design models, one of the most comprehensive is the IDM (Bolchini and Paolini 2004b), which focuses more on the communication (in terms of dialogical exchanges, as we have seen presenting the hypertext structure) between the user and the site, than on the technical solutions to be provided.

IDM is a comprehensive yet usable design model enabling designers to shape the user–website dialogue in order to devise the site structure, navigation and presentation strategies to be supported (see Figure 4.3).

IDM foresees the applications in terms of *kinds of topics* (what the site is about; what the main types of content are, such as print, artistic movement, printing techniques, etc.); *dialogue acts* (how different kinds of topics are actually recounted to the user, e.g. each print may have an introduction, a big image and an in-depth comment); and *relevant relations* the user can exploit to navigate from one topic to another (e.g. from a given picture the user can navigate to the technique used to make that picture). A further design choice is the definition of the *groups of topics*, that is how the user can access, choose and be guided to the exploration of the topics (e.g. reproductions of paintings may be organized by 'masterpieces', by 'theme', or by an 'index of all paintings').

Once the designer has made these basic decisions about how the dialogue strategy on the site should be sustained by the user, page design can be sketched.

4.4.2 Communication between non-technical and technical people

In communication exchanges between clients – or their representatives, who commission the website – and technical people who design and build it, many problems and misunderstandings can arise. The reason is quite simple: literate humans are quite well equipped from an early age to read and interpret a house plan; the same cannot be said, however, in relation to website description. Moreover, there are very different experiences of, and presuppositions (as well as prejudices) about, websites, so that communication cannot rely on a shared common ground, but needs a continuous bridging effort to solve and fix possible meaning misalignments.

In Table 4.2, a synopsis of the most frequent communication difficulties is presented.

1 All the possible misunderstandings due to an inadequate judgement about the interlocutor belong to this area. The most frequent are the following:

a   A mistake about the interlocutor him/herself. A careful under-
     standing of who is who on both sides is needed in order to know
     who has the right and the power to do what, and to allow a
     smooth process of website planning and development.

b   A second problem is the underestimation of the interlocutor's
     role and importance, a sort of stereotyping activity: 'analysts/
     developers cannot understand real problems', and the like.

c   The saying 'Can't see the wood for the trees' well describes
     another possible mistake: that of focusing too much on details,
     forgetting the overall picture.

d   Clients and analysts/developers belong to different 'communi-
     ties of practices' (Wenger 1998; Wenger et al. 2002). Thus,
     they need to develop a common understanding of the involved
     issues: goals, problems, constraints, and so on; without it, many
     misunderstandings can take place.

e   Sometimes people think it is necessary not only to understand
     their interlocutors (which is fine), but also to do their job,
     which often means pretending to be an expert in new and
     unknown areas.

f   When one thinks s/he is supposed to do the other's job, s/he
     could decide just to remain silent, waiting for the other to do
     her/his work. This can lead to an abrogation of responsibility
     for the development process.

Table 4.2 Frequent difficulties in communication between technical and non-
technical people

Area	Possible misunderstanding
1 Interlocutors	a Mistaking the interlocutor
	b Not recognizing the importance of the interlocutor's role
	c 'Can't see the wood for the trees'
	d Thinking that the interlocutor thinks and works exactly like we do
	e Thinking that it is necessary to think like the interlocutor does
	f Dumbness or shyness
2 The world and its representations	a Simulation
	b Dissimulation
	c Utopia of the double
3 The time factor	a Haste
	b Indecision

Source; Cantoni and Piccini 2004.

2   Significant misunderstandings can be found regarding the relationship between the website and the reality it is supposed to represent.

a   Simulation occurs when the website pretends to represent a reality that does not exist, for instance by exaggerating it.

b   The other side of the coin is dissimulation: in this case a website does not try to present something that does not exist, but tries to hide something that actually does exist. It is the case that some companies try to paper over their weaknesses by using a website. If a company is weak in customer care, it may offer many customer care features on its website to compensate for the unhappy reality, hence adding a technology without touching where the real problems are, in culture, values and processes.

However, it must be remembered that websites can also *emphasize* deficiencies in the companies they try to represent. In brief: the web can reinforce strengths, but can also exacerbate weaknesses.

c   Another relevant misunderstanding can occur when conceiving a website: the utopia of the double. In this case, a sort of perfect virtual reproduction of the real organization is sought. While in the previous two instances the website was an unfaithful representation of reality – presenting a reality that does not exist – in this case it tries to reproduce or mirror the reality itself, producing a sort of 1:1 map of a territory: it does not add or leave aside anything, but is completely useless by virtue of adding too much irrelevant information rather than adding value.

This misunderstanding of how websites function is largely due to low website publishing costs, which encourage companies to continuously add contents and functionalities, and to the excuse – already mentioned – of publishing for everybody: 'There must be someone somewhere who is interested in this!' (Examples might include a picture of every employee, or the historical series of quarterly reports since the company was founded, or comics about the business, and so on and so forth.)

3   In communication exchanges between clients and analysts/developers, the time factor is a crucial one. Two different problems could arise: haste and indecision.

a   As a website is something virtual, there is the danger of thinking that it does not take time to be designed, produced, tested and published; hence there is the concomitant excessive hurry among companies to get websites online.

b   The opposite case happens when – in order to reach perfection – a website is continuously rebuilt, without ever being published.

4.4.3 Maintenance tasks

A detailed description of all the necessary maintenance tasks needed to run a successful website goes far beyond the scope of this chapter, and depends also largely on the kind of business concerned. However, a summary of the process helps to understand what is needed to make the websites you access enjoyable, readable, current, engaging, useful, information rich or, on the other hand, tedious, repetitive, alienating and redundant. Once a website has been properly designed, developed and tested, and goes online, maintenance activities start. They can be summarized according to their connection with the different elements in WCM; namely:

• *contents and services*: ensuring new relevant contents and services are added, old – unused and/or obsolete – ones are removed;
• *accessibility tools*: data backups, due to hardware, operating systems and applications' upgrades, software upgrade, due to new browsers' functionalities, or new programming languages, etc.; changes in the graphic interface required either by new devices (e.g. new screens are used, wider and with a higher resolution; new tags are available), or by new visual communication trends;
• *managers*: continuous training activities to renew the skills of producers, refining of organization (workforce) and/or procedures (work-flow) to better fit the website's activities;
• *users*: providing timely feedback to users, interacting with them, analysing their usages, upgrading website usability, promoting the website in order to widen its reach (these issues will be dealt in the following chapter);
• *world/market*: constantly analysing the concerned sector on the web, to catch trends and new opportunities, and to avoid failures. In particular, benchmarking: learning by the 'best in the class' in their business.

High-order maintenance activities are usually accompanied by evaluation strategies, in order to promote continuity. Furthermore, that continuity is a matter of transforming communication in relation to changing contexts.

Communication in general, of course, is to be analysed, assessed and evaluated in given communication contexts and from the viewpoint of its addressees: receivers are at the very core of every communication act and process (Cantoni and Di Blas 2002). To stress this point also in website communication, the fourth WCM element (users) and the fifth one (*ecological context* of a website) are presented and discussed in the next chapter, along with one of the key tools of internet users: the search engine.

5

CONCEPTUALIZING
USERS OF THE INTERNET
Traces and search engines

Users are the 'why' when a website is conceived, developed, run, promoted and evaluated; without them, these activities do not make any sense. In this chapter, the following issues will be presented: how web design is implemented to reach the intended audience: web promotion (5.1.1); how to analyse the actual website usages, mainly through log file analysis (5.1.2); and how to assess and evaluate website usability (5.1.3). The fifth WCM element is also presented here: the *ecological context* of a website: how it is inserted and connected with the web itself (5.2), dealing with the issues of proximity (5.2.1), history (5.2.2) and authority (5.2.3).

Special attention has to be devoted to internet search engines: they mediate the relationship between the web and its users, helping the latter to find relevant answers to their informational and operational needs (5.3).

5.1 USERS

5.1.1 Web promotion

In order to promote the knowledge and the use of a website, reaching the intended public, many activities are carried out by website managers (Haig 2000; Holtz 2002; Roberts 2003). They are organized depending on whether (potential) users are offline (in the real world) or online. In the case of online users a distinction has to be made between the

Table 5.1 Strategies of web promotion

Offline	Integration of website and e-mail address into every communication by the company/institution Dedicated commercials	
Online	First visit	Search engines Banners and interstitials Other kinds of backlinking
	Following visits	Dedicated mailing lists 'Push' services

first visit and the following ones; Table 5.1 summarizes the overall picture.

When one is considering these factors it is as well to remember that not everything occurs online. Offline promotion is still important in web use: ultimately, all web users live in the real world.

First of all we need to understand the integration of online communication with offline communication: both are just different media/channels of communication, issued by a particular subject: e.g. a company/institution. Offline and online complement and reinforce each other, rather than cancelling each other out. Thus, in corporate communication, many things bear the 'electronic stamp' of the company/institution: stationery, business cards, forms to be filled in, invoices, answering machine messages, gadgets, uniforms, posters, radio and TV advertisements, vehicles, flyers, press releases, and so on and so forth. Where does the internet fit in all of this? In brief: wherever the company/institution name appears, there is an increasing tendency for its website address to be present.

Where online communication is concerned, search engines are the most powerful tool to procure a first visit, while dedicated mailing lists are the most important for inviting users to come to a site again and again. Due to their importance, and to their intrinsic communicative relevance, search engines will be dealt with and discussed later in this chapter; here, some other strategies used to procure the first visit are presented.

Although of very different kinds, all strategies consist in giving a link towards the promoted website where prospective users/clients are supposed to navigate; linked elements supposedly catch users' attention and convince them to leave their present position and jump to the target website. So, in general, every kind of backlink is targeted at getting a first visit; actually – in very specific cases – they could also help in getting the subsequent ones, too, e.g. on portals, where people go just to avoid remembering or bookmarking a website they already know – let us say, for instance, an airline's website, or one with train timetables.

The most common and known backlink vehicle is the banner: a graphic element, often animated. While in the first period of the web's development these garnered much attention, and seemed to be the best online promotion strategy, users have become more aware of the meaning of the different elements in a web page, hence developing a more selective attention. This then helps them concentrate only on the relevant items, leaving banners almost outside the scope of their interest (rather like commercial breaks on television). Today, if banners are put in relevant places, where potentially interested users navigate, they get clickthrough from about 1 per cent of the visitors. That is why new kinds of banners, increasingly aggressive, of many different shapes and behaviours, with a wider use of multimedia features have been created, such as skyscraper banners, interstitials, pop ups, flying images, expanding graphics. Due to this significant decrease in *clickthrough* ratio (how many times a linked element is clicked out of the total number of visits: 1 per cent means that one visitor out of 100 selects the concerned element), many websites – mainly portals – have (partially) abandoned a business model based on the number of exposed banners.

Also a different payment model is emerging: banners are not funded depending on the number of exposures, but on the number of click-throughs. A quite similar model is used in the affiliation (or referral) programs. In this case, a website exposes a link to another website that offers goods or services that complement its own, but are outside its core business. For instance, a website devoted to informing mothers of newborn babies about healthcare issues could feature a link to a website that sells nappies online. In this case, a win-win situation can arise for the website: on the one hand, the second website is not a competitor of the first one; indeed, it could offer a useful service to its users. On the other hand, users will not perceive the link as being a distraction, but as an added value. Affiliation programs usually adopt one of the following three cost models: *pay per click* – as above for banners; *pay per lead* – the referred website pays only if the user is responsible for a certain action: for instance, subscribing to a mailing list or filling in a questionnaire; *pay per transaction* – payment is due only if users buy something (usually it is a given percentage of the transaction amount).

Paid links (to ensure a first visit) can be bought on mailing list messages, offering products/services likely to be relevant to their readership. A mailing list run by a website is the best means to maintain a contact over time with its visitors: they are notified when new information items (or the like) are available, and invited to come back and visit; moreover, website managers can gain useful information about their users: e-mail addresses plus other data. In some cases, the core service is a mailing list, while the website just offers stable information, such as how to subscribe, who publishes it, how much it costs (if anything).

Mailing lists, in general, are lists of e-mail addresses, used to diffuse messages. They could allow for different communication patterns, usually 'many to many' (everyone is allowed to send messages to all the subscribers), or 'one to many' (only the manager can send messages). The second type is the most diffused, and is analogous to a newsletter or a corporate newsletter in the real world.

A good quality mailing list fits some strict communicative requirements:

- It clearly states the kind of messages that are sent (both the content and the format: pure text, HTML, with attached files), their frequency, and how data provided by subscribers – their e-mail address and all other required data – are treated (*privacy statement*).
- It is 'opt-out': it is possible to unsubscribe at any time, instructions on how to do so are presented in each message and the procedure is simple. After the unsubscription, often one more message is allowed, clearly stating that the procedure was correct and effective.
- It is 'opt-in': e-mail addresses are to be used only by permission (as in permission marketing), so that nobody receives messages without having explicitly given his/her consensus. When subscription is processed via an online form, in order to check that the input address has been provided by the owner of it, a confirmation procedure is often applied (double opt-in): the system sends an e-mail to the address, asking for a confirmation: unless it is given, subscription is not effective (a similar procedure is sometimes followed also for unsubscription).

As in direct and permission marketing, mailing lists are a very effective and efficient communication strategy, helping companies/ institutions to keep in touch with their public; they also allow for many kinds of customization: messages can be tailored according to specific user profiles.

Moreover, mailing lists are not expensive to manage (they do not require printing, envelopes, stamps) and allow for a continuous update of the list: incorrect addresses are automatically removed, while receivers can easily unsubscribe if not interested any longer. As we mentioned in Chapters 1 and 2, when dealing with e-mail and the 'deadly duo', spam and viruses, although they are a powerful means of communication, mailing lists are put in danger by intrinsically poor quality (neither opt-in nor opt-out) and by every kind of spam.

Another important way of distributing new information items, and even of syndicating them, is provided by RSS technology, already presented in Chapter 2.

5.1.2 Analysis of usages

In the electronic world, everything leaves a trace, a sort of footprint; this is due mainly to technical reasons: merely by keeping a register of all the processes a system has, the system can take a step back: bugs can be fixed, system recovery can be made possible. Also web servers – the hardware and software required to run a website – record their own activities, compiling a 'log-file' (Stout 1997; Sterne 2002; Inan and Kean 2002). Although there are slightly different syntaxes, depending on the different web servers, a log file consists of a pure text file, with a line for each single server call; for instance, a line could be as follows:

> 192.168.70.211 – [01/Nov/1999:10:11:30 +0100] 'GET /sito/index.htm HTTP/
> 1.1' 200 3617 'http://www.lugano-tourism.ch/Home/Header.htm' 'Mozilla/4.0
> (compatible; MSIE 4.01; Windows NT)'

recording the user IP number; date and time of the access:

> 01/Nov/1999:10:11:30 +0100;

request:

> 'GET /sito/index.htm HTTP/1.1';

status code:

> 200 [meaning that the transaction was OK];

transmitted bytes:

> 3617;

referring page, the page clicking on which the user accessed the website:

> 'http://www.lugano-tourism.ch/Home/Header.htm';

and, information about the user's browser and operating system:

> 'Mozilla/4.0 (compatible; MSIE 4.01; Windows NT)'.

The log file records every file transaction (hit); this means that a single web page could correspond to more than one hit, each for every single image, or other separated elements.

While specific technicalities are not to be discussed here, the 'communication' side of this has to be stressed: website managers, in fact, can get hugely relevant pieces of information about their users by analysing web server activity. Of course, log files are not interpreted directly by website managers, but through dedicated programs that compile data, extrapolate the relevant facts and visualize them in due form. The most relevant insights (from a communicative point of view) that a website publisher can gather are:

- *Users and user sessions*, usually counted as follows: each unique IP address is considered a user, and a request from that same IP address over 30 minutes after the last request adds to the user-session count. In order to get the exact user numbers an identification procedure has to be followed, or – but with less precision – visitor ID cookies are employed. First-time visitors, or visitors coming again can be measured, hence studying their loyalty towards the website.
- *Fruition activities*, which pages/media or services were accessed most frequently? Which ones less frequently? What are the most common usage patterns? What is the user behaviour on a given page: is that a site entry, a site exit or a single access one? What are the most followed links on a given page? etc.
- *Time factors*, knowing website traffic according to months, days of the week and hours. This information can be of great value to understanding the kinds of users that visit the site: do they access it in office time or during the night? In working days or during weekends? Also effectiveness of promotion campaigns can be assessed: e.g. if a peak is recorded (or not) after a TV campaign. Also the average time spent on the website can be measured.
- *Space factors*, although there is a quite large uncertainty margin, users' locations can be inferred by their IP number, knowing where the corresponding internet service provider is located.
- *Referring resources*, if a user accesses the website being referred by another website, this can be recorded, allowing the website managers to determine from what other resources they get the most relevant income; in particular, it is also possible to detect, when the referrer is a search engine, what was the query (e.g. 'http://www.google.com/search?q=cantoni+tardini&[other parameters]', meaning that the referred user was looking for 'cantoni+tardini' on Google).

- *Technical data*, many technical data can be interpreted also from a communicative point of view, for instance status code 206 means 'only partial content delivered, the requested file was not completely downloaded to the user'. This could indicate a slow server, or an unbalanced ratio between needed download time and the page added value (relevance) as perceived by the user. Users' operating systems and browsers can provide useful information on their equipment, in order not to provide over-elaborated services (e.g. using languages/functions not supported by their available browsers).

When interpreting log file data a website manager will have goals, make hypotheses and test them. Moreover, data could be biased according to many factors: user sessions could seem more numerous due to automatic systems' accesses (e.g. search engines' crawlers); the same could be said about session time, geographical locations, access time (time is connected to the web server time zone, not to the user's one), and so on.

If log file data are to be carefully analysed and interpreted, they are not the only available data to assess and evaluate a website's activity. For instance, other information can be gathered through java scripts (e.g. installed plug-ins, screen width, dimensions of the used window), and access data could also be processed by a third service provider. Additionally, usages data are integrated with data concerning the specific services offered by a website: how many subscriptions/unsubscriptions? How many products/services sold? (And which ones? When? To whom? etc.) How many e-mail interactions? And so on.

5.1.3 Usability

Usability has been defined by ISO, in the framework of *Ergonomic Requirements for Office Work with Visual Display*, as being the '[e]xtent to which a product can be used by specified users to achieve specified goals with effectiveness, efficiency and satisfaction in a specified context of use' (ISO 1998: n. 11). In fact, once the web has become a widely distributed medium, the issue of its ease of use has become of the utmost importance. While there is not space here to provide a deeper discussion on this issue (see Cantoni *et al.* 2003; Nielsen 1993, 2000; Nielsen and Mack 1994; Nielsen and Tahir 2002; Lim *et al.* 1996), it is important to frame it in the WCM approach, where it can be defined as being:

> the adequacy of contents/functionalities (pillar I) and accessibility tools (pillar II), between themselves and with respect to the users (pillar IV) and

the relevant context (world). However, this adequacy has to be measured taking into consideration the goals of people who commission, project, develop, promote and run the website (pillar III).

(Cantoni *et al.* 2003: 7–8)

This means 1) that accessibility tools are to be exactly what they are supposed to be; 2) that contents/functionalities and accessibility tools are to fit users' requirements; 3) that in order to guarantee usability, the needs and goals, the expectations, the education and the previous and similar experiences of both publishers and users are all to be considered.

Two main approaches are adopted when measuring usability (Triacca *et al.* 2004): one moves from a set of usability criteria (heuristics), to be employed by expert evaluators; the other asks a group of users, representative of the target, to navigate the website, and studies their navigation. The first one goes a deductive way, while the other takes an inductive route. One of the most illuminating sets of usability criteria has been proposed by Nielsen and Mack. This involves:

1   visibility of system status;
2   match between system and the real world;
3   user control and freedom;
4   consistency and standards;
5   error prevention;
6   recognition rather than recall;
7   flexibility and efficiency of use;
8   aesthetic and minimalist design;
9   help users recognize, diagnose, and recover from errors;
10   help and documentation.

(Nielsen and Mack 1994: 30)

Clearly, the extent to which websites might deviate from such stringent usability requirements indicates that internet communication is by no means foolproof and demands circumspection on the part of designers. Put another way, usability relies heavily on an understanding of the world that users inhabit.

5.2 RELEVANT CONTEXT/WORLD

Although from a technical standpoint the web is a flat structure, where everything can be just a click away from everything else, users shape it according to their actual navigations and perceptions, creating a complex and rich geography with diverse degrees of proximity and distance. This landscape will be explored in the following section, identifying three different paths: proximity (5.2.1), history (5.2.2) and authority (5.2.3).

5.2.1 Proximity

On the web, physical *contiguity* among websites is not a possibility and might even be considered meaningless; however, two main kinds of proximities can be found: a navigational and a psychological one. Navigational proximity occurs when an item is linked to another, or when both are linked through a third one; distance can thus be measured by the number of clicks necessary in order to move from one item to another, without directly typing the address in the URL space on the computer display.

Psychological proximity occurs when different items belong, in the user's perception, to the same (or similar) paradigm, a paradigm being a set of items grouped by their having a common aspect. For instance, Yahoo! (www.yahoo.com) and Google (www.google.com) are search engines, hence belonging to the same paradigm; Weather.com (www. weather.com) and BBC World (www.bbcworld.com) provide the weather forecast service; Yahoo! (www.yahoo.com) and Maps.com (www.maps.com) provide city maps, etc. While it is impossible to have a full and objective picture of such connections, it is indeed possible to reconstruct a partial sketch of it. Two paths can be followed.

One way is through search engines, in particular those that take into consideration *link popularity*: the later part of this chapter will present this in more detail, explaining that link popularity is based only on technical elements – a mere automatic tool can analyse it – that are supposed to represent actual human behaviours. The second way is through a mapping of actual users' navigations, studying where they go.

The biggest effort on the internet to map actual users' navigations is carried out by Alexa (www.alexa.com). Its subscribers are given, through a bar plugged into the browser, pieces of relevant information while navigating. Among the data provided, there is information addressing the question 'which other sites do users visit who have visited this one?'. In order to be able to provide such detail, Alexa monitors and records all the navigations of its millions of subscribers (actually, only the navigations on freely accessible websites, not on intranets, or secured websites). So, when users are visiting a given website, Alexa can compile the second most visited website by people who visited the one in question, the second most visited one after that, and so on. This kind of information is very useful, because it represents real usage patterns, thus mapping websites' psychological proximity.

In fact, Alexa is owned by Amazon (www.amazon.com), which offers a very similar service to people who visit its online bookshop, presenting, together with a book, sundry associated information: 'people who bought this book, also bought . . .', again, a way of mapping psychological proximity based not on inference, but on actual clients' behaviours. Alexa's service has been provided also to non-subscribers, through menus integrated both in Internet Explorer and Netscape Navigator, and is also accessible through the Alexa website.

The privacy issue remains one of the most relevant concerns in services like this one that record users' activities for further analysis: users are entitled to be made aware of what is recorded, why, and how those data are going to be used/stored and/or cancelled. It is worth mentioning that in 2001 Alexa itself had to pay out in a legal privacy dispute of precisely this nature (due to problems caused by version 5.0 of the software: see www.pages.alexa.com/settlement/).

5.2.2 History

As we have seen and discussed in section 4.2.1, the default internet perception is that of simultaneity between message fruition and message production; moreover, website managers can remove at any moment pages and items they do not want to be available any longer, thus producing a sort of ever-changing geography without any history. The internet resembles, then, a realm of mere presence: both in space – everything is just there, without distance – and in time – there is neither past nor future, but only an instantaneous present; it is a sort of technologically produced and always vanishing *hic et nunc* (here and now).

The consequences for the audiences/users are similar to those of radio and television (as well as newspapers), but in a more textual environment: contents tend to be just consumed, like physical goods, in an endless consumption activity without reflection; *reflection* – in fact – needs both a spatial and a temporal distance, where also psychological distance can find some room.

Among the epistemological consequences of this is the underestimation of previous knowledge. Or, to reiterate – the history disappears and the here and now dominates. This supplants the circular process of interpretation (the hermeneutical process of building on prior knowledge: see, for instance, Gadamer 2005) with a simple 'additive' one, where the newer piece of knowledge simply *replaces* what preceded it, and renders the preceding at the same time false and useless, as well as technologically inaccessible (de Kerckhove 1995, 1997; Levy 1997; Castells 2003).

Some search engines actually offer a backup copy of indexed pages, in case those pages are not available online. However, they try to remove from their indexes every obsolete item and backup, leaving just the last visited version of their indexed pages. Since 1999, a partial reconstruction of the history of the web has been made possible by the Wayback Machine (www.archive.org). This service, created by Alexa, records huge amounts of web pages, offering all the pages according to the date they were recorded, thus making it possible to solve the apparent temporal mono-dimensionality of a website into a timeline. Although incomplete (recorded data start in 1996 and depend on many random circumstances), the Wayback Machine is a very useful tool for anybody who wants to study the web, its history and geography, and belongs to the same class of endeavour as the great efforts being made in order to preserve and make accessible audio-video archival materials.

5.2.3 Authority

Items in psychological proximity are also implicitly organized by individuals and groups according to a judgement of value: they are coloured depending on the level of trust they (are supposed to) deserve and also in terms of the usefulness they provide for different needs. Here again we find the technical flatness of the web giving birth to a rich landscape of mountains and seas, with a continuous negotiation – inside every user and among them – of contour lines. In this perspective, the internet has re-proposed a situation similar to that which occurred when radio emerged (see Gackenbach and Ellerman 1998: 9–15): the same receiving set and the same procedure allowed access to the programmes of broadcasting stations that were very different with regard to the quality of their contents and the target public they addressed. How, then, was it possible to distinguish high-quality stations from low-quality ones? The hierarchy of sources the press had established suddenly appeared to be disrupted, in an undifferentiated jumble of words, sounds and programmes. Analogously, in the internet everything can be accessed by means of the same software (the browser), in a seemingly flat and indistinct network. However, in respect of the internet – as well as in the early days of radio – high-quality providers tended to emerge and to gain a good reputation over time.

Gackenbach and Ellerman describe the issue of quality emergence in the following way:

> The panic caused in the eastern United States by the 1938 Orson Welles's broadcast of 'The War of the Worlds', a dramatized invasion of earth by

Martians, was the culmination of radio's two-decade flirtation with the ineffable. But this broadcast was also a turning point in the credibility of radio as a medium of truth. [. . .] Today we are ambivalent about the people's medium, 'The Net'. When someone tells us, 'I found it on the Net', we are still powerfully compelled to accept and believe. On the other hand, we now know that there are no guarantees of truth value for anything on the Net.

(Gackenbach and Ellerman 1998: 13)

In fact, the veracity of sources is always changing, in a context where many old and new players try to be perceived as their fields' leaders, and people and groups entrust and distrust sources according to many different criteria and reasons. The emergence of a sources hierarchy has been paralleled by a reduction of websites offering identical services: as long as the most accredited players are emerging in each field, other players stop competing on the same field. Websites that still want to offer a given service (e.g. in order to keep visitors loyal), find it better to buy such a service through the major players (syndication – an example might be all the second-hand bookshops whose orders are now managed by Amazon.com): through syndication service providers are able to widen their reach, while at the same time concentrating on their core business.

The means by which sources are ranked, then, within a generally perceived hierarchy, is of the utmost importance for users. It may be that there is no absolute means to identify the value of internet sources, although there have been certain rules of thumb that have been applied, sometimes taken over from the reputation of previous media. The BBC website (www.bbc.co.uk), for example, not only takes on the mantle of trust that has been associated with it internationally since at least the Second World War, but it is also acknowledged to be one of the best websites in terms of content and design. Apart from this, though, users have to rely on other means for evaluation (see section 4.2.1; see also Alexander and Tate 1999) and, in turn, to guide their use of the internet. Obviously, among the most important of these are search engines.

5.3 INTERNET SEARCH ENGINES

In the previous section, we have presented websites from a communication point of view; one of the pillars that constitute websites concerns users, i.e. a group of people who access and visit the website in order to find relevant information, to make use of an online service, and so on. This section will be entirely dedicated to presenting one of the main tools for online promotion of websites, namely search engines; as already stated earlier in this chapter, internet search engines are of the utmost importance in order to ensure users' first visits, i.e. in order to get new clients to access the website for the first time. In fact, this sort of brokering service – mediating between senders' and addressees' interests – is necessary to help the web fulfil its goals, both from a communicative and a business viewpoint. Not being accessible through search engines could amount to being censored, hence the relevance of the search engines' issue not only as a knowledge management challenge, but also as a big challenge from the point of view of communication rights.

In this section we will first introduce how internet search engines work (5.3.1), then describe a significant turn that they have embarked on in order to be more effective (5.3.2), and finally present some examples related to the most known and used search engines (5.3.3).

5.3.1 How internet search engines work

The huge amount of information available on the internet makes it difficult for both website publishers and users to communicate effectively: publishers need to make their websites visible and stand out in the mass of available information. Search engines are among the main tools that allow publishers to make their websites stand out and for users to find information they are looking for; without search engines the only way to find a web resource would be that of knowing the exact URL of the resource itself, or being referred by other known resources or experts.

Search engines are services that allow users to make full-text searches on the content of web pages; basically they consist of big databases that archive web pages, index them and present them to users who request them. Under the name of 'search engines', two different kinds of systems are commonly acknowledged: directories and proper search engines.

Directories are big archives where websites are classified in a tree structure: every website that enters the directory is assigned to one (or more) category or sub-category. Ideally, categories should be exhaustive, i.e. they should cover all human knowledge, and should be reciprocally exclusive, i.e. one category should not overlap with another. As a consequence, every website should be allowed to be assigned to at least one category, whatever its content is. In fact, very often websites are assigned to more than one category, thus making the directories areas far from mutually exclusive. For instance, in a directory the website of the Louvre museum could be made accessible under the category Art, and/or under the category France, and/or under the category Tourism, and so on. Actually, the branches of a directory tree are defined and instantiated differently by different directories, according to opportunistic reasons;

usually due to economic factors – tourism could be a first-level branch, while biology could be deeply indented – to the number and quality of available resources – the more resources there are in a field, the more branches are needed – and to cultural imperatives: religion, for instance, could be considered as a stand-alone branch, or as being connected with or dependent on culture and/or leisure, and/or lifestyles.

Directories have two main characteristics:

1   they are managed by human editors who decide whether or not to insert the website in the directory's database and – if so – decide to which category (or categories) it is to be assigned;
2   they index websites, and not single web pages.

In contrast, proper search engines index single web pages, and do it automatically. According to SearchEngineWatch (www.searchenginewatch. com), which is probably the best observer of the field, the major internet search engines, i.e. those that are either well known or well used, are Google (www.google.com), Yahoo! (which is the web's oldest directory, but in 2002 integrated also crawler-based listings; see www. yahoo.com), Ask Jeeves (www.ask.com), AllTheWeb (www.alltheweb.com), AOL Search (aolsearch.aol.com), HotBot (www.hotbot.com), and Teoma (www.teoma.com). The major directories are Yahoo!, Dmoz – Open Directory Project (www.dmoz.org), and LookSmart (www.looksmart. com) (see Sullivan 2004).

Directories and search engines may collect websites and web pages of any field, or only of one or more specific fields, thus presenting themselves as a specialized access to a well-defined subject field, for instance: news, finance, kids, and so on, or again of one or more specific linguistic or geographic areas. Furthermore, they may index not only websites, but also newsgroups messages, images, audio and videos, blogs, and so on. The general working of internet search engines can be divided into three main activities: 1) spidering; 2) indexing; 3) responding (see Figure 5.1). We are now going to explain each of these in more detail.

5.3.1.1 Spidering
The first activity of an internet search engine is that of gathering web pages to create a database of web resources. Basically, internet search engines gather web resources in two ways: 1) by spidering the web; and 2) by allowing submission of websites to the database.

1   *Spiders,* or *web crawlers,* are robots (i.e. pieces of software) that surf the web in order to find web pages to be inserted into the search engine's

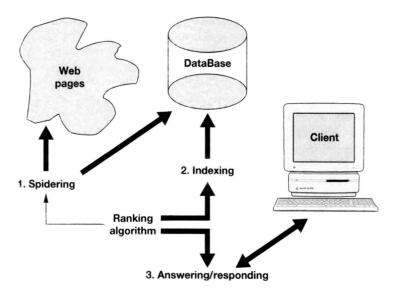

Figure 5.1 The general working of internet search engines

database. Spiders go through the web randomly or according to given instructions, following links and fetching web pages to feed the database. Once a spider gets to a website, it reads the information contained in it, follows the links available in the website, and returns all the information to the search engine's database. Periodically, the spider goes back to the same site in order to check any new information, changes and updates that it could present. Concretely, when spiders get to a website, they first look for a file called *robots.txt*: this file – if provided – must be placed in the website's root directory, and tells the spider which files or areas of the website (if any) should not be spidered and indexed; robots.txt can only forbid something, it cannot give any positive order to a spider. In this way, websites' administrators can specify which parts of the site are off-limits to robots and disallow access to those pages. According to the instructions of this file (if available) and to its own instructions, the spider follows the website's links and downloads the site's web pages to the search engine's database.

2   Most search engines allow websites' publishers to submit websites and web pages to their database on the publishers' own initiative. In these cases, it is not the search engine that autonomously fetches the resources to feed the database, but it is websites' publishers that propose their websites/web pages be inserted in the search engine's database. The

submission of websites and web pages to a search engine can be made automatically or manually, i.e. by people who submit web pages one by one in the search engine's database.

5.3.1.2 Indexing

Once the information pieces are loaded in the database, they have to be indexed in order to be made available for users' requests. Web resources are indexed on the base of a ranking algorithm, which controls the ranking of presentation of the resources to the users' requests. Thus in this phase, web resources are first catalogued according to some criteria, then ranked to be presented to possible users' searches. The ranking algorithm used to index the web resources and present them to users' requests varies from one search engine to the other, but they rely basically on two kinds of criteria:

1   Criteria based on *intrinsic factors*: these are elements that are deducible from the web resources themselves, such as their URL, the name of the website, the titles of its pages and other information deducible from the source code with its tags and meta tags. Search engines get information about a web page from these elements, and, according to their criteria, they catalogue the page into their indexes, and assign it some keywords to make it accessible to users' searches.

2   Criteria based on *extrinsic factors*: these are those elements that cannot be found at all in the web page source code or in its URL, elements through which it is possible to capture some information about the publishers and the users of the website; we will come back to these elements later.

Criteria based exclusively on intrinsic factors are often insufficient in offering relevant answers to users' queries. This is the case for the following: (a) the impossibility for automatic tools to fully understand the actual meaning of a web page, and for users to completely express their information needs through keywords, and (b) the unfair competition by which web managers who want their websites be ranked first use spam or pay fees to search engines even though their websites are not completely relevant for search engine users.

(a)   First, a gap between syntax and semantics often occurs: the formal correspondence of the keywords of the indexed web pages with those typed in by the users does not guarantee the correspondence between such keywords and the real content of the web pages. This problem –

related to the exact correspondence between indexed web resources and users' queries – is due to the limits of the algorithms of computational linguistics (Zampolli 1995), which cannot fully take into account, for instance, the problem of synonymy – two terms having the same meaning – and homonymy – one term having many meanings. For instance, if one types in the text box of a search engine the keyword [mercury], the search engine is not able to understand whether the user needs information about the planet, about the Roman god, about the chemical substance, about the make of vehicle, or about the English pop singer Freddie Mercury (1946–91); as a result, it will present to the user all the pages containing information about all these different topics (and many others). Of course, the user can do more precise searches, refining them using the operators presented in section 5.3.1.3 (e.g. s/he could type in the keywords ['Freddie Mercury'], or [mercury planet], or [mercury vehicles], and so on). However, this does not solve the problem on the search engine side. These can, and actually do, work towards bettering their algorithms, integrating new features and aspects of natural language engineering, but cannot fully reach the goal of understanding the meaning of web pages and users' queries.

In order to solve this intrinsic problem, and to better match users' needs, meta tags were developed. Meta tags are tags that are not intended to be interpreted by browsers, and whose values are devoted to describing the web page in its entirety (hence the 'meta' name). Their goal is that of providing sound and useful information about the actual content of a resource. Let us explain this through an example: in an encyclopedia, usually entries devoted to presenting a person (e.g. Plato), present his/her name only once, and afterwards refer to the name only using its initials (e.g. P.). Moreover, other items, not devoted to that single person, could mention his/her name many times (e.g. Plato being mentioned many times in Aristotle's biography); hence the paradox of having the keyword 'Plato' only once in a text completely devoted to him, while being present many times in a text fully devoted to Aristotle. Through meta tags, the author could label the first item as being thoroughly devoted to Plato (although his name appears only once in its actual wording); authors are then entitled to meta-describe their resources, hence making them more suitable for human searches.

While meta tags are very useful and important in areas where all the players share the same cognitive map(s) and commitment to loyal description (for instance in intranets, or in specific areas of the web, where there is room for a Web of Trust: see the Semantic Web Activity of the W3C: www.w3.org/2001/sw/), elsewhere, if they are not properly used, they become useless. And in fact, after a first enthusiastic implementation of meta tags in their search algorithms, search engines had to reduce or even to completely cancel the importance they gave to most meta tags, due to their purposely being false or exaggerated. This inequitable behaviour is referred to as a kind of search engine spamming. We have then to enter the second area of problems: those due to human will.

(b)   Another kind of spamming is *URL spamming*: the regular submission of a large number of pages by one website to the indexes in the hope of showing up very frequently in their result pages.

Generally speaking, spamming is the sending of electronic junk mails or the posting of junk newsgroup messages. Usually, spam is e-mail advertising sent to a mailing list or to a newsgroup (see section 2.3.3). The origin of the term is debated: some take the term back to a Monty Python sketch featuring an eatery that serves only: 'Spam spam spam spam, spam spam spam spam, lovely spam, wonderful spam . . .', to mean an endless repetition of worthless text; others claim the name is taken directly from the luncheon meat Spam, to which it has some common features:

> [N]obody wants it or ever asks for it. No one ever eats it; it is the first item to be pushed to the side when eating the entrée. Sometimes it is actually tasty, like 1 per cent of junk mail that is really useful to some people.
>
> (www.webopedia.com/TERM/s/spam.html)

The phenomenon of URL spamming is strictly related to the very nature of websites, since they behave as attractors of the attention of search engines in order to reach as many readers as possible (Andersen 1998). A few years ago, AltaVista devoted one page to URL spamming, where the problem was clearly explained in this way:

> Trying to fool search engines into including pages that don't truly match queries, or ranking marginally relevant pages very high on result lists, is one form of 'spamming'. Spamming degrades the value of the index and is a nuisance for all. The logic that leads people to try such tricks is rather bizarre. I figure everybody searches for the word 'sex'. I don't have any sex at my site, but I want people to stumble across my site. So I'm going to put the word 'sex', three thousand times as comments. And any time that anybody searches for 'sex', my pages will show up first.
>
> (www.help.altavista.com/adv_search/ast_haw_spam)

5.3.1.3 Responding

The third phase of the activity of an internet search engine is more concerned with the users' side: it is the phase of responding to the user's requests or searches. Also the activity of responding is based on the ranking algorithm of the search engine, since the visualization of the information given by the search engine to the user's request depends on the ranking algorithm used.

Let us now show the working of internet search engines through an example, starting from this last phase. A student needs to have some information about the English writer Gilbert Keith Chesterton (1874–1936). S/he connects to the website of the (fictitious) search engine SearchEngineX, and types in the provided field box the keywords [Gilbert] and [Chesterton]. In less than one second s/he gets back a list of about 50,000 results. What has happened? The search engine looked in its database for all the documents that matched the keywords typed by the student, found about 50,000 documents, and presented them to the student in an established order, according to its ranking algorithm. It is worth remembering here that the student's search did not actually take place directly over the internet, but s/he searched through the index created by SearchEngineX, i.e. through its database. This is the reason why it is possible that some of the 50,000 results received by the student are no longer available: they could be, for instance, 'dead links', i.e. links that are no longer linked to any page. This can occur because the website has updated and changed its pages, while SearchEngineX has not yet updated its index, an activity that search engines, by means of their spiders, do periodically.

By typing in the keywords [Gilbert] and [Chesterton], the student found all the pages available in SearchEngineX's index that contained both keywords; as a matter of fact, search engines usually have the Boolean operator 'and' automatically included, and search for the documents that contain all the keywords typed by users. The student could also exclude one or more words from his/her search, by adding the minus sign ([–]) before the word to be excluded; for instance, if the student needed to find all the documents concerning Chesterton, except those concerning his Father Brown stories, s/he could type in [Gilbert Chesterton –Father –Brown], and the result would have included all the documents containing the keywords [Gilbert] and [Chesterton] and not containing the keywords [Father] and [Brown].

Search engines have a list of words that are automatically excluded from a search: the so-called *stop-list*. This list includes common words and characters, such as articles and prepositions, which are ignored during the search phase because they would slow down the search without improving its results. If the user needs to include these words in his/her search, s/he can add a plus sign ([+]) before the word: for instance, if one were searching information about the movie Star Wars – Episode I, in order not to have the 'I' sign excluded from the search, s/he could type in: [Star Wars Episode +I]. In this case, the search engine will include also the 'I' sign in the search. As an alternative, a whole phrase can be searched for, by putting quotation marks around the phrase to be searched: ['Star Wars Episode I']. In this case, the search engine searches for all the pages containing exactly this sequence of words; of course, if one document contains the phrase [Star Wars started with Episode I], this document will not appear in the results of the search.

Finally, searches with the 'or' operator can be made as well: for instance, if one wants to find information about the Pope, one can type the keywords: ['Benedict XVI' or 'Joseph Ratzinger']. As a result, all the documents containing the exact phrase [Benedict XVI] and all the documents containing the exact phrase [Joseph Ratzinger] will be presented.

5.3.1.4 Metasearch engines
In addition to search engines and directories, a third kind of tool for searching the web has to be mentioned: *metasearch engines* (or *metacrawlers*). They look exactly like search engines, but actually they do not have a database of their own, since they do not perform the activities of spidering the web and indexing the web resources. Metasearch engines just respond to users' requests, presenting results of users' searches, which they draw from some selected search engines. According to Search EngineWatch, the major metasearch engines are Dogpile (www.dogpile.com), Vivisimo (www.vivisimo.com), Kartoo (www.kartoo.com), Mamma (www.mamma.com) and SurfWax (www.surfwax.com) (see Sherman 2005).

5.3.2 The pragmatic turn of internet search engines

In what follows, we are going to describe an important development that has occurred in the functioning of internet search engines in the last few years: borrowing the term from the linguistic tradition, we will call it the 'pragmatic' turn of search engines.

5.3.2.1 Syntactics, semantics and pragmatics
In his 'Foundations of the Theory of Signs' (1938), semiotician Charles W. Morris (1901–79) distinguished three branches within the semiotic field: syntactics (or syntax), semantics and pragmatics. Since semiotics is

the science of signs, Morris defined syntactics as the study of 'the formal relation of signs to one another', semantics as the study of 'the relations of signs to the objects to which the signs are applicable', i.e. their *designata*, and pragmatics as the study of 'the relation of signs to interpreters' (Morris 1938: 6). Let us explain this through a seemingly simple example, after Cantoni and Di Blas (2002: 18–22): the Italian code of traffic lights (which is almost identical with many others). The code of traffic lights can be seen as a semiotic system that has three main states:

1 the red light is on, the amber and green lights are off;
2 the amber light is on, the red and green lights are off;
3 the green light is on, the red and amber lights are off.

Basically, state 1) means 'Stop!', state 2) means: 'Attention! Red is going to light up', state 3) means: 'Go!'. All other system states can be seen as a tool for controlling whether the traffic light is working: when no light is on, as well as when red and green lights are on at the same time, or in other similar cases, it is as if the system means: 'the traffic lights are not working correctly'.

This code of traffic lights defines also which sequences of states are allowed and which are not: for instance, it establishes that after the green the amber must light up, the red after the amber, and the green after the red; in this code only these sequences are allowed. In the UK and Switzerland different states are possible (namely, red + amber is allowed, with the meaning: 'Get ready! Green is going to light up'), and different sequences are allowed: after the green light, amber must light up, then red, then red + amber, then green again, and so on. The interpretation of the code can vary depending on the context of use: for instance, if one is going up to a crossing with the green light and one realizes that on the other side a big truck is arriving at full speed with no intention of observing the red light, it is likely one will stop in spite of the green light.

Going back to Morris' distinction, the fact that every state has a definite meaning is a matter of semantics, i.e. a matter of relation of signs (the red, green and amber lights) with the objects to which they are applicable (the actions they require of drivers according to the highway code); the fact that some sequences of states are allowed and others not is a matter of syntactics, i.e. of relation of signs to one another; finally, the fact that the code may be interpreted differently depending on the context of use is a matter of pragmatics, i.e. of relation of signs to people who interpret them. In the following paragraphs, this distinction will be applied to the working of internet search engines, and will help us understand an important change that has occurred in the last few years.

5.3.2.2 The need for a pragmatic turn of internet search engines

The claim of this section is that internet search engines are now taking into account more and more the behaviour of people who publish and use websites, while at first they focused their attention almost exclusively on some syntactic and semantic features of web pages. The recent evolution of search engines over the internet can be seen as evidence of the importance of a pragmatic approach to electronic communication, i.e. of the importance of adopting a sound communicative point of view in studying electronic communication, as already observed at the beginning of Chapter 4. The issues we are concerned with here have to do with the criteria followed by search engines to regulate website submission to their indexes, to rank resources and to present the results of a query to their readers.

At first, search engines usually allowed free website submission, trying to compete on the field of completeness; their main objective was to have in their database as many web pages as possible, in order to be sure of offering to their users all the possible resources that matched their queries. Nowadays the huge results they give to almost every query are becoming more and more a problem for their users, creating a situation that many call *information overload*: the user gets so many resources and so many documents back from the search engine that s/he is flooded with information and is not able to understand which ones are really relevant and useful to him/her and which to select (see section 4.2.1).

For this reason, search engines have recently started to put restrictions on the possibility of a website being indexed. This change is due to the fact that if a high number of indexed pages helps fulfil the need for *recall* – all the pages that meet a given query are indexed – it reduces at the same time the chance for *precision* – only the relevant pages are presented to the user, and in a proper order (ranking) (Cantoni and Tardini 2003: 238). Earlier (5.3.1.2), two kinds of criteria were singled out, according to which indexed web pages can be ranked and presented to readers: criteria based on intrinsic factors and criteria based on extrinsic factors. The former rely mainly on *syntactical* features of the indexed pages, i.e. they rely on a formal correspondence between signs, namely the keywords typed in by the users and some textual elements contained in the indexed pages; or on *semantics*, as long as meta tags provide trustful semantic information about the actual resource's content. The latter rely on pragmatic elements, i.e. on elements that do not directly concern the content of the pages, but mainly the context where they are used, in particular the behaviour of the publishers and the readers of the web pages. These elements can provide some information about the real interest and the real motivation of publishers, by assessing, for instance, how often they update their pages, how much they are willing to pay to have actual communications on their websites, and so on; they can also provide some information about the readers' interest in a resource, by assessing, for instance, the popularity of a resource in the community of its users.

Thus, search engines are trying harder to take into account extrinsic (pragmatic) elements, which help to assess not only a formal correspondence between queries and indexed web pages, but also the actual communities behind the web resources they have indexed: that of publishers and that of readers (users). In other words, it is clearly recognizable in the evolution of search engines that there is a shift from purely syntactic/semantic to pragmatic criteria for the indexing and the presentation ranking of web pages. Both strategies, it is to be underlined, have the same goal: that of better matching, semantically, users' queries and search engines' answers. Some of these extrinsic strategies meant to increase relevance will now be presented. In particular, examples of search engines that use strategies centred on what the publishers do will be presented, and then examples of search engines using strategies centred on what users/readers do.

5.3.3 Pragmatic strategies of internet search engines: some examples

If we go back to the search engine schema, we can find pragmatic strategies in all the three main activities carried out by an internet search engine. Let us present them in the same order.

5.3.3.1 Pragmatics in spidering
To improve the quality of indexed web pages, a search engine can decide to reduce the number of spidered items – according to certain criteria. In particular, the most adopted strategies are:

- not allowing automatic submissions;
- accepting (only) paid submissions.

Both are targeted at assessing the senders' commitment: are they really interested in having their web pages visited by the search engine users?

In the first case – stopping automatic submissions – the search engine does not ask for money, but for time; to feed a new resource one has to demonstrate s/he is a human being, who is devoting his/her time to this.

For instance, MSN adopts the following strategy: to submit a URL one has to interpret a sequence of letters, and copy it into a form; if the sequence is correct (it is written in a way only a human being can decipher) the submission is allowed (a similar strategy was used also by AltaVista).

Money is a quite clear testimony of commitment, although a gross one. So some search engines ask for a payment in order to spider a given website, or to spider it on a given frequency in time: the idea behind it is that if you pay to be in a search engine, you must have something interesting to say; or, conversely, if your website is just rubbish, the payment will at least alleviate the harm for the search engine owners of the site appearing in the index.

Also directories have adopted this strategy: in this case, if a producer wants his/her website to be considered in a given period, s/he has to pay, without being assured that the website will be listed in the directory. This, for instance, is the policy applied by Yahoo! to commercial websites; once added, they have to pay a yearly fee to remain in the directory. Again, this is a strategy to pre-check (indirectly) the quality of a website through the commitment of its publisher. Needless to say, it is also a strategy to fund search engines.

5.3.3.2 Pragmatics in indexing

While every ranking algorithm has to take into account computational linguistic rules – to match keywords, and to assess their relative relevance in a given corpus, it can also embed pragmatic rules, to ensure a higher level of relevance. The most used pragmatic strategy here is that adopted by Google: the so called 'link popularity'. This is how it is explained by Google itself:

> PageRank [the ranking algorithm used by Google] relies on the uniquely democratic nature of the web by using its vast link structure as an indicator of an individual page's value. In essence, Google interprets a link from page A to page B as a vote, by page A, for page B. But, Google looks at more than the sheer volume of votes, or links a page receives; it also analyzes the page that casts the vote. Votes cast by pages that are themselves 'important' weigh more heavily and help to make other pages 'important.'
>
> Important, high-quality sites receive a higher PageRank, which Google remembers each time it conducts a search. Of course, important pages mean nothing to you if they don't match your query. So, Google combines PageRank with sophisticated text-matching techniques to find pages that are both important and relevant to your search. Google goes far beyond the number of times a term appears on a page and examines all aspects of the

page's content (and the content of the pages linking to it) to determine if it's a good match for your query.

(www.google.com/technology)

Actually, link popularity allows the re-interpretation of the apparently flat link structure of the WWW rather as a hierarchical one. It has introduced an automatic strategy to reconstruct a hierarchy of sources. In this scenario, the web is considered as an ecological system itself, and not as being just a casual collection of pages.

It has to be stressed that link popularity is a double indicator: it indicates explicitly a judgement of interest – usually a positive one (like a 'vote') – carried out by the person who links a website to another website; but it indicates also, inferentially, paths of actual usages: the more backlinks a website has, the more visits it is likely to receive. The ranking algorithm can also use the active part of an external backlink to assess the content of a given page. Here an interesting phenomenon occurs: while in a single page it is possible to lie by spamming search engines in many ways without sidetracking a human reader, it is much less likely that external links lie on the content of the target linked page. If they did, they would sidetrack both a search engine and a human reader. Moreover, in order to decide whether or not to select a link, one's judgement lies mainly with the content of the link itself; hence, when adding a link, publishers are likely to word it in a suitable format, to enable sound choices by readers.

If link popularity infers usages, click popularity – another strategy implemented by search engines – measures them. Click popularity has been used to correct the result of the ranking algorithm through the feedback given (involuntarily) by search engine users. Let us pretend that all the users entering the keywords ['Cristoforo Colombo'] do not click on the third result offered by a search engine: it can measure their clicks – and the time they spend on a given website before coming back to the results page of the search engine – and use them to correct/integrate this feedback to better its ranking algorithm.

Another use of click popularity is made by search engines that offer a pay per ranking service. If a given item is not clicked by users, search engines can discard it, even though the link has made a good cash bid. This strategy is, for instance, implemented by the AdWords service by Google (www.adwords.google.com). Items that are not selected on a given frequency by users are excluded automatically by the service. This approach matches quite well the interests of a search engine – if people do not click on items, the search engine does not get paid. It also matches the interests of its users: if they do not click, it means that an item is not relevant for them; hence by removing it the search engine ensures a better service to its users.

Another extrinsic element that can be embedded into the ranking algorithm is time/currency: resources that are more frequently/recently modified can be considered of higher quality than those published or updated earlier. Money is used also as a pragmatic indicator by ranking algorithms. A website's publisher can bid on given keywords, so that the web page s/he submitted has a good position when those keywords are submitted to the search engine (e.g. www.overture.com). In this case, the rank is just based on the amount of the bid: the more you bid, the higher you go in the rankings. In the case of identical bids, the search engine could award the better position to the web page that was submitted earliest (which, in the case of inflation and international exchange rate fluctuations, invariably means, again, that it paid more). As already mentioned earlier, money is not a direct and deeply relevant way of assessing website quality, nor is the relevance of a given web page for certain keywords; but money can offer a reasonable approximation of quality, at least in business areas, while, at the same time, offering an interesting business model to the search engines themselves. In addition, it can be complemented by other strategies, like click popularity and/or human review.

There is a common agreement in judging a search engine that if it offers paid links, this is to be declared to the users. If they offer non-paid results – so-called 'organic' results – mixed with paid ones, they must be distinguishable. For economic reasons, some operators do not show the amount of single bids. Integrating bids into a search engine algorithm has an intrinsic limit: only the best bidders can take advantage of it: if 100,000 people bid on the same keywords, only items which end up being in the first page are usually selected, while for all the others bidding becomes simply useless. As a result, the struggle to get the first positions is quite fierce, and items in top positions are frequently exported through syndication agreements.

Alexa, presented in section 5.2.1, provides a service similar to that offered by a search engine: provided the user knows at least a relevant resource, it suggests other similar ones, based on the pragmatic indicator of actual web navigations. Alexa offers, in fact, a service that is in between the ranking algorithm layer – it ranks websites according to their being visited by sub-groups in the same community – and the presentation layer: it can be implemented in the browser through a link or through a bar, and takes into account the website one is actually accessing.

5.3.3.3 Pragmatics in responding

When answering a user's question, a search engine can take into account contextual items, hence customizing results according to explicit and/or implicit indications given by the user. In particular, implicit information can be inferred about the user's language and nation, so that the search engine offers a specific interface. Search engines that also index news items consider the moment in which they are accessed, selecting only the more recent leads. Previous customizing choices done by the users can be taken into account by a search engine, hence 'packing' results according to its users' requests. While answers based on geographic information are usually explicitly elicited by users, through their entering a reference in space when doing a search, or through a customization choice, mobile technologies are opening huge possibilities to fully and transparently integrate user's spatial coordinates into the elements a search engine considers when compiling its answers.

In conclusion, then, we can see that search engines are not just a matter of comfortably facilitating users' communication with and through the internet. They are also electronic devices that overwhelmingly serve the interests of business and commerce. One of the chief ways in which they do this is by electronically 'conceptualizing' users, evaluating patterns of internet use and registering traces of users' behaviour. As such, search engines are like so many other so-called 'consumer benefits', such as the supermarket loyalty card. Rather than giving customers points that can be redeemed for discounts at a store, loyalty cards are primarily involved in recording consumption patterns, with each use of such a card helping to record the EPOS (Electronic Point of Sale) details that inform the strategies of store chain managers. This kind of understanding of internet audiences – electronically 'reading off' from their 'behaviour' – is, in its way, crude. However, it differs little from many other means by which businesses understand their audiences. What is absent from such accounts are the predilections and ideological baggage that all groups of users carry. The audience can thus be seen as a commodity rather than as a community with a number of complexly related imperatives. The next chapter will be devoted to exploring this second sense in which internet users can be conceptualized.

6

INTERNET

Communities and practices

Very simple and naive questions such as 'where is the internet now?' or 'what is the current state of the internet?' cannot – of course – get any complete answer, any more than questions such as 'what is happening now in the world?'. Nonetheless – as it happens in the real world, for instance with press agencies – it is possible to study events and trends in special areas (for an aggregator of field research on the internet, see www.clickz.com/stats). Selecting particularly relevant areas of the internet, and approaching them from the communicative point of view is the goal of this chapter. As we have already discussed, human communication is an ecological system, where the impact of new technologies requires a reorganization of the system itself. In this chapter, as part of a wider consideration of the users of the internet, we focus on how the mass media as a whole are changed by the internet (6.1). When such changes occur, it is invariably the case that they are changes closely bound up with media use and the social organization that is associated with such use. In fact, as mass media were at the same time an effect and a cause of a certain kind of social organization, also electronic media and the internet give birth to (and are promoted by) new social organizations: so-called virtual communities. The nature of these will be explored in their inner nature (6.2) and in a paradigmatic instance: that of video and online games (section 6.2.7).

Communication technologies also shape, together with communities, every aspect of human life. In this chapter, three relevant fields are briefly outlined: first of all how the internet impacts onto social and political communities and organizations, giving birth to the so-called eGovernment (6.3); second, the very place where a society organizes and hands over its knowledge – as well as learning and scientific communities – is deeply affected by the internet: eLearning (6.4); third, all economic activities, be they concerned with the production and exchange of physical goods or of services, make use of the internet and are changed by it (6.5).

6.1 MASS MEDIA IN THE TIME OF THE INTERNET

In this section we will try to briefly describe the reconfiguration the world of mass media has been exposed to thanks to the worldwide success of the internet; journalism, radio and television cannot be the same after the diffusion of the internet, since they have been obliged to confront this new information technology.

Generally speaking, the emergence and the growing diffusion of the internet constitute a situation of convergence with the already existing mass communication technologies, as we pointed out in Chapter 1. This convergence seems to go in both directions: on one hand, the internet is being incorporated into other mass media, in particular acting as a new and very important information source for them; on the other hand, the internet tends to include the existing media as an extra channel for the information they broadcast. We will analyse in more detail the way the internet is used as an information source by mass-media professionals in section 6.1.1 and the way it includes the other mass media as a broadcasting channel in section 6.1.2.

6.1.1 The internet as an information source

As already observed in section 5.2.3, the internet has reconfigured the issue of sources hierarchy. Since everything can be accessed by means of the same software (the browser), in a seemingly flat and indistinct network, it is not easy to distinguish the high-quality and trustworthy websites from the others. The issue of the credibility of web information sources is one of the main concerns when dealing with the relationship between the internet and the other mass media. A survey conducted in 1999 in North America about print media in cyberspace – which became an annual survey involving broadcast media, as well – pointed out that 'credibility of information has emerged as a significant issue' and that 'journalists find Web sites to be sorely lacking in credibility' (Ross and Middleberg 2000: 4). Only trade association websites were seen as more credible than not credible, while the least credible internet sources were message boards and chat groups. Nonetheless, the same survey revealed that most journalists (in particular, magazine reporters) used web forums and Usenet newsgroup messages as sources for their articles, especially if the information could be confirmed elsewhere. The same finding emerged in the 2001 and 2002 surveys, which confirmed that there was enormous dissatisfaction among journalists with the quality, and even the veracity, of information offered to them by corporations, but their dissatisfaction had not yet been converted into action (see Middleberg and Ross 2002). This outward contradiction shows that, 'despite reservations, the Internet is too good a tool to be ignored by the journalists' and that 'the Internet has become woven into the fabric of modern journalism' (Middleberg 2001: 29–30).

This claim is confirmed by other findings of the same surveys: in 1998 48 per cent of print journalists went online at least once a day, in 1999 this figure went up to nearly 75 per cent; in the same year broadcast journalists used online resources even more frequently than print ones (Ross and Middleberg 1999). In 1999 only 1 per cent of sample respondents said they never went online, while the year before there were about 5 per cent; print journalists use the internet mostly to search articles and to gather reference materials, but the reading of online publications and the search for online images is growing as well (Ross and Middleberg 2000). In 2001, for the first time e-mail turned out to be the preferred method used by journalists when working with new or unknown sources; again, in 2001, 'also for the first time, journalists covering breaking stories say they are more likely to turn first to a corporate Web site than to a live source at the company or in the community' (Middleberg and Ross 2002: 4).

Going back to the issue of the credibility of online sources, a few words need to be said about the theory of *agenda setting*. In its simplest formulation, the theory, framed in 1972 by Max McCombs and Donald Shaw (McCombs and Shaw 1972; Shaw 1979), states that the issues and the events mass media assign more salience to are taken up by the public. The basic concept is that of *salience*, which indicates the degree of significance of an issue in the agenda according to the perception of the public, of the mass media or of the politicians. The main challenge in the agenda-setting process is to understand why the salience of a topic changes in the different agenda (Dearing and Rogers 1996; González Gaitano 1999).

Acknowledging what Bernard Cohen argued about the press, we could assert that the basic idea of the theory is that mass media usually do not succeed in telling people what to think, but they are extraordinarily able to tell them what to think about (see Cohen 1965: 13). In other words, mass media provide a selection of the issues and of the events to be presented to the public, thus determining what the public talks about and the comparative salience of the issues. This point is crucial and could be one of the reasons for the (partial) failure of the personal-ization of online information services: what online information services seem not to have taken into account is exactly the importance of the agenda-setting function of the mass media; somehow, it is as if the general public did not ask the mass media: 'tell me what is happening in the world', but: 'tell me what is important for me to know in order to be accepted in the society I'm living in'. Roughly speaking, it is as if members of the general public were not interested in the possibility of choosing the information to receive, but in receiving the information that is salient and relevant for social life. Of course, the issue of the credibility of the information sources here again plays an essential role.

6.1.2 Mass media on the internet

Still in 1999 Ross and Middleberg found that broadcast

> stations have been slow to establish Web sites, and to showcase news over promotional material. Of the Web sites affiliated with local broadcast tele-vision stations, only a small fraction take full advantage of the capabilities of the Internet by offering 'real news'.
>
> (Ross and Middleberg 1999: 3)

Only three years later the situation looked very different, and the integration of online and offline information was accelerating: newsroom operations began to be shared between online reporters/editors and offline print/broadcast staffs (more in magazines than in newspapers and broadcasters), and for the first time the number of print news organizations that routinely allowed their websites to scoop their print publications equalled the number of those that did not allow scooping at all; Middleberg and Ross could conclude that 'Web readership now often rivals or surpasses print readership. The Web is not an incremental add-on to readership, viewership or profitability. Increasingly, it is the soul of a publication' (Middleberg and Ross 2002: 4). Moreover, original content on websites increased as well, in particular for newspapers, thus showing that more journalism jobs were becoming online only.

It is interesting to see in the last part of this section what print and broadcast mass media do with their websites: the commonalities and the differences between offline publications and the corresponding websites, the additional services offered by online publications, the business model they adopt, and so on. Recent research conducted by the European

Journalism Observatory (EJO – www.ejo.ch) about information on the internet showed that the current trend of information websites, both in Europe and in the US, is to adopt a blended model, where some contents need to be paid, while others are free. The typical model can be described as follows: the website of a newspaper presents a selection of free news and funds this through advertising; on the same website readers can then download and read online the edition of the day of the newspaper, access the newspaper's archive and a series of services, which may be either directly linked to the newspaper's core business or not: these services are usually available for a fee. This model has been adopted, though with some differences, by most European newspapers and magazines, such as the Spanish *El Mundo* (www.elmundo.es), the French *Le Monde* (www.lemonde.fr), the German *Der Spiegel* (www.spiegel.de) and the Italian *Il Corriere della Sera* (www.corriere.it). Important exceptions to the blended model are the *Wall Street Journal* (www.wsj.com), which is the initiator of the model of all information for a fee, the *New York Times* (www.nytimes.com) and the news section of the BBC website (www.news.bbc.co.uk), which, in contrast, provides all information for free (for a more detailed presentation of the major newspapers and magazines on the internet, see Corti 2004). Generally speaking, it must be noted that because of the value of the information it is easier to demand a fee for financial websites than for general information websites; however, the general trend for free online information towards a blended model is confirmed by the fact that the market of online paid content is continuously growing: according to research conducted by the Online Publishers Association (OPA – www.online-publishers.org), in 2003 US consumers spent 18.8 per cent more on paid content than in 2002, and in 2002 even 95 per cent more than in 2001 (OPA 2004).

What are the main advantages information websites offer when compared to other mass media? We can single out five areas where online information presents a clear added value:

1   Multimedia: online information sources can offer information coded through different media: texts, audio, pictures, photos, animations, movies; they can, for instance, integrate radio programmes with images and movies, and TV programmes with written texts.
2   Interaction: information websites can offer a higher level of interactivity than any other mass medium, allowing users to interact both with the website's system and with other people through the website.
3   Persistence: online information can be easily archived, re-used and left continuously accessible to readers.

4 In-depth studies: the ease of online publishing makes it possible also to provide in-depth analyses and studies of given information, and to make them always available to readers.

5 Immediacy: online information can be easily updated at any time and can be used just-in-time.

Let us now describe in more detail what are the typical contents offered by newspapers and magazines websites:

*   Of course, they offer information articles, which can be the same as the articles of the paper editions, as is the case of the *Financial Times* (www.ft.com), but usually they are different; the difference may vary depending on whether the editorial staff of the website is the same as that of the offline version, or is partially or completely different.

*   Information websites always offer updates in real time on the latest news; this is surely one of the main added values of online information services, when compared to print ones.

*   Newspapers and magazines websites very often provide the possibility of accessing the archive of the old articles published in the paper version; this service usually requires the registration and the payment of a fee. Moreover, archives are usually made searchable by means of internal search engines.

*   Information websites furnish their services with multimedia contents, such as photographs, videos, animations, audios, and so on; this is another important difference with offline editions.

*   Very often websites provide added value services such as yellow pages, job offers, maps, online games, real estate advertisements, newsletters, and so on. The role of games and diversions for information websites must be highlighted here: very important newspapers, such as *The Times* (www.timesonline.co.uk) and the *New York Times*, provide the possibility of subscribing only to their online crosswords, a 'must' their readers evidently cannot give up; furthermore, crosswords have been specifically the first service for which the online version of *The Times* required the payment of a fee (Corti 2004).

*   Information websites usually also provide interactive features, ranging from online surveys and polls, to thematic forums moderated by their most famous journalists, to live events, such as video chat conversations with well-known political, TV, cinema or sport personalities.

One major feature of communication that the internet has brought to the fore in its impact on existing media is the idea of 'communities' of users. One of the examples earlier, that of crossword enthusiasts, demonstrates that supplementary internet services have stressed some of the predilections of media users. While it may have been relatively difficult to establish that the crossword was an integral part of newspapers' attraction for their readers, the internet serves to identify this need more clearly. Indeed, it even identifies communities of crossword enthusiasts.

6.2 VIRTUAL COMMUNITIES

It is not easy to define what a community is; though in everyday life the concept of 'community' is widespread, and probably nobody would have any difficulty to list intuitively to which communities s/he belongs. Nevertheless, the concept is very problematic in scientific analyses, partly because of its strongly interdisciplinary nature. Generally speaking, a community can be intended as a group of persons who share something more or less decisive for their life, and who are tied by more or less strong relationships. It is worth noticing here that the term 'community' seems to have only favourable connotations: as observed in 1887 by Ferdinand Tönnies, the German sociologist who first brought the term 'community' into the scientific vocabulary of the social sciences, 'a young man is warned about mixing with bad society: but "bad community" makes no sense in our language' (Tönnies 2001: 18; see also Williams 1983b).

6.2.1 Between virtuality and reality: paradigmatic and syntagmatic communities

Two main ways of considering communities can be singled out:

1   communities as a set of people who have something in common;
2   communities as a group of people who interact.

In the first sense, we speak, for instance, of the community of the Italians, of the community of English-speaking people, of the community of paediatricians, and so on. The members of such communities usually do not know each other, they do not communicate with *all* the others, but they have the perception of belonging to the community, they are aware of being part of it. According to anthropologist Anthony Cohen, such communities are symbolic constructions: rather than being structures, they are entities of meaning, founded on a shared conglomeration of normative codes and values that provide community members with a sense of identity (see Cohen 1985).

In a similar way, Benedict Anderson defines modern nations as 'imagined communities':

> In an anthropological spirit, I propose the following definition of the nation: it is an imagined political community – and imagined as both inherently limited and sovereign. It is *imagined* because the members of even the smallest nation will never know most of their fellow-members, meet them, or even hear of them, yet in the minds of each lives the image of their communion. [. . .] In fact, all communities larger than primordial villages or face-to-face contact (and perhaps even these) are imagined. Communities are to be distinguished, not by their falsity/genuineness, but by the style in which they are imagined.
>
> (1991: 5–6)

These kinds of communities can be regarded as symbolic, imagined, or, in a broad sense, virtual.

The distinction we have sketched above is very well illustrated by an example provided by Aristotle (384–22 BCE). In his *Politics* (3.1.12), the Greek philosopher tells that, when Babylon was captured by an invading army of Persians, in certain parts of the city the capture itself had not been noticed for three days. This is the reason why Aristotle considers Babylon not a *polis*, but an *ethnos*. In fact, according to Aristotle, what distinguishes the *polis*, i.e. the perfect form of community (see *Politics* 1.1.1), from the *ethnos* is the presence of interactions and communications among the citizens: in a *polis* citizens speak to each other, they interact and communicate, while in an *ethnos* they just have in common the same walls. Thus, the *ethnos* can be considered as an imagined community, since its members do not share a history of facts, events, texts and interactions.

Borrowing the linguistic terminology of the structuralist tradition, we can name the two different typologies of communities: 'paradigmatic' and 'syntagmatic' communities. The former are characterized by sharing or similarity: members of paradigmatic communities are usually similar in some way, they share similar interests or similar features. The syntagmatic communities, on the contrary, are characterized by differences of function that facilitate combination: the interactions among the members are built up through the combination of different elements that carry out complementary, but different functions.

6.2.2 Communities and communication

Syntagmatic communities rely mainly on communication exchanges. Indeed, the concept of 'community' is strictly related to that of 'communication', as is shown by the common root of the words. Community and communication entail each other, being each a necessary condition for the existence of the other. On the one hand, communities are built and maintained through communicative processes, which can take place both within a community and towards the outside. In the former case, communication is necessary to increase the common ground among community members; in the latter, communicative processes have the twofold aim of delineating the boundaries of the community and of guaranteeing the communication between the community and the outside world. On the other hand, even a minimal form of community must exist in order to make any communicative event possible; every communicative act presupposes that among the interlocutors a more or less extended common ground exists, where the communication could root and flower, like a seed in rich soil. Communication processes and communities are now undergoing a critical phase, due to the exploitation of new powerful communication technologies, such as CMC, and to the progressive changing of traditional forms of communities, which were characterized by a strong cultural homogeneity and by certain slowness in changes.

6.2.3 Computer mediated communication and virtual communities

New communication technologies have always given rise to the emergence of new forms of communities: 'virtual communities' are the new kind of communities that emerged thanks to CMC. As with the concept of 'community', it is very difficult to give a precise definition of what a virtual community is. Clear evidence of this difficulty is the fact that for a couple of years many web services that host virtual communities have been calling them 'groups' rather than 'communities'. For instance, in June 2002 MSN announced to all its users the change of the name from communities to groups; the decision was explained by saying that 'groups' is rapidly becoming the most common term for this kind of service, and that 'groups' is clearer, more precise, and even easier to type in. Even so, we can supply a provisional definition of a virtual community as *a group of people to whom interactions and communications via computer play an important role in creating and maintaining significant social relations.*

Two different situations that represent the relationship between social groups and CMC can be singled out: on one hand, there are groups that have formed thanks to CMC, and on the other, there are groups that already existed in the real world and employ CMC as a further means for communication. In the former case, through the computer, new social relations are created among people who had no previous mutual relationships; in the latter, already constituted groups, organizations, associations and communities use electronic technologies and virtual environments to foster and increase their communication processes. Ulrike Lechner and Beat Schmid have identified two processes that correspond to the two possible relations between media and communities: *facilitation* and *constitution*:

> Media constitute communities by facilitating communication among community. We distinguish two cases: 1) a community may design a medium to employ it for communication. The community may decide on the organization it implements on the medium; 2) a community may be constituted by employing the same medium. The need for coordination in employing the same medium may let a common logical space and an organization emerge.
>
> (Lechner and Schmid 2000)

The difference between the two situations is essential, since it reaches to the very root of communities, namely the level of the shared experience of their members. In the case of online-constituted communities the initial common ground is nearly absent. Since this kind of community usually emerges around a common interest, often the field of the world that is initially shared is reduced to nothing but the object of interest and the employed technology. The expression 'virtual communities' in its original sense referred to this kind of community.

If we regard the community as a set of people who use a medium, another concept enters the fray: *appropriation*. By appropriation we mean the process through which the users of a system appropriate the system structures, employing them in unforeseen ways in order to reach their goals, to carry out their tasks, and to create new common meanings; a well-known and emblematic example of this process of appropriation is the use of *emoticons*. Such a process is of the greatest importance for the emerging of well-delineated social structures however localized and small: 'Social organization emerges in a dynamic process of appropriation in which participants invoke structures to create meanings in ways that researchers or system designers may not foresee. Those innovative uses may, in turn, impact the structures' (Baym 1998: 51).

Thus, the process of appropriation contributes a great deal to make a well-defined community out of a group of people who use the same technology. As we have seen, CMC and virtual communities are strictly connected, interdependent on each other. One of the earliest and most known definitions of virtual communities, given by Howard Rheingold (2000: xx), stressed this aspect: 'Virtual communities are social aggregations that emerge from the Net when enough people carry on those public discussions long enough, with sufficient human feeling, to form webs of personal relationships in cyberspace.'

Nancy Baym emphasizes the importance of communicative interactions for the emerging of virtual communities as well; she defines them as 'new social realms emerging through this on-line interaction, capturing a sense of interpersonal connection as well as internal organization' (Baym 1998: 35). Jan Fernback and Brad Thompson (1995) stress also the spatial aspect of virtual communities: 'We assert our own definition of on-line community: social relationships forged in cyberspace through repeated contact within a specified boundary or place (e.g., a conference or chat line) that is symbolically delineated by topic of interest.'

To sum up the issue, the main features of virtual communities can be singled out. They require:

- a shared communication environment;
- interpersonal relationships that emerge and are maintained by means of online interaction;
- a sense of belonging to the group;
- an internal structure of the group;
- a symbolic common space represented by shared norms, values and interests.

6.2.4 Critical issues in virtual communities

In this section, three basic concepts will be introduced, which are the three constituent factors of communities: 1) belonging; 2) identity; 3) interest (Tardini and Cantoni 2005).

1   *Belonging* is a key concept in communities: first of all, a community is belonged to. Belonging to a community may be more or less intense, involving more or less awareness, be more or less voluntary; one community may request a formal subscription, whereas, in other communities belonging may depend only on the feeling of their members. For instance, belonging to a family (the basic form of community) involves

awareness but is not voluntary; belonging to the European Community may not often be apparent to its citizens; and so on. In this perspective, the Social Network Analysis approach studies the structure of social networks through an analysis of the social relationships and of the communication flows among their members. One of the units of analysis of this approach is the strength of ties among individuals, which are usually divided into *strong* and *weak* ties:

> [W]eak ties are generally infrequently maintained, nonintimate connections – for example, between co-workers who share no joint tasks or friendship relations. Strong ties include combinations of intimacy, self-disclosure, provision of reciprocal services, frequent contact, and kinship, as between close friends and colleagues.
>
> (Garton *et al.* 1999: 79)

According to these studies, electronic communities would rely mainly on weak ties, i.e. on not very frequent contacts, on the absence of emotional proximity, and on the lack of a tradition of mutual help. Thus, the feeling of belonging to the community would be weak as well; furthermore, the lack of proximity, of physical copresence and of the sharing of the same territory does not foster this feeling of belonging to the community. In fact, the issue of belonging is critical with regard to virtual communities:

> [W]hat is the nature of individual members' commitments to them? In the physical world, community members must live together. When community membership is in no small way a simple matter of subscribing or unsubscribing to a bulletin board or electronic newsgroups, is the nature of interaction different simply because one may disengage with little or no consequence?
>
> (Jones 1995: 11)

Of course, there are examples of online communities where the members' engagement reached very deep and intimate levels; however, the issue of belonging to online communities remains critical.

2   In virtual environments, *identity* assumes an enormous importance:

> Identity plays a key role in virtual communities. In communication, which is the primary activity, knowing the identity of those with whom you communicate is essential for understanding and evaluating an interaction. Yet in the disembodied world of the virtual community, identity is also ambiguous.

Many of the basic cues about personality and social role we are accustomed to in the physical world are absent.

(Donath 1999: 29; see also Burnett
and Marshall 2003: 61–80)

In fact, in the virtual world everybody can assume the identity s/he wants, can change and disguise his/her own, can assume more identities at once, and so on. This can have far-reaching consequences, as shown by Peter Steiner's well-known cartoon (Figure 6.1).

Online identities ultimately have a semiotic/linguistic nature, being the outcome of language; identities that are built in cyberspace coincide with the assertions that a user makes about him/herself:

"On the Internet, nobody knows you're a dog."

Figure 6.1 'On the Internet, nobody knows you're a dog'
Source: *The New Yorker*, 5 July 1993, p. 61.

> We reduce and encode our identities as words on a screen, decode and
> unpack the identities of others. The way we use these words, the stories
> (true or false) we tell about ourselves (or about the identity we want people
> to believe us to be) is what determines our identities in cyberspace.
>
> (Rheingold 1993: 61)

In virtual environments even the name, which is one of the main identification marks in the real world, leaves space for fictions and deceptions:
in many environments users must choose a nickname or an avatar that
will appear for them in online interactions. Sherry Turkle presents some
consequences of this phenomenon:

> When people can play at having different genders and different lives, it isn't
> surprising that for some this play has become as real as what we conven-
> tionally think of as their lives, although for them this is no longer a valid
> distinction. [. . .] The anonymity of most MUDs (you are known only by the
> name you give your characters) provides ample room for individuals to
> express unexplored parts of themselves. [. . .] MUDs imply difference, multi-
> plicity, heterogeneity, and fragmentation. Such an experience of identity
> contradicts the Latin root of the word, *idem*, meaning 'the same'. But this
> contradiction increasingly defines the conditions of our lives beyond the
> virtual world.
>
> (Turkle 1995: 14, 185)

3   Most virtual communities arise originally as discussions about a
topic of *interest*, and get to gather persons or groups who have common
ideas and interests. The sharing of a common interest is one of the
main features of those communities that cannot rely on geographical
proximity:

> But if 'communities' are no longer defined by their geographic boundaries,
> how, then, do we define them? [. . .] Shared interests and self-identification
> of belonging to a group are viable alternatives. [. . .] 'Communities of inter-
> est' [are] bound together by choice rather than geography.
>
> (Clodius 1997)

This feature of online communities has been seen by some authors to
have its negative aspects: since virtual communities emerge from the
free and spontaneous aggregation of persons with unanimous views, they
risk being very homogeneous and self-referential, they have few internal
dynamics, and tend to behave like closed groups, where differences are
excluded, and only similarities are dealt with. In this perspective, some

authors talked of 'neo-tribalism', and compared gatherings around a topic of interest, typical of virtual communities, to tribal gatherings around a totem (see Maffesoli 1995; Maldonado 1997). However, the notion of interest remains pivotal with regard to online communities: in fact, since they do not have any physical boundaries that delimit them, their boundaries are only symbolic, and are represented precisely by the topics of interest people discuss and by any keywords that may be supplied in order to describe the community. In the next section, starting from the notion of interest, a semiotic approach to virtual communities will be sketched.

6.2.5 A semiotic approach to virtual communities

According to semiotician Yuri Lotman, 'every culture begins by dividing the world into "its own" internal space and "their" external space'; this is the main function of the boundary, which he defines as 'the outer limit of a first-person form' (Lotman 2001: 131). Analogously, virtual communities delimit their semiotic space through the topics of interest and the keywords, which have the function of outlining the relevant field of communication of the community, i.e. of establishing the topics members are allowed to discuss.

In this perspective, topics of interest and keywords can be seen as two basic elements that delineate what Lotman called the *semiosphere* of a culture (or, in our case, of a community). Lotman coined the term by analogy with the concept of 'biosphere', which was coined in its turn in the early twentieth century by Russian scientist Vladimir Vernadsky:

> By analogy with the biosphere (Vernadsky's concept) we could talk of a semi-osphere, which we shall define as the semiotic space necessary for the existence and functioning of languages. [. . .] Outside the semiosphere there can be neither communication, nor language. [. . .] The semiosphere is the result and the condition for the development of culture; we justify our term by analogy with the biosphere, as Vernadsky defined it, namely the totality and the organic whole of living matter and also the condition for the continuation of life.
>
> (Lotman 2001: 123–5)

We can see this principle in action regularly on the internet. For instance, Classic Movies (groups.msn.com/ClassicMovies) is an online community that gathers together movie fans from all over the world. This is the description of the community given by the founder:

> We're a community that celebrates Hollywood from the early days of the
> silents through the New Hollywood Era of the early 80's. Join us in 2005 as
> we focus on comedies from the silents through the 80's!
>
> Though we celebrate all old movies, we have a yearly theme: we're half-
> way through Comedy! Join us now and learn about cinematic history! When
> applying, be sure to tell a bit about yourself!

And these are the keywords provided by the founder: 'movies, classics, Clark Gable, Marilyn Monroe, silent films, westerns, classic films, classic movies'. The description, the general topic of interest, and the keywords can be considered as the elements that outline the semiosphere of the community: beyond these semiotic boundaries, no communicative event is allowed to take place inside the community.

In a certain sense, these keywords act as passwords to the community: those not interested in movies, classics, Clark Gable, and so on, are not allowed to access the community; or rather, they can physically access the community, but take no real part in it, they do not really belong to the community. In this case, the keywords act as the passwords that users must enter in order to access reserved areas of web services or limited-access websites. In virtual communities, whoever speaks of something different than the topic of interest, i.e. whoever writes 'off topic' messages, is usually 'glared' at (sometimes 'flamed') and put aside, and his/her messages do not receive any answer. In this perspective, keywords are the keys that open the doors of the community, both in a physical sense, as in the case of the passwords that allow the access to a website, and in a semiotic sense, as with the keywords that outline the semiosphere of a community and disclose the understanding of its semiotic world (see Tardini 2003).

The distinction between paradigmatic and syntagmatic communities sketched in section 6.2.1 can be applied to online communities as well. In fact, if virtual communities are to be seen as social relationships that emerge in cyberspace through online interactions, then they are to be considered syntagmatic communities. But in cyberspace we can easily come across paradigmatic communities as well. Let us present some examples.

First of all, virtual communities are made up also of people who do not really interact. This phenomenon goes under the name of *lurking*:

> *Lurkers* are people who access a chatgroup and read its messages but do
> not contribute to the discussion. The motives include newbie reluctance to
> be involved, academic curiosity (researching some aspect of Internet
> culture), or voyeurism. Some manuals refer to lurking as 'spying'.
>
> (Crystal 2001: 53)

The same holds true for discussion forums and virtual communities as well.

Furthermore, the term community occurs often in the virtual world also in another sense: it is often employed to refer to the regular visitors of a website as well as to the habitual users of a web service, i.e. to the stable community that is recognizable behind a hypertext in general. For instance, a web service such as Alexa (see section 5.2.1) relies so much on the behaviours of the community of its users, that Alexa itself refers to them as 'the collective Alexa community' and 'the community of Alexa Toolbar users' (www.pages.alexa.com/company/technology.html?p=Corp_W_t_40_L1). These kinds of online communities are paradigmatic: in this case users normally do not interact with each other, but only with the same website; moreover, they usually have no perception of being part of a community. This use of the term 'community' is comparable to the concept of imagined communities and to the Aristotelian notion of *ethnos*.

We have seen in the last chapter that internet users can be conceptualized as commodities; hence 'communities', of almost any sort, represent targetable groups for marketers.

6.2.6 Community marketing

Communities of users of a website or web service are turning out to be a very powerful tool for online marketing. Community marketing is the promotion of a brand, business, product, service, and so on, through the creation, the support and the fostering of social ties among the persons interested in the product/brand, i.e. through the creation of a community of clients. Online communities are so suitable for this kind of marketing that some companies developed dedicated community sites devoted to Customer Relationship Management (CRM), where a strong tie with their active or potential clients could be created. In such community sites, companies can interact with their clients and make their clients interact with each other (see Montagna 2004).

For instance, big motor brands, such as Harley Davidson, Porsche, Ducati and Ferrari, have created a mass myth that has also a great experiential value for people who own their products; these companies, which rely strongly on the clients' feeling of belonging to a group, invested a lot in creating online sites that act as a fast and updated point of reference for their clients; see, for instance, www.harley-davidson.com and www.owners.ferrari.com.

In other words, the effort of companies that invest in community marketing is to create a syntagmatic community out of the paradigmatic community of their clients: from the imagined community of all persons who own a Ferrari it is possible to make a syntagmatic community of Ferrari owners who interact with one another, share information, experiences, and so on. In the virtual world, even the level of the paradigmatic community is interesting, since companies can monitor the behaviour of their clients who access their websites and can easily have feedback from them by interacting via e-mail, web forms, and so on. However, creating a syntagmatic community out of all of a company's clients can improve the feeling of belonging to the group, thus making the brand more successful and the clients more faithful and attached to the brand.

A possible case for more focused targeting, and certainly a more internet-based community, is that of online gamers. Internet videogame playing communities demonstrate quite nicely some of the features of internet communities that we have tried to describe, particularly in relation to the concept of identity.

6.2.7 Online videogames

Online videogames provide a very rich ground for studies on virtual communities: communities of online players have been explored since the early studies about virtual communities, for instance in MUDs, and are nowadays among the most significant and representative online communities.

Generally speaking, a game can be defined, after Johannes Huizinga, as

> a voluntary activity or occupation executed within certain fixed limits of time and place, according to rules freely accepted but absolutely binding, having its aim in itself and accompanied by a feeling of tension, joy and the consciousness that it is 'different' from 'ordinary life'.
>
> (Huizinga 1950: 28)

Videogames are very significant forms of new media, since they 'are indivisible from the dissemination and popularisation, and even the development, of personal computing, its software and interfaces, its practices and meanings. The relationship between the emergence of home/ personal computers and videogames is tangled and complex' (Lister *et al.* 2003: 263). Videogames are 'any forms of computer-based entertainment software, either textual or image-based, using any electronic platform such as personal computers or consoles and involving one or multiple players in a physical or networked environment' (Frasca 2001).

Some of the observations made about videogame players that follow may be applicable to such players in general; however, note that in this section we will refer only to videogames that *involve multiple players in a networked environment*. After Newman (2004) and Ciofi and Graziano (2003), online videogames can be roughly divided into a few main genres: Strategy and Simulation, including Real Time Strategic (RTS) Games and 'God Games'; First Person Shooter (FPS – the genre most played in the internet); Role Playing Games (RPG); MUDs, that rely mainly on a textual interface (see 2.1.1); Massive Multiplayer Online Role Playing Games (MMORPG), which represent the last generation in computer role-playing games. Online videogames provide several directions for studies in the different fields of CMC: we mainly mention here the issues of interaction and interactivity, narrative and narrativity, space and cyberspace (see Newman 2004). Only in the last few years have computer-game studies as a whole tried to constitute themselves as an independent field of studies (see Aarseth 2001).

In relation to gaming, we will come back to one issue that is closely related to virtual communities: identity (see also section 6.2.4). According to James Paul Gee (2004), the relationship that exists between the player and the play gives rise to three different identities:

1 The *real person*, i.e. the player's real world identity, which does not vanish when playing, but, on the contrary, affects the choices and the decisions that are made during the play.
2 The *virtual character*, i.e. the identity the player assumes in the game's virtual world, which is usually represented on the internet by an avatar (see section 2.1.1).
3 The *projective identity*, an intermediate identity that is a sort of bridge between the real person and the virtual character. As a matter of fact, the real person projects his/her real world identity on the virtual one, and on the other side the virtual identity allows to emerge in the real person desires and aspirations concerning the virtual character. Eva Liestøl describes the projection of one identity on the other this way:

> When playing I am 'transformed' into the player. The task demands my attention and requires active participation. To stay in the game, reach the goal of each and every episode, get into the next, and finally win, I must do what must be done. [. . .] But as Gadamer suggests, I can also detach myself from the immediate and 'physical' behavior of the player and engage in interpretative actions. At this level, and as I reenter the fictional universe of the game, or rather reflect on the temporal and sequential trail my playing produced, I need no longer to overcome the immediate

> obstacles of my mission but to decode the enigmatic representations of
> this universe.
>
> (Liestøl 2003: 354; reference is to Gadamer 2005)

At the levels of the real person's and the virtual character's identities, two different virtual communities can be outlined:

1   The *playing community*, i.e. the community of the virtual characters, who interact in the game's world with other characters to build cities, fight with *npcs* (*non playing characters*, i.e. characters played by the system/computer), kill monsters and common enemies or kill each other, and so on; the whole community of characters that are present at a given moment in the virtual world can, of course, be divided into different groups of people who 'really' interact in specific virtual spaces.
2   The *players' community*, i.e. the community of the real persons who interact with other persons who are interested in the same game; these communities are very popular and active, and are functional to the game itself, since they can shape and modify the game's environment, by building new objects, new spaces, new game levels, which can be integrated in the game.

Talking of *Doom*, one of the most well-known online videogames, Bolter and Grusin describe the social space of computer games:

> With *Doom* you can play with one or more networked partners, with whom
> you share the work of eliminating monsters, and, if you get in the way of
> the other players' weapons, you too can be eliminated. *Doom* defines
> community as a community of killers, the high-tech version of a tribe of
> paleolithic hunters. Like MUDs and MOOs [MUD Object Oriented], *Doom*
> is socially shared in another sense. It allows experienced users to build new
> architectural 'levels', in which the game of destruction can continue. There
> is an entire community of such users on the Internet who construct and
> share the vast environment that Doom has become.
>
> (Bolter and Grusin 1999: 102–3)

Both the 'community of killers' and the community of experienced users of a game are *communities of practice*, i.e. 'groups of people who share a concern, a set of problems, or a passion about a topic, and who deepen their knowledge and expertise in this area by interacting on an ongoing basis' (Wenger *et al.* 2002: 4). Three basic aspects are characteristic of communities of practice: a mutual engagement, a joint enterprise, and a shared repertoire among their members (Wenger 1998: 73–82).

Communities of practice are always syntagmatic communities; however, playing communities can be intended as paradigmatic as well, when the whole virtual environment is taken into consideration, with all the players connected to it in a given moment. In the category of paradigmatic communities can be inserted also all gaming communities in general, i.e. those communities of people who connect to a website or web service and play a game hosted in the website, such as poker, crosswords, sudoku, and so on. This kind of community is entirely similar to the communities of the visitors of a given website.

Having considered a pursuit that, while far from frivolous, is more associated with a community of leisure, we will now turn to three more serious areas of social life. The existing common practices (and the corresponding communities) associated with these areas have been strongly challenged by new communication technologies. Thus, in the internet age, we stand on the threshold of a new era of eGovernment (6.3), eLearning (6.4) and eCommerce (6.5).

6.3 eGOVERNMENT

This section is divided as follows: first, definitions of eGovernment will be presented and discussed, underlying its importance for, and impact on, social and political life (6.3.1); then a high-level eGovernment map will be offered, depicting its many application areas (6.3.2); a third section is devoted to a specific close-up, presenting a five-layer model of eGovernment websites (6.3.3).

6.3.1 An eGovernment definition and some related issues

Many definitions have been proposed for *eGovernment*, showing at the same time the importance of this subject, its vitality and novelty, as well as the fact that no single discipline studies it; but it is rather an application domain, explored by many sciences, with different approaches, peculiar languages and traditions.

In order to approach the eGovernment definition issue, let us read the proposal by OECD, which presents a wide spectrum of viewpoints:

> There are many definitions of e-government, and the term itself is not universally used. The differences are not just semantic and may reflect priorities in government strategies. The definitions fall into three groups:

- E-government is defined as Internet (online) service delivery and other Internet-based activity such as e-consultation.
- E-government is equated to the use of ICTs in government. While the focus is generally on the delivery of services and processing, the broadest definition encompasses all aspects of government activity.
- E-government is defined as a capacity to transform public administration through the use of ICTs or indeed is used to describe a new form of government built around ICTs. This aspect is usually linked to Internet use.

Definitions and terms adopted by individual countries have shifted, as priorities change and as progress is made towards particular objectives. This is as it should be; the area is a dynamic one and policies and definitions need to remain relevant. In the context of the OECD E-Government Project, the term 'e-government' is defined as:

OECD Definition of E-Government: The use of information and communication technologies, and particularly the Internet, as a tool to achieve better government.

(OECD 2003: 23; see also Wyld 2004: 20)

Although the most visible eGovernment side is that connected to the improvement of communication between public administration and citizens (or businesses), through a reduction of distance and a wider range of services offered, the impact of ICT on governments has a much greater impact on the very nature of government (Eifert and Püschel 2004).

Every eGovernment activity, in fact, is likely to have an impact on rights, laws, privacy, participation, and so on, hence requiring a complex and holistic approach; in particular, experiments and trials can be conducted if and only if all legal issues have been solved, a case that makes this field among the most delicate ones. The strong connection between eGovernment and government goes in both directions: while eGovernment needs a re-setting of legal and structural organization to be implemented, new public management finds in eGovernment relevant opportunities to enhance public administration, meeting the requests for more effectiveness, efficiency and transparency.

Among the most crucial issues in eGovernment, those of participation, security and privacy, reliability and authority are to be mentioned here. First of all, ICTs offer opportunities for democratic participation: citizens and concerned bodies can access information, interact, even vote, through them. But this is a double-edged sword: the other side is the possibility of setting aside wide areas of the population – those who do not have access, for economic or cultural reasons, to the electronic world (see the issue of the digital divide, both within and among countries, in section 1.5.2). There is also the possibility of losing the link between public administration – becoming just virtual – and people, who could feel the advent of the worst kind of bureaucracy, without any human understanding and flexibility whatsoever.

The issues of privacy and security are closely connected with the previous aspects: as long as machines are given personal data and the power of elaborating and exchanging them, data security becomes of the utmost importance along with personal privacy. If they do not, democratic power and rules can be in danger. If data access has to be strictly regulated according to the laws (and dedicated laws are to be elaborated and implemented), also data integrity and reliability are to be ensured. In fact, data corruption or loss can dramatically damage people, and hinder them from the exercise of their personal rights.

6.3.2 An eGovernment map

The many areas converging – and sometimes conflicting – under the eGovernment umbrella, could be summarized under four main sections (Eppler and Cantoni 2005):

- *Technology*: here the WCM approach can be very useful in understanding its many facets.
- *Budget*: eGovernment could help reduce and optimize expenses, but no doubt it adds new costs, in addition, almost always public administration has to maintain a double system (the previously used one and that allowed by ICTs and the internet).
- *Stakeholders*: eGovernment has a great impact onto the ways people do things (both in public agencies and among businesses and citizens); expectations and fears could be quite different in different communities, and require to be analysed and met/overcome.
- *Laws and regulations*: as in every field, the internet raises issues that require new legal instruments in order to be properly dealt with.

These areas can be conceived as planets orbiting the same eGovernment star, as depicted in Figure 6.2.

The four eGovernment 'planets' can help in taking into account the great complexity of eGovernment projects and processes, while, at the same time, stressing their areas of constraints; all of them can be further adapted to the three main eGovernment application areas, those of government-to-citizens (G2C), government-to-businesses (G2B) and government-to-government (G2G).

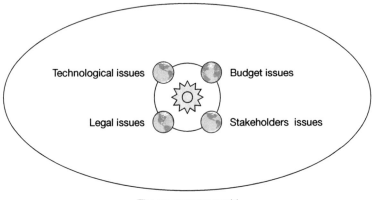

The government world

Figure 6.2 The four eGovernment planets

In addition, a given eGovernment system is not something that can stay in itself, it has to be interpreted and understood inside the eGovernment world, in an ecological perspective.

6.3.3 The case of eGovernment websites

As we have seen in previous chapters, websites play a major role in the internet. In the eGovernment field, a Web Measure Index has been proposed by the *UN Global E-government Readiness Report* (2004: 16–18): it is

> based upon a five-stage model, ascending in nature, and building upon the previous level of sophistication, of a state's online presence.
>
> For the countries which have established an online presence, the model defines stages of e-readiness according to a scale of progressively sophisticated citizen services. Countries are ranked in consonance with what they provide online.
>
> The web measure assessment model does not assess the quality of services by design. As such, any discretionary ratings are eliminated from the quantitative web measure and the e-government readiness indices minimizing the bias inherent in combining qualitative assessments with quantitative measures.
>
> (UNDESA 2004: 16)

The five stages are emerging presence, enhanced presence, interactive presence, transactional presence and networked presence. Let us analyse them in more detail:

1 *Emerging presence*: at this level the information offered online is limited, basic and mostly static; governments are typically present through an official website, a national portal or an official homepage, with some archived information, documents and links to ministries and departments, regional or local governments and branches, etc.

2 *Enhanced presence*: at this level, some enhanced capabilities are offered, such as search functionalities, help features and site maps, but information still remains one-way.

3 *Interactive presence*: at the third level 'the online services of the government enter the interactive mode with services to enhance convenience of the consumer such as downloadable forms for tax payment, application for license renewal' (UNDESA 2004: 17). These services typically include the possibility of downloading forms, audios and videos, the possibility of contacting government officials via e-mail, fax, telephone and post, and so on. Usually, the website is updated regularly.

4 *Transactional presence*: this stage 'allows two-way interactions between the citizen and his/her government' (UNDESA 2004: 17), such as paying taxes, applying for ID cards, certificates, permits, and other similar interactions; furthermore, citizens are able to pay for relevant public services or expenses such as fines for motor vehicle violations, taxes and fees for postal services, through their credit, bank or debit cards.

5 *Networked presence*: the highest stage is characterized by a close integration of G2G, G2B and G2C (and their reverse) interactions:

> The government is willing and able to involve the society in a two-way dialogue. Through employing the use of web comment forms, and innovative online consultation mechanisms, the government actively solicits the views of people acting in their capacities as consumers of public services and as citizens. Implicit in this stage of the model is the integration of consultation and collective decision making.
>
> (UNDESA 2003: 14)

The increased movement towards eGovernment is inevitable. Like telephone call centres that now exist for the major businesses, from the point of view of the business or provider, it is cheaper and more efficient than previous, personnel-heavy modes of interaction. As the model suggests, however, there are many threats to be circumvented (in addition to advantages to be welcomed). Indeed, it might be argued that eGovernment could *prevent* the maintenance of a common good and create an anti-bureaucracy community.

The internet's role in social life, therefore, is not straightforward. It involves threats as well as opportunities if insufficient thought is given to internet applications. Let us now consider other areas of social life. As with eGovernment, the internet deeply changes the fields of education and training, opening up new opportunities, as well as creating new challenges.

6.4 eLEARNING

If we go back to the three levels proposed by the OECD definition of eGovernment, we can rephrase them to outline eLearning, as being:

- internet (online) education and training;
- the use of ICTs in education and training;
- the capacity to transform education and training through the use of ICTs.

In fact, the definition of eLearning offered in EU documents integrates all the above-mentioned layers: 'the use of new multimedia technologies and the Internet to improve the quality of learning by facilitating access to resources and services as well as remote exchanges and collaboration' (CEC 2001: 2); while in the ASTD Learning Circuits, it is defined as: 'Term covering a wide set of applications and processes, such as Web-based learning, computer-based learning, virtual classrooms, and digital collaboration. It includes the delivery of content via Internet, intranet/extranet (LAN [Local Area Network]/WAN [Wide Area Network]), audio- and videotape, satellite broadcast, interactive TV, CD-ROM, and more' (www.learningcircuits.org/glossary).

In general, when digital information and communication tools are integrated into the learning/teaching experience, we enter in the eLearning field (Rossett 2002). However, in education and training, the *continuum* between the extreme points – from not using digital media at all until using them extensively – can be segmented into quite different scenarios. Let us study them adopting two different points of view: the first one (6.4.1) takes into account the recent history of eLearning, paying specific attention to the different names used to indicate it, while the second one (6.4.2) proposes some relevant parameters useful to draw a map of the eLearning territory. A third section (6.4.3) will be devoted to briefly presenting the case of eLearning impact on higher education.

6.4.1 eLearning from different perspectives

Many terms have been used to indicate the integration of digital media in teaching/learning processes: their presentation can help us better understand different opportunities, scenarios of use, and approaches that have emerged in recent years (Adelsberger *et al.* 2002).

Table 6.1 presents the most used ones (in alphabetical order).

CBT – Computer Based Training, to start with, was intended to mean every use of computers in the teaching/learning experience; for instance PLATO, a system developed in the early 1960s at the University of Illinois, whose

> basic idea was to offer a central computer with courseware and use the material from a (then very rudimentary) terminal. However, the fact that all students accessed the same computer allowed for some communication between participants, for keeping track of scores and other statistical information, including feedback on the quality of the courseware.
>
> (Maurer 2002: 2)

The terms *based* and *training* stress the role of the technology itself, and an approach indebted to behaviourism.

CAI – Computer Assisted Instruction put less emphasis on the role of technology, which assists teaching instead of being its base; the educational approach remains quite teacher/instructor centred.

Table 6.1 The most used acronyms for new media in education

Acronym	Computer/ Electronic/ Technology/ Web	Assisted/ Based/ Enhanced/ Supported	Blended/ Collaborative/ Distributed/ Language	Education/ Learning/ Teaching/ Training
CAI	Computer	Assisted		Instruction
CAL	Computer	Assisted		Learning
CALL	Computer	Assisted	Language	Learning
CBT	Computer	Based		Training
CSCL	Computer	Supported	Collaborative	Learning
eLearning	Electronic		Learning	
TBDL	Technology	Based	Distributed	Learning
TEL	Technology	Enhanced		Learning
WBT	Web	Based		Training/ Teaching
–	Technology			Educational
–			Blended	Learning

CAL – Computer Assisted Learning (with its fellow acronym CALL: Computer Assisted Language Learning) adopts the learner's point of view. In general, the use of *learning* instead of *training* (or *teaching*), and a reduced emphasis on technological tools, are found where psycho-pedagogical approaches other than behaviourism are taken (e.g. cognitivism, constructivism, humanistic and so on).

While TEL and TBDL shift their attention from computer to technology in general, the second one emphasizes distance learning, and the use of different channels.

eLearning (or e-Learning) – whose definition we already met earlier – was introduced applying the same structure as eCommerce, and seems to offer a more neutral tool to mean a wide variety of activities and approaches, hence its fortune.

Blended Learning refers to a combination of online and FTF learning.

6.4.2 Mapping eLearning: some relevant parameters (ABCST$_2$U)

In order to better understand the many activities/experiences eLearning makes possible, a set of relevant parameters is to be taken into account; they will help in mapping the eLearning space, as well as in tracing the right position of a specific experience, and in planning a new one, considering the whole eLearning picture (Botturi 2006).

Although no single set of parameters has yet emerged in the international debate (Cantoni and Rega 2004; Bates and Poole 2003), the following presents some among the most considered ones, and those specific to define eLearning when compared to other learning experiences: Assistance, Blend, Communication, Space, Time, Technology, Use of media, hence the acronym: ABCST$_2$U; actually, if listed in a different order and with small changes, the same parameters could be combined to form the acronym: THAT MUSIC: TecHnology, Assistance, Time, Media Use, Space, Integration (or blend), Communication.

Let us now present ABCST$_2$U elements in more detail:

- *Assistance*: according to this parameter, eLearning activities can be situated along a continuum, which starts from self-learning, without any kind of assistance, up to a personalized assistance. Human assistance can be offered in three different areas: technical, psycho/pedagogical and on the taught contents. The first case covers all the problems the learner can encounter when dealing with technologies. A second assistance layer deals with the learning experience itself. While almost all learners have an extensive experience in learning in FTF settings, or on the job, the vast majority do not have any experience at all in learning through a computer and a computer network. This means that they have not yet developed and tested strategies to *make the best of it*; on the contrary, they are in danger of wasting time, losing motivation or feeling lost (see ASTD and The Masie Center 2001). To cope with this situation, and to acquire the new abilities and strategies, a dedicated assistance can be of great help. Subject matter help is the third assistance layer, i.e. the possibility of interacting with a domain expert.

- *Blend*: digital media can be integrated in the teaching/learning practice and experience in many ways, to form lots of different configurations (Collis 2002; Masie 2002). While, at first, their use seemed to configure a special case in itself, in recent times online learning – i.e. eLearning where everything is mediated by digital media – is finding its place in a much more complex and rich landscape, allowing room for a continuum between online learning itself and education without any use of digital media (let us say, for example, learning how to swim in a swimming pool, or horse riding).

- *Communication*: if compared with previous distance learning, based mainly on books, readers and letters, eLearning offers many more communication opportunities, allowing distant learners to interact with teachers and within their different groups. eLearning has fostered collaborative learning, and allows for the kind of class groups that were previously completely impossible (Dillenbourg 1999). An important aspect to be considered is the distance between the expert and the learner. The latter does not learn only by what the teacher says (and can convey online through written or other media), but also by watching the teacher's behaviour: in a sense, the expert embodies the knowledge s/he teaches (Dufeu 1994; Cantoni 2003; Curran 1976). Embodiment covers aspects such as patterns of reasoning and discussing, weighting of different opportunities and hypotheses, existential coherence, and the like. Once learning is mediated (by books as well as by digital media) this kind of learning takes place, but on a smaller scale.

- *Space*: while eLearning can also occur in FTF situations (syntopic – in these cases digital media are used to enrich in presence communication), its applications are usually found in distance learning, where the act of producing the teaching message happens in a space different from its fruition (asyntopic). The internet offers the real possibility of building classes completely independent from space constraints: let us think, for example, of the possibility an international company has to organize some training activities involving all professionals across the planet.

- *Time*: time is closely connected with space, and impacts onto physical and psychological setting. eLearning activities can be synchronous – when the educational message is produced and received in the same point in time – or asynchronous, where its fruition happens later on. If asynchronous, it can be atemporal or temporal. In the first case, learners completely control the time and pace of their learning (as happens, for instance, also when reading a book), while in the second case the learning experience has to take place in a given temporal framework, although this is fairly flexible. An online module on how to fix a printer problem – which one can access when the problem occurs – offers an atemporal framework, while an online university course – which students can access and study when they want, but which starts on a given date and ends at the end of the term – offers an asynchronous but temporal eLearning experience. Both space and time (partial) independence allows for great eLearning flexibility: learners can study at very different paces, and according to many different scenarios. This kind of flexibility and accessibility, of course, must not be misunderstood as constituting a panacea for every learning problem (Cantoni and McLoughlin 2004). On the contrary, as mentioned earlier regarding blend, it means usually a greater effort on the part of the learner, who has to take more responsibility for her/his learning activities; the less external structure there is, the more internal motivation is needed.
- *Technology*: every computer and internet technology can be integrated in eLearning activities. In particular (Bates 1999): e-mail, presentational software, audio and video conferences, digital, interactive and business television, multimedia CD/DVD-ROM, software for simulations and the web. The internet, integrating all other technologies, offers a wide spectrum of educational opportunities (Mioduser *et al.* 1999, 2000); it can be used as information provider, communication facilitator, creation environment, teacher resource centre and for instruction delivery. In fact, to support eLearning experience over the net, dedicated pieces of software have been developed, called Learning Management Systems (LMS); they usually support four different areas of activity: 1) content management, 2) communication, 3) evaluation and 4) class management.
- *Use of media*: eLearning benefits from the convergence of different media through digitization: every digital format can be adopted to enrich an eLearning experience, and to meet different learning styles.

6.4.3 The case of higher education

There is a large body of literature on the use of eLearning in higher education (Reeves and Laffey 1999; Oliver and Herrington 2001; Coimbra Group 2002; van der Wende and van de Ven 2003; Lepori and Succi 2003; Lepori and Rezzonico 2003). However, we are not able to go into this literature here except to offer a brief outline of what characterizes online as opposed to offline learning. Hopefully, this will also help shed some light on the character of the internet as a whole.

Tony Bates (2001) suggests classifying the different eLearning activities in higher education, as in Figure 6.3. If we imagine a continuum between no online learning and fully online learning, it manifests itself as a simple taxonomy:

1　FTF classroom teaching: 'traditional' activities involving teacher and students in the same place (syntopic) and at the same time (synchronous);
2　technology-enhanced FTF teaching: such as classroom lectures but supported by online materials or software simulations;
3　mixed mode (reduced FTF + online) teaching: here some activities, for example questions or exercises, are completely delegated to the new technologies;
4　distance education: courses or degree programmes developed completely as 'distance'; enrolment, fee payment, lessons, communications, and examinations are managed from a distance with new technologies (Lepori *et al.* 2005).

At the same time, eLearning weakens the distinction between presence and distance education (hybridization). This phenomenon has two different dimensions: first, the distinction between presence teaching and distance learning is becoming increasingly blurred since 'hybrid' delivery

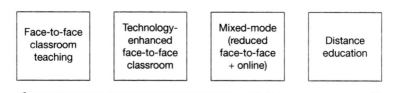

Figure 6.3 Continuum of online learning applications
Source: Bates 2001. With permission.

modes are diffusing in both domains. Second, hybridization means that the markets for distance education and for education of university students on campus are no longer clearly separate. Besides the traditional distance education universities (based on textbooks and surface mail, such as the Open University and the Fernuniversität Hagen), which have introduced ICT in their courses, we find a whole range of virtual universities offering courses or degrees to non-residential students (Guri-Rosenblit 1999). These include dual-mode universities (offering both on campus and distance degrees), mixed-mode universities (where students attend both presence and distance-learning classes), extension services, distance educational degrees presented by campus university consortia, and new virtual universities based on ICT (Guri-Rosenblit 2001). In other words, some campus-based universities are developing new educational programmes targeted to non-campus students for accessing new potentially profitable markets (especially in corporate training), finding a niche in an increasingly competitive environment, or responding to social and political pressures (Lepori and Succi 2003; Cantoni and Succi 2002).

Educational institutions as well as companies have considered eLearning due to the fact that they usually have in place the suitable technological infrastructure and competencies. They thus maximize their return on technological investments while the travelling costs a company has to pay for training its employees are significantly reduced.

The wide diffusion of eLearning programmes has, however, raised questions of quality: is the eLearning experience a poorer learning experience if compared with others? While it is impossible to compare learning and eLearning in themselves, since their success depends on many different factors (Russell 1999), attempts have been made to set out the parameters of quality eLearning (e.g. ECC by ASTD (workflow. ecc-astdinstitute.org), EFQUEL (www.qualityfoundation.org), EQO (www.eqo.info) and Phipps and Merisotis 2000).

The issue of quality, needless to say, is also among the most important when approaching the relationship between the internet and its business applications.

6.5 eBUSINESS AND eCOMMERCE

The internet has greatly impacted on business settings and processes, offering new and great opportunities as well as threats and challenges. In this section we will discuss how a company can integrate the internet (in every sense that this process can be interpreted) in its business and especially in its transactions with internal and external clients

(6.5.1). A map of different internet business models is presented (6.5.2), and the case of trust on the internet is discussed (6.5.3).

6.5.1 Companies in internet times

Every company and institution – be it for profit or not for profit – is deeply affected by the internet and can turn this to useful ends. If electronic and digital technologies have entered companies over the last decades, creating a completely different shape in production, distribution, administration and so on, networks – and especially the internet – have pushed the change even further. The connected enterprise is innervated by electronic sensors and communication streams, which, at the same time, strengthen its unity – people in different places can communicate and have access to the same data in real time – and alter its hierarchy: communication flows through channels unavailable before. Companies can set themselves up on the internet in different ways, from just opening an 'electronic shop-window' to integrating the internet in each of their activities and processes.

The first step is to put in the electronic world a link to the physical company, usually through a simple website that presents the company, outlines its activities and gives its contacts in the real world: physical address, how to get to sites in the physical world, telephone, fax, opening times, and the like. As we have already seen when studying websites, a company adding an e-mail address to its external communications means more than just presenting itself on the internet: it entails working to a certain extent, offering the service of receiving e-mail messages and processing and answering them.

Once a company decides to make a more extensive use of the opportunities offered by the internet, it moves from simply *being there*, to *operating* in it. Internet-based services can stay inside the company: mainly for knowledge management, communication and internal training, or can be projected towards the external world: interacting with prospective or actual customers, selling products/services, buying materials. While intranets and extranets are used for the in-company scenario or for some business-to-business (B2B) activities, external activities are hosted on the open internet.

According to Sloman (2002: 17), internet impact onto companies can be seen along a line, which goes from the dissemination of information (eInformation), to electronic transactions (eCommerce), to a pervasive all-embracing embedded use (eCompany), up to a deep reframing of markets and industries (eConomy). These four steps – which, of course, go in parallel – can touch the company at different levels, from its production processes to employee management, to supply chain (eProcurement), customer connections (E-CRM), to marketplace. This process can be seen as an integration process, where internet opportunities are deeply integrated into every company activity; the internet does not any longer affect just one or more company's parts, but is effectively and efficiently integrated everywhere, becoming part of the company itself.

6.5.2 A map of internet business models

Let us now go into more detail regarding the eCommerce issue. If we go back to the late 1990s, this term was coined to imply that the internet was initiating a completely different kind of commerce and economy (also: new economy), and some players tried to accredit themselves as being capable of performing miracles, offering profits never seen before. The dotcom dream vanished a few months afterwards, when the market realized that the new economy was not something completely different from the previous one, and that the internet was deeply impacting on the market, but not subverting its basic rules; in particular, a foundation in the single business was still needed: the internet was not a magic wand that could transform all of business into a single (internet) model.

A map of different internet business models is offered by Rappa (2004), who distinguishes them as shown in Table 6.2.

In the brokerage model, the internet service pulls together vendor and buyers, be it a B2B or a business-to-consumer (B2C) relationship. The broker itself charges for the service it provides, usually a percentage of the transaction amount. It is to be underlined that B2B activities account for the largest part of eBusiness activities: in fact, they allow for massive exchanges and build upon already existent business relationships.

The advertising model replicates on the internet what happens in mass media: commercials are sold depending on the medium's audience. Actually, while initially many players thought it could be largely profitable, advertisements (especially banners and similar tools) on the internet were much less effective than expected. The costs of advertising on the internet therefore fell drastically. New opportunities are being explored in paid positioning on search engines (as we discussed in detail in Chapter 5), where adverts' relevance is ensured by their connection with an actual search performed by a user. Every movement on the internet leaves traces, which can be used – and sold – in order to better understand the market, and target specific groups: this is the business of specialized companies, which acquire, analyse and sell data on usages (see also Chapter 5).

Table 6.2 Internet business models

Brokerage model	Buy/sell fulfilment
	Demand collection system
	Auction broker
	Transaction broker
	Distributor
	Search agent
	Virtual marketplace
Advertising model	Portal
	Classifieds
	User registration
	Query-based paid placement
	Contextual advertising
	Content-targeted advertising
	Intromercials
	Ultramercials
Infomediary model	Audience measurement services
	Incentive marketing
	Metamediary
Merchant model	Virtual merchant
	Catalog merchant
	Click and mortar
	Bit vendor
Manufacturer (direct) model	Purchase
	Lease
	License
	Brand integrated content
Affiliate model	Banner exchange
	Pay-per-click
	Revenue sharing
Community model	Open source
	Public broadcasting
	Knowledge networks
Subscription model	Content services
	Person-to-person networking services
	Trust services
	Internet services providers
Utility model	Metered usage
	Metered subscriptions

Source: Rappa 2004.

Merchant and manufacturer models differ due to the fact that in the latter it is the same company that produces and sells goods and/or services. Selling goods on the internet depends on many factors, among which are the company image, the type of goods being sold, its delivery (selling physical goods over the internet is very demanding from the point of view of logistics), modalities of payment, related services.

In general, when goods are easily identifiable and not very expensive, and when related services are good (such as substitution and/or assistance), the internet market works better for B2C exchanges, e.g. travel tickets, books, CD-ROMs, electronic devices and similar goods embody those facilitating aspects. A special case is when the good/service can be also delivered via the internet itself, as for software and music, or internet-based services; in this case eCommerce is the natural solution, although not the only one.

The affiliate model – already presented in Chapter 5 – is based on the possibility of referring one's website visitors to services offered by a third party, while getting revenues depending on the number of referred visitors, the kind of activities they perform on the visited websites or on the amount of their transactions. The community model, on the other hand, 'is based on user loyalty. Users have a high investment in both time and emotion. Revenue can be based on the sale of ancillary products and services or voluntary contributions' (Rappa 2004).

In subscription and metered models, goods and services are offered on a subscription basis, or depending on actual consumption.

6.5.3 The case of trust

Internet diffusion and use is forcing people to develop new strategies to assess and evaluate the credibility and trustworthiness of an internet player: while we are quite well equipped to distinguish a good economic player in the real world, strategies to cope with the internet-mediated market players are being socially negotiated, and are still to become widely diffused.

Trust is a fundamental keyword in the internet market: people will not buy and sell over the internet unless they feel comfortable and secure. If technical security is an issue that cannot be covered here (for coverage, see Yourdon 2002) then trustworthiness requires a brief discussion, being closely related to communication quality.

Research carried out by the Web Credibility Project at the University of Stanford (Fogg 2002) has studied how people evaluate a website's credibility; the research involved more than 2,500 people and focused on websites in the following areas: eCommerce, entertainment, finance, health, news, non-profit, opinion or review, search engines, sports and travel (see Table 6.3).

Data in this study show that

> e-commerce sites stand out from other types of sites in four ways. First, issues of *name recognition and reputation* were mentioned more often by

Table 6.3 How often participants commented on various issues when evaluating the credibility of websites

	Percentage (of 2,440 comments)	Comment topics (addressing specific credibility issue)
1	46.1	Design look
2	28.5	Information design/structure
3	25.1	Information focus
4	15.5	Company motive
5	14.8	Information usefulness
6	14.3	Information accuracy
7	14.1	Name recognition and reputation
8	13.8	Advertising
9	11.6	Information bias
10	9.0	Writing tone
11	8.8	Identity of site operator
12	8.6	Site functionality
13	6.4	Customer service
14	4.6	Past experience with site
15	3.7	Information clarity
16	3.6	Performance on test by user
17	3.6	Readability
18	3.4	Affiliations

Source: Fogg *et al.* 2002: 23.

Note: Categories with less than 3 per cent incidence are not in this table.

people evaluating e-commerce sites, compared to the overall mean for this type of comment (25.9% compared to 14.1% overall). Next, comments about *customer service* were also relatively more frequent (16.7% compared to 6.4%). On the other side of the scale, compared to the overall mean, e-commerce sites received far fewer comments about information bias (2.6% vs. 11.6%). One final difference [. . .] has to do with comments [. . .] classified as '*general suspicion.*' These comments would include things like 'It just makes me suspicious,' and 'I'm always wary of these type of sites.' These types of comments appeared in 9.4 percent of all the comments in this study. The 'general suspicion' comments appeared more often when people evaluated e-commerce sites, in 17.2 percent of the comments people made.

(Fogg 2002: 63)

The issue of trust, then, is a 'threat' to eCommerce and prevents us from envisioning a future where one 'never needs to leave one's computer screen'. Where trust is lacking, users will revert to other communication channels: these involve leaving the space of the computer and interacting with interlocutors in a different way.

In this chapter we have explored communities and practices allowed, generated and promoted by the internet. On the one hand, we have seen that the internet is a communication technology that is capable of stimulating the growth of communities, from those involved in the relatively frivolous pursuit of online gaming to those brought into classes of communities of learning through the opportunities offered by electronic distance pedagogy. On the other hand, we have seen the way in which the internet, while having transformative potential, is usually some way away from thoroughly revolutionizing certain practices at all levels. eCommerce has been a case in point. A few concluding remarks are still to be made in the last chapter of the book.

CONCLUSION

In this volume we tried to introduce the internet from the point of view of communication, regarding it primarily as a very powerful communication tool, which it indeed is. Comparing the internet with the other technologies of the word currently available and considering it as the last step in the development of all other communication technologies, the main communicative features of this medium can be outlined:

1   The internet allows a great *convergence* of previous media: digitized texts can be combined with (digital) images, sounds, movies, graphics, etc.
2   Digital texts can be *modified* and *reproduced very easily*. Yet, where presentation is concerned, the electronic world seems very *fragile*: physical supports are not strong, hardware and software standards change at a very fast pace, requiring a continuous upgrading of every digital collection.
3   The internet, like many other technologies of the word, has become accessible to large groups of a society, thus raising the issue of alphabetization or *digital literacy*: non-professional people can take their digital pictures, shoot (digital) movies, write and print texts, or publish them over the internet.
4   The internet allows for almost instant *bi-directional* and *multi-directional communications*, at a global level.
5   Internet documents require hardware and software to be accessed and interpreted, i.e. to be communicated: in the digital realm, *obsolescence* is so fast that some supports used only a few years ago are

no longer available, and files codified in 'old' operating systems and programmes cannot communicate anything any more.

Due to these and other features, the internet has dramatically changed the way we communicate: thanks to *e-mail* we can have the same immediacy as with fax and in addition the possibility of attaching all kinds of documents to the message (but with more problems concerning the legal value); *websites* combine the chance of reaching wide audiences, typical of other mass media, with the possibility of allowing much more interaction on the audience's side; *chat and messenger systems* allow written (as well as audio and video) synchronous communications; *blogs* allow instant publishing and diffusion over the net; and so on.

Since communication permeates all other social practices, the changes in the way we communicate bring about changes in most social practices: for instance, the way we can access, edit and share documents (movies, songs, images, texts or any other kind of documents) is changed, as well as the way we relate to government, we access health, banking or other public services, the way we work, we play, we learn, we buy and sell, we meet unknown people, and so on.

What about the future? It is very difficult to predict what the development of the internet will be, because of the many different factors that affect the development and the diffusion of every technology. However, some trends may be – with a little dose of risk – hazarded:

1 *The internet and the web*: the future should provide a larger convergence of the internet with other media (telephone – VoIP, TV, radio, cinema, etc.), and a larger integration of them into the web.

2 *The internet and the computer*: the integration of the internet with the other media could even move the internet gradually away from the computer: right now other supports provide access to the internet, such as TV (webTV), mobile phones, Personal Digital Assistants (PDAs), and domotics systems; in the future, this trend could increase, with a strong emphasis on mobility (and with a connection to localization technologies).

3 *The internet and literacy*: the internet will continue to spread, thus allowing the access to information for more and more people, and increasing digital literacy.

4 *The internet and access to information*: however, this will not automatically solve the problem (or even: this will enlarge it) of the digital divide, i.e. of also enabling access to the internet for people who, for different reasons – such as the social status or the geographical area – currently cannot access it; on the contrary, the gap between

who can access the internet and who cannot runs the risk of becoming even deeper.

5   *The internet and communities*: the internet will become more and more an important interaction and communication tool for communities of practice; services for hosting communities may probably make their way towards specifically targeted groups rather than generic community building.

6   *The internet and the senses*: the internet currently relies on sight and hearing; actually, some advanced virtual environments are trying to take into account also other senses, namely touch and smell, in order to make the virtual reality more and more immersive and to enhance the users' feeling of being present in the virtual environment. Will the internet be able to integrate these senses as well?

As a communication tool, the internet is immensely powerful. It might also seem to be, already, the pinnacle of human achievements in the sphere of communication technology. However, as this list suggests, the internet's position as one of the foremost instances of CMC is only really the beginning.

FURTHER READING AND RESOURCES

In this section we suggest some further reading and some resources related to the issues dealt with in the previous chapters, which in our opinion are worth reading and consulting in order to have a more in-depth outlook of the presented concepts. Of course, this list does not pretend to be either complete or exhaustive; it just aims at providing some suggestions to let the reader take a step forward in the world of the internet. In fact, the best resource to have an accurate knowledge of the internet is . . . the internet itself; we hope that this book helps the reader to move towards a more aware and effective use of it.

COMMUNICATION TECHNOLOGIES: HISTORICAL PERSPECTIVES

Berners-Lee, T. (2000) *Weaving the Web. The Original Design and Ultimate Destiny of the World Wide Web by Its Inventor*, with M. Fischetti, New York: Harper Collins.
> The story of the invention of the WWW told by its inventor; Berners-Lee reflects also on the impact of the WWW and tries to predict its future directions.

Fidler, R. (1997) *Mediamorphosis. Understanding New Media*, Thousand Oaks, CA: Pine Forge Press.
> The text provides a theoretical and historical context to help place media technology developments in their proper perspective. It offers a useful analysis of the diffusion, evolution and mutual relationships and influences of communication technologies in their given contexts, in a process the author names 'mediamorphosis'.

Gillies, J. and Cailliau, R. (2000) *How the Web was Born. The Story of the World Wide Web*, Oxford: Oxford University Press.
A detailed story of the birth of the WWW, one of the major components of the internet. With a useful timeline at the end of the book.

Hafner, K. and Lyon, M. (1998) *Where Wizards Stay Up Late. The Origins of the Internet*, New York: Touchstone.
A very detailed story of the birth and the early years of the internet, with many 'behind the scenes' anecdotes.

McLuhan, M. (1964; 3rd edn 2001) *Understanding Media. The Extensions of Man*, London; New York: Routledge.
A milestone in the field of studies on the relationship between communication technologies and cultures. As observed in Chapter 1, McLuhan's provocative findings have often been criticized; however, his work remains a key reference point in this field.

Nyce, J.M. and Kahn, P. (eds) (1991) *From Memex to Hypertext: Vannevar Bush and the Mind's Machine*, San Diego, CA: Academic Press.
This book offers a complete collection of Vannevar Bush's writings about the Memex, the machine that is commonly regarded as the origin of the concept of 'hypertext'.

Ong, W.J. (1982; 3rd edn 2002) *Orality and Literacy. The Technologizing of the Word*, London; New York: Routledge.
A classic study on the relationship between the 'technologies of the word' and the societies in which they spread. It focuses in particular on the social and cultural consequences of two of the major technologies of the word, namely writing and printing from movable type.

Rogers, E.M. (1995) *Diffusion of Innovations*, 4th edn, New York: The Free Press.
The starting point for diffusion theories. It explains how innovative ideas and technologies spread within a community of users via the given communication channels.

Wardrip-Fruin, N. and Montfort, N. (eds) (2003) *The New Media Reader*, Cambridge, MA; London: MIT Press.
It offers a wide collection of the most influential works that contributed to create the history of new media. With a CD-ROM containing videos, programs and electronic documents from the history of new media.

Winston, B. (1998) *Media Technology and Society. A History: From the Telegraph to the Internet*, London; New York: Routledge.
A detailed history of the evolution of media technologies and of their impact on society. Notable for the way in which the argument eschews technological determinism.

COMPUTER MEDIATED COMMUNICATION: TECHNOLOGICAL AND THEORETICAL ASPECTS

Alexander, J.E. and Tate, M.A. (1999) *Web Wisdom: How to Evaluate and Create Information Quality on the Web*, Mahwah, NJ: Lawrence Erlbaum Associates.
A comprehensive introduction to the issue of information quality on the web.

Bolchini, D., Arasa, D. and Cantoni, L. (2004) 'Teaching websites as communication: a "coffee shop approach"', in L. Cantoni and C. McLoughlin (eds) *Proceedings of ED-MEDIA 2004*, Norfolk, VA: AACE, 4119–24.

Bolter, J.D. (2001) *Wrtiting Space. Computers, Hypertext, and the Remediation of Print*, Mahwah, NJ: Lawrence Erlbaum Associates.
In this classic book (1st edition: 1991), Bolter regards hypertext as the new writing space created by digital media.

Burnett, R. and Marshall, P.D. (2003) *Web Theory. An Introduction*, London; New York: Routledge.
A comprehensive and critical introduction to the theories of the internet and the WWW from a sociological and cultural perspective.

Cantoni, L. and Paolini, P. (2001) 'Hypermedia analysis. Some insights from semiotics and ancient rhetoric', *Studies in Communication Sciences*, 1 (1): 33–53.
An interesting approach to the concept of hypertext, which takes into account earlier studies and offers interesting insights based on ancient rhetorical studies.

Cantoni, L., Di Blas, N. and Bolchini, D. (2003) *Comunicazione, qualità, usabilità*, Milan: Apogeo.
The paper and the book (in Italian) offer a presentation of the WCM, which is featured also in the current book (see Chapters 4 and 5).

Crystal, D. (2001) *Language and the Internet*, Cambridge: Cambridge University Press.
An in-depth analysis of the communicative and linguistic aspects of the internet and of online conversations. The author's thesis is that 'netspeak' is a radically new linguistic medium that cannot be ignored.

Delany, P. and Landow, G.P. (eds) (1994) *Hypermedia and Literary Studies*, Cambridge, MA; London: The MIT Press.

Gackenbach, J. (ed.) (1998) *Psychology and the Internet: Intrapersonal, Interpersonal, and Transpersonal Implications*, San Diego, CA; London: Academic Press.

An overview of the main psychological aspects of internet use: it examines how the internet affects our understanding of who we are, and the way we communicate and work.

van der Geest, T.M. (2001) *Web Site Design is Communication Design*, Amsterdam; Philadelphia, PA: John Benjamins.
A good presentation of the approach to websites as communication tools rather than as purely technological artefacts.

Inan, H. and Kean, M. (2002) *Measuring the Success of Your Website: A Customer-centric Approach to Website Management*, Frenchs Forest: Longman.
Two interesting books presenting different strategies and metrics for measuring the success of a website.

Landow, G.P. (ed.) (1994a) *Hyper/Text/Theory*, Baltimore, MD; London: The Johns Hopkins University Press.

Landow, G.P. (1997) *Hypertext 2.0*, Baltimore, MD; London: The Johns Hopkins University Press.
The starting point to theoretical studies about hypertext: these three works introduce the concept of 'hypertext' linking it to literary studies and critical theories; these works offered the first cues for reflection about this new form of textuality.

Lister, M., Dovey, J., Giddings, S., Grant, I. and Kelly, K. (2003) *New Media: A Critical Introduction*, London; New York: Routledge.
A comprehensive introduction to new media from sociological, cultural, historical and theoretical perspectives.

Middleberg, D. (2001) *Winning PR in the Wired World. Powerful Communications Strategies for the Noisy Digital Space*, New York: McGraw-Hill.

Nielsen, J. (1995) *Multimedia and Hypertext. The Internet and Beyond*, Cambridge, MA: AP Professional.
A classic work about multimedia and hypertext. It proposes a well-known partition of hypertext's architecture.

Nielsen, J. (2000) *Designing Web Usability: The Practice of Simplicity*, Indianapolis, IN: New Riders Publishing.

Nielsen, J. and Mack, R. (1994) *Usability Inspection Methods*, New York: J. Wiley & Sons.
Two classic books about web applications' usability by Jakob Nielsen, the pioneer in the field: they deal with usability from the point of view of designing usable websites and of inspecting web applications' usability respectively.

Panwar, S., Mao, S., Ryoo, J.D. and Li, Y. (2004) *TCP/IP Essentials. A Lab-Based Approach*, Cambridge: Cambridge University Press.
An interesting approach to the very technical core of the internet: the TCP/IP protocols.

Roberts, M.L. (2003) *Internet Marketing: Integrating Online and Offline Strategies*, New York: McGraw-Hill/Irwin.
Two interesting books, among many others, about the issues of web marketing, web promotion and online public relations.

Sterne, J. (2002) *Web Metrics. Proven Methods for Measuring Web Site Success*, New York: J. Wiley & Sons.

Wood, A.F. and Smith, M.J. (2001) *Online Communication. Linking Technology, Identity and Culture*, Mahwah, NJ; London: Lawrence Erlbaum Associates.
An exhaustive introduction to online communication from a sociological perspective.

Yourdon, E. (2002) *Byte Wars. The Impact of September 11 on Information Technology*, Upper Saddle River, NJ: Prentice Hall.
It offers an interesting overview of the problems concerning the security of the internet.

INTERNET: COMMUNITIES AND PRACTICES

Bates, A.W. (1999) *Managing Technological Change: Strategies for Academic Leaders*, San Francisco: Jossey-Bass.

Bates, A.W. and Poole, G. (2003) *Effective Teaching with Technology in Higher Education: Foundations for Success*, San Francisco: Jossey-Bass.
Anthony Bates' works, offering a complete introduction to the main questions raised by the introduction of eLearning in the context of higher education.

Cantoni, L. and Schulz, P. (eds) (2003) Special issue 'New media in education', *Studies in Communication Sciences*, March.
It presents a series of interesting papers, best practices and case studies in the overlapping areas of communication, education and new media.

Eifert, M. and Püschel, J.O. (eds) (2004) *National Electronic Government. Comparing Governance Structures in Multi-layer Administrations*, London; New York: Routledge.
It provides a comprehensive comparison among national eGovernment structures in some countries (Britain, Finland, France, Germany, Japan, Australia, United States).

Fogg, B.J. (2002) *Persuasive Technology: Using Computers to Change What We Think and Do*, London: Morgan Kaufmann.
An interesting introduction to the issue of web trust (i.e. of being credible on the web), a pivotal aspect of eBusiness and eCommerce.

Jones, S.G. (ed.) (1998) *Cybersociety 2.0. Revisiting Computer-Mediated Communication and Community*, Thousand Oaks, CA; London; New Delhi: Sage.
Two collections, among others, of the main earlier studies on the cultural aspects of 'cybersociety' and virtual communities.

Kiesler, S. (ed.) (1997) *Culture of the Internet*, Mahwah, NJ: Lawrence Erlbaum Associates.

Klang, M. and Murray, A. (eds) (2005) *Human Rights in the Digital Age*, London; Sydney; Portland, OR: GlassHouse Press.
An interesting overview about human rights in the digital age: the book examines the role played by digital technologies in both the exercise and suppression of human rights.

Middleberg, D. and Ross, S.S. (2002) *The Middleberg/Ross Media Survey. Change and its Impact on Communications, 8th Annual National Survey*, New York: Middleberg and Associates.
The eighth report by Don Middleberg and Steven S. Ross, who have been analysing the relationship between the internet and the other mass media (print and broadcast) since the early 1990s.

Preece, J. and Maloney-Krichmar, D. (eds) (2005) Special theme 'Online communities', *Journal of Computer-Mediated Communication*, 10 (4), available online: www.jcmc.indiana.edu/vol10/issue4.
This issue of the online *Journal of Computer-Mediated Communication* is dedicated to the special theme of online communities in its manifold aspects: design, theory and practice.

Rappa, M. (2004) 'Business models on the web', *Managing the Digital Enterprise*, available online: www.digitalenterprise.org/models/models.pdf.
This paper presents a map of the different business models made available by the diffusion of the internet.

Rheingold, H. (2000) *The Virtual Community. Homesteading on the Electronic Frontier*, revised edition, Cambridge, MA; London: The MIT Press.
The starting point for virtual communities (1st edition: 1993): Rheingold's classic book tells in a very conversational way the story of his pioneer experience in a virtual community.

Rossett, A. (ed.) (2002) *The ASTD E-Learning Handbook*, New York: McGraw-Hill.
A collection of more than 50 articles on the state of eLearning, providing a wide presentation of case studies, best practices and strategies.

Turkle, S. (1995) *Life on the Screen. Identity in the Age of the Internet*, New York: Simon & Schuster.
The classic book on the issue of identity in the virtual world.

UNDESA (2003) *UN Global E-government Survey 2003*, available online: www.unpan1.un.org/intradoc/groups/public/documents/un/unpan 016066.pdf.

UNDESA (2004) *UN Global E-government Readiness Report 2004. Towards Access for Opportunity*, available online: www.unpan1.un.org/intradoc/ groups/public/documents/un/unpan019207.pdf.
Two important reports made by a UN agency, monitoring the current situation and trend in eGovernment activities.

Since 1987 the ACM Special Interest Group on Hypertext, Hypermedia and the Web has run a Conference on Hypertext and Hypermedia, whose proceedings present the most recent and updated trends in the field of hypertext studies (see: www.sigweb.org).

ONLINE RESOURCES

AACE (Association for the Advancement of Computing in Education): www.aace.org
It organizes three-yearly conferences, publishes five academic journals and offers a wide Digital Library.

Clickz Network – Internet Marketing Solutions for Marketers: www. clickz.com
One of the most important online resources for web marketing and web promotion, providing news, expert advice and opinions, stats, events and conferences, and so on.

Game Studies: www.gamestudies.org
A cross-disciplinary online journal dedicated to games research, focusing in particular on aesthetic, cultural and communicative aspects of computer games.

ITU – International Telecommunication Union: www.itu.int
On this website some important reports and resources on the state of the 'information society' are available (see, for instance, ITU 2003a, 2003b; Utsumi 2001).

Journal of Computer-Mediated Communication: http://jcmc.indiana.edu
An online quarterly publication, published since 1995, covering the issue of CMC in all its many different aspects.

The MASIE Center: www.masie.com
The website of one of the most important centres that study and analyse the main issues related to the adoption of eLearning in the context of businesses and governments.

Search Engine Watch: Tips About Internet Search Engines & Search Engine Submission: www.searchenginewatch.com

The most important online observatory on search engines, which provides updated information on their world and useful tips on how to use them effectively.

United Nations Information and Communication Technologies Task Force: www.unicttaskforce.org
The UN ICT Task Force website provides interesting reports on the state of the 'information society'.

Useit.com – Jakob Nielsen on Usability and Web Design: www.useit.com
Nielsen's website on usability and web design offers many resources: reports, conferences, tutorials, courses, and so on.

Webopedia – Online Computer Dictionary for Computer and Internet Terms and Definitions: www.webopedia.com
A very interesting and complete resource concerning all the technical aspects of CMC and its different tools.

W3C – the WWW Consortium: www.w3.org
It 'develops interoperable technologies (specifications, guidelines, software, and tools) to lead the Web to its full potential' (see Chapter 2 for other standardization bodies concerned with the internet).

REFERENCES

All online references were checked 15 December 2005.

Aarseth, E.J. (1994) 'Nonlinearity and literary theory', in G.P. Landow (ed.) *Hyper/Text/Theory*, Baltimore, MD; London: The Johns Hopkins University Press, 51–86.

—— (1997) *Cybertext. Perspectives on Ergodic Literature*, Baltimore, MD; London: The Johns Hopkins University Press.

—— (2001) 'Computer game studies, year one', *Game Studies. The International Journal of Computer Game Research*, 1 (1), available at: www.gamestudies.org/0101/editorial.html.

Adelsberger, H.H., Collis, B. and Pawlowski, J.B. (eds) (2002) *Handbook on Information Technologies for Education and Training*, Berlin; New York: Springer.

Alexander, J.E. and Tate, M.A. (1999) *Web Wisdom: How to Evaluate and Create Information Quality on the Web*, Mahwah, NJ: Lawrence Erlbaum Associates.

Andersen, P.B. (1998) 'WWW as a self-organizing system', *Cybernetics & Human Knowing*, 5 (2): 5–42, available online: www.imv.au.dk/~pba/Homepagematerial/publicationfolder/WWWSelfOrg.pdf.

Anderson, B. (1991) *Imagined Communities: Reflections on the Origin and Spread of Nationalism*, London: Verso.

Aristotle, *Politics*.

Armani, J. and Rocci, A. (2003) 'Conceptual maps in e-learning. How map based interfaces help the contextualization of information and the structuring of knowledge', *Information Design Journal*, 11 (3): 171–84.

ASTD and The Masie Center (2001) *E-Learning: 'If We Build It, Will They Come?'*, Alexandria, VA: ASTD.

Augustine of Hippo, St, *Retractationes*.

Austin, J.L. (1962) *How to Do Things with Words*, 2nd edn, Cambridge, MA: Harvard University Press.

Baran, P. (1964) 'On distributed communications', Memorandum RM-3420, RAND Corporation, available online: www.rand.org/publications/RM/RM3420/.

Barfield, L. (1993) *The User Interface. Concepts and Design*, Reading, MA: Addison-Wesley Publishing Company.

Barthes, R. (1974) *S/Z*, New York: Hill & Wang.

Bates, A.W. (1999) *Managing Technological Change: Strategies for Academic Leaders*, San Francisco: Jossey-Bass.

——— (2001) *National Strategies for E-learning in Post-secondary Education and Training*, International Institute for Educational Planning, Paris: UNESCO.

——— and Poole, G. (2003) *Effective Teaching with Technology in Higher Education: Foundations for Success*, San Francisco: Jossey-Bass.

Baym, N.K. (1998) 'The emergence of on-line community', in S.G. Jones (ed.) *Cybersociety 2.0. Revisiting Computer-Mediated Communication and Community*, Thousand Oaks, CA; London; New Delhi: Sage, 35–68.

Benjamin, W. (1973) 'The work of art in the age of mechanical reproduction', in W. Benjamin, *Illuminations,* edited and with an introduction by H. Arendt, London: Fontana Press, 211–44.

Benveniste, É. (1973) *Problems in General Linguistics*, Miami, FL: University of Miami Press.

Berners-Lee, T. (2000) *Weaving the Web. The Original Design and Ultimate Destiny of the World Wide Web by Its Inventor*, New York: Harper Collins.

Bettetini, G., Gasparini, B. and Vittadini, N. (1999) *Gli spazi dell'ipertesto*, Milan: Bompiani.

Blasi, G. (1999) *Internet. Storia e futuro di un nuovo medium*, Milan: Guerini Studio.

Bolchini, D. and Paolini, P. (2004a) 'Goal-driven requirements analysis for hypermedia-intensive web applications', *Requirements Engineering Journal*, special issue, 9: 85–103.

——— and ——— (2004b) 'Dialogue-based design for multichannel interactions', in M. Matera and S. Comai (eds) *Engineering Advanced Web Applications*, Proceedings of Workshops in Connection with the 4th International Conference on Web Engineering ICWE '04, Munich (Germany), May 2004.

———, Arasa, D. and Cantoni, L. (2004) 'Teaching websites as communication: a "coffee shop approach"', in L. Cantoni and C. McLoughlin (eds) *Proceedings of ED-MEDIA 2004*, Norfolk, VA: AACE, 4119–24.

———, Paolini, P. and Di Blas, N. (2002) 'Web as dialogue. Interpreting navigational artifacts as dialogic structures', TEC-lab Editorial Report TR02.3, University of Lugano.

Bolter, J.D. (2001) *Wrtiting Space. Computers, Hypertext, and the Remediation of Print*, Mahwah, NJ: Lawrence Erlbaum Associates.

—— and Grusin, R. (1999) *Remediation. Understanding New Media*, Cambridge, MA; London: The MIT Press.

Botturi, L. (2006) 'E2ML. A visual language for the design of instruction', *Educational Technologies Research & Development*, 54 (3).

Brennan, S.E. (2002) 'Visual co-presence, coordination signals, and partner effects in spontaneous spoken discourse', *Journal of the Japanese Cognitive Science Society*, 9: 7–25.

—— and Ohaeri, J.O. (1999) 'Why do electronic conversations seem less polite? The costs and benefits of hedging', *Proceedings of the International Joint Conference on Work Activities Coordination and Collaboration (WACC '99)*, New York: ACM Press, 227–35.

Brown, P. and Levinson, S.C. (1978) *Politeness: Some Universals in Language Use*, Cambridge: Cambridge University Press.

Brusilovsky, P. (1997) 'Efficient techniques for adaptive hypermedia', in C. Nicholas and J. Mayfield (eds) *Intelligent Hypertext: Advanced Techniques for the World Wide Web*, Berlin: Springer Verlag, 12–30.

Bühler, K. (1982 3rd edn) [1934] *Sprachtheorie: die Darstellungsfunktion der Sprache*, Stuttgart; New York: Fischer.

Burnett, R. and Marshall, P.D. (2003) *Web Theory. An Introduction*, London; New York: Routledge.

Bush, V. (1933) 'The inscrutable thirties', in J.M. Nyce and P. Kahn (eds) (1991) *From Memex to Hypertext: Vannevar Bush and the Mind's Machine*, San Diego, CA: Academic Press, 67–79; originally published in *Technology Review*, 35 (4): 123–7.

—— (1945) 'As we may think', in N. Wardrip-Fruin and N. Montfort (eds) (2003) *The New Media Reader*, Cambridge, MA; London: The MIT Press, 37–47; originally published in *Atlantic Monthly*, 176 (1): 101–8; and in *Life*, 19 (11), September 1945; available at: www.ps.uni-sb.de/~duchier/pub/vbush/vbush-all.shtml.

—— (1959) 'Memex II', in J.M. Nyce and P. Kahn (eds) (1991) *From Memex to Hypertext: Vannevar Bush and the Mind's Machine*, San Diego, CA: Academic Press, 165–84: originally published as a manuscript, Vannevar Press: MIT Archive.

—— (1967) 'Memex revisited', in J.M. Nyce and P. Kahn (eds) (1991) *From Memex to Hypertext: Vannevar Bush and the Mind's Machine*, San Diego, CA: Academic Press, 197–216; originally published in V. Bush (1967) *Science is Not Enough*, New York: William Morrow, 75–101.

Cantoni, L. (1999) 'Benjamin Lee Whorf ed Émile Benveniste', in G. Bettetini, S. Cigada, S. Raynaud and E. Rigotti (eds) *Semiotica I. Origini e fondamenti*, Brescia: La Scuola, 315–43.

—— (2002) 'Lingua', in F. Lever, A. Zanacchi and P.C. Rivoltella (eds) *La Comunicazione. Il dizionario di scienze e tecniche*, Turin: RAI-ERI.

—— (2003) 'Il Counseling-Learning/Community Language Learning (C-L/CLL) di Charles A. Curran nella glottodidattica umanistica', in C.A. Curran, *Il Counseling-Learning nelle lingue seconde, con un saggio introduttivo di Lorenzo Cantoni*, Perugia: Guerra Edizioni, 7–82.

—— and Di Blas, N. (2002) *Teoria e pratiche della comunicazione*, Milan: Apogeo.

—— and McLoughlin, C. (eds) (2004) *Proceedings of ED-MEDIA 2004 – World Conference on Educational Multimedia, Hypermedia & Telecommunications* (21–26 June; Lugano, Switzerland), Norfolk, VA: AACE.

—— and Paolini, P. (2001) 'Hypermedia analysis. Some insights from semiotics and ancient rhetoric', *Studies in Communication Sciences*, 1 (1): 33–53.

—— and Piccini, C. (2003) 'Websites as communication. The "coffee shop approach"', in G. Poncini, F. Frandsen and W. Johansen (eds) *5th ABC [The Association for Business Communication] European Convention. Communication in Business: Meeting the Challenges of a Changing World*, Lugano: USI.

—— and —— (2004) *Il sito del vicino è sempre più verde. La comunicazione fra committenti e progettisti di siti internet*, Milan: FrancoAngeli.

—— and Rega, I. (2004) 'Looking for fixed stars in the eLearning community: a research on referenced literature in SITE Proceeding Books from 1994 to 2001', in L. Cantoni and C. McLoughlin (eds) *Proceedings of ED-MEDIA 2004*, Norfolk, VA: AACE, 4697–704.

—— and Succi, C. (2002) *Swiss and EU Universities Facing the Issue of eLearning Quality. A Qualitative and a Quantitative Research*, Ronneby, Sweden: Netlearning 2002.

—— and Tardini, S. (2003) 'La svolta pragmatica dei motori di ricerca in internet', in A. Giacalone Ramat, E. Rigotti and A. Rocci (eds) *Linguistica e nuove professioni*, Milan: FrancoAngeli, 234–44.

—— and Vittadini, N. (2003) 'L'ipertesto digitale', in G. Bettetini, S. Cigada, S. Raynaud and E. Rigotti (eds) *Semiotica II. Configurazione disciplinare e questioni contemporanee*, Brescia: La Scuola, 321–51.

——, Di Blas, N. and Bolchini, D. (2003) *Comunicazione, qualità, usabilità*, Milan: Apogeo.

Castells, M. (2003) *The Internet Galaxy. Reflections on the Internet, Business, and Society*, Oxford: Oxford University Press.

Cavallo, G., Chartier, R. and Cochrane, L.G. (2003) *A History of Reading in the West (Studies in Print Culture and the History of the Book)*, Amherst, MA: University of Massachusetts Press.

CEC (2001) *Communication from the Commission to the Council and the European Parliament, The eLearning Action Plan: Designing Tomorrow's Education*, COM(2001)172, Brussels, 28 March.

Cicero, *De oratore*.

——, *Rhetorica ad Herennium*.

Cicognani, A. (1998) 'On the linguistic nature of cyberspace and virtual communities', *Virtual Reality*, 3: 16–24.

Ciofi, R. and Graziano, D. (2003) *Giochi pericolosi? Perché i giovani passano ore tra videogiochi online e comunità virtuali*, Milan: FrancoAngeli.

Clark, H.H. (1996) *Using Language*, Cambridge: Cambridge University Press.

—— and Brennan, S.E. (1991) 'Grounding in communication', in L.B. Resnick, J.M. Levine and S.D. Teasley (eds) *Perspectives on Socially Shared Cognition*, Washington, DC: APA Books, 127–49.

Clodius, J. (1997) *Creating a Community of Interest. 'Self' and 'Other' on DragonMud*, paper presented at the Combined Conference on MUDs, Jackson Hole (Wyoming), 15 January, available at: www.dragonmud.org/people/jen/mudshopiii.html.

Cobley, P. (2001) 'Structuralism, structuralist', in P. Cobley (ed.) *The Routledge Companion to Semiotics and Linguistics*, London; New York: Routledge.

Cohen, A. (1985) *The Symbolic Construction of Community*, New York: Routledge.

Cohen, B. (1965) *Foreign Policy in American Government*, Boston, MA: Little, Brown.

Coimbra Group (2002) *European Union Policies and Strategic Change for eLearning in Universities*, Brussels, available at: www.flp.ed.ac.uk/HECTIC/HECTICREPORT.PDF.

Collis, B. (2002) *Flexible Learning in a Digital World*, London: Kogan Page.

COM (2002) *eEurope 2005: An Information Society for All*, Brussels, available at: www.europa.eu.int/information_society/eeurope/2005/all_about/action_plan/index_en.htm.

Corti, A. (2004) *L'informazione su Internet. Inizia l'era della concretezza*, European Journalism Observatory, available at: www.ejo.ch/analysis/newmedia/corti_integrale_it.pdf.

Coseriu, E. (1981) *Sincronia, diacronia e storia. Il problema del cambio linguistico*, Turin: Boringhieri.

Crystal, D. (2001) *Language and the Internet*, Cambridge: Cambridge University Press.

Curran, C.A. (1976) *Counseling-Learning in Second Languages*, Apple River, IL: Apple River Press.

Daley, E. (2003) 'Expanding the concept of literacy', *Educause Review*, 38 (2): 33–40, available at: www.iml.annenberg.edu/downloads/news_articles/erm0322.pdf.

Dearing, J.D. and Rogers, E.M. (1996) *Agenda-Setting*, Newbury Park, CA: Sage.

Deibert, R.J. and Villeneuve, N. (2005) 'Firewalls and power: an overview of global state censorship of the internet', in M. Klang and A. Murray (eds) *Human Rights in the Digital Age*, London; Sydney; Portland, OR: GlassHouse Press, 111–24.

Delany, P. and Landow, G.P. (eds) (1994) *Hypermedia and Literary Studies*, Cambridge, MA; London: The MIT Press.

Di Blas, N. and Paolini, P. (2003) 'Do we speak to computers? How linguistics meddle with the web', in A. Giacalone Ramat, E. Rigotti and A. Rocci (eds) *Linguistica e nuove professioni*, Milan: FrancoAngeli, 221–33.

Dillenbourg, P. (1999) *Collaborative Learning: Cognitive and Computational Approaches*, Amsterdam: Pergamon.

Doglio, D. and Richeri, G. (1980) *La radio. Origini, storia, modelli*, Milan: Mondadori.

Donath, J.S. (1999) 'Identity and deception in the virtual community', in M.A. Smith and P. Kollock (eds) *Communities in Cyberspace*, London; New York: Routledge, 29–59.

Drezner, D.W. (2004) 'The global governance of the internet: bringing the state back in', *Political Science Quarterly*, 119 (3): 477–98, available at: www.danieldrezner.com/research/egovernance.pdf.

Dufeu, B. (1994) *Teaching Myself*, Oxford: Oxford University Press.

Eco, U. (1979) *A Theory of Semiotics*, Bloomington, IN: Indiana University Press.

Eifert, M. and Püschel, J.O. (eds) (2004) *National Electronic Government. Comparing Governance Structures in Multi-layer Administrations*, London; New York: Routledge.

Engelbart, D. (1962) *Augmenting Human Intellect. A Conceptual Framework*, Summary Report AFOSR-3233, Menlo Park, CA: Stanford Research Institute, available at: www.bootstrap.org/augdocs/friedewald 030402/augmentinghumanintellect/AHI62.pdf.

—— and English, W. (1968) 'A research center for augmenting human intellect', in N. Wardrip-Fruin and N. Montfort (eds) (2003) *The New Media Reader*, Cambridge, MA; London: The MIT Press, 233–46; originally published in *AFIPS [American Federation of Information Processing Societies] Conference Proceedings*, 33, part 1, Fall Joint Computer Conference, 395–410.

Eppler, M.J. (2003) *Managing Information Quality. Increasing the Value of Information in Knowledge-intensive Products and Processes*, Berlin: Springer.

—— and Cantoni, L. (2005) 'Information quality in e-Government', in J. Castro and E. Teniente (eds) *Proceedings of the CAiSE '05 Second International Workshop on Information Quality* (13–17 June, Porto, Portugal), Heidelberg: Springer, 251–64.

——, Helfert, M. and Gasser, U. (2004) 'Information quality: organizational, technological, and legal perspectives', *Studies in Communication Sciences*, 4 (2): 1–15.

Erickson, T. (ed.) (1999) 'Persistent conversation', *Journal of Computer-Mediated Communication*, 4 (4), available at: www.jcmc.indiana.edu/vol4/issue4/.

Esselink, B. (2000) *A Practical Guide to Localization*, Amsterdam; Philadelphia, PA: John Benjamins.

European Parliament (2000) *Presidency Conclusions*, Lisbon European Council 23 and 24 March, available at: www.europarl.eu.int/summits/lis1_en.htm.

Fagerjord, A. (2003) 'Rhetorical convergence. Studying web media', in G. Liestøl, A. Morrison and T. Rasmussen (eds) *Digital Media Revisited. Theoretical and Conceptual Innovation in Digital Domains*, Cambridge, MA; London: The MIT Press, 295–325.

Fernback, J. and Thompson, B. (1995) *Virtual Communities: Abort, Retry, Failure?*, available at: www.well.com/user/hlr/texts/VCcivil.html.

Fidler, R. (1997) *Mediamorphosis. Understanding New Media*, Thousand Oaks, CA: Pine Forge Press.

Fogg, B.J. (2002) *Persuasive Technology: Using Computers to Change What We Think and Do*, London: Morgan Kaufmann.

Foley, J.P. (ed.) (2002) *Ethics in Internet*, Pontifical Council For Social Communications, available at: www.vatican.va/roman_curia/pontifical_councils/pccs/documents/rc_pc_pccs_doc_20020228_ethics-internet_en.html.

Frasca, G. (2001) *Videogames of the Oppressed: Videogames as a Means for Critical Thinking and Debate*, Master's thesis (Georgia Institute of Technology), available at: www.ludology.org/articles/thesis/FrascaThesisVideogames.pdf.

Fuller, K.E. (2001) 'ICANN: the debate over governing the internet', *Duke Law and Technology Review*, 2, available at: www.law.duke.edu/journals/dltr/articles/2001dltr0002.html.

Gackenbach, J. and Ellerman, E. (1998) 'Introduction to psychological aspects of internet use', in J. Gackenbach (ed.) *Psychology and the Internet: Intrapersonal, Interpersonal, and Transpersonal Implications*, San Diego, CA; London: Academic Press, 1–26.

Gadamer, H.G. (2005) *Truth and Method*, 2nd edn, London; New York: Continuum International Publishing Group.

Garton, L., Haythornthwaite, C. and Wellman, B. (1999) 'Studying on-line social networks', in S. Jones (ed.) *Doing Internet Research. Critical Issues and Methods for Examining the Net*, Thousand Oaks, CA; London; New Delhi: Sage, 75–105.

Gatti, M.C. (1992) *Dalla semantica alla lessicologia: introduzione al modello Senso-Testo di I.A. Mel'čuk*, Brescia: La Scuola.

Gee, J.P. (2004) *What Video Games Have to Teach Us about Learning and Literacy*, New York: Palgrave Macmillan.

van der Geest, T.M. (2001) *Web Site Design is Communication Design*, Amsterdam; Philadelphia, PA: John Benjamins.

Gillies, J. and Cailliau, R. (2000) *How the Web was Born. The Story of the World Wide Web*, Oxford: Oxford University Press.

González Gaitano, N. (1999) 'L'agenda-setting 25 anni dopo (1972–1997)', *Sociologia della comunicazione*, XIV (27): 183–205.

Graham, G. (1999) *The Internet: A Philosophical Inquiry*, London; New York: Routledge.

Guri-Rosenblit, S. (1999) *Distance and Campus Universities: Tensions and Interactions*, Paris: Pergamon.

—— (2001) 'Virtual universities: current models and future trends', *Higher Education in Europe*, 26 (4): 487–99.

Hafner, K. and Lyon, M. (1998) *Where Wizards Stay Up Late. The Origins of the Internet*, New York: Touchstone.

Haig, M. (2000) *E-PR. The Essential Guide to Public Relations on the Internet*, London; Milford, CT: Kogan Page.

Hall, M. (2002) 'Give your users the power of the press with weblogs and wikis', *Intranet Journal*, 16 December, available at: www.intranet journal.com/articles/200212/ij_12_16_02a.html.

Harris, R. (2001a) 'Paradigm (paradigmatic)', in P. Cobley (ed.) *The Routledge Companion to Semiotics and Linguistics*, London; New York: Routledge, 233.

—— (2001b) 'Syntagm, syntagmatic', in P. Cobley (ed.) *The Routledge Companion to Semiotics and Linguistics*, London; New York: Routledge, 273.

Havelock, E.A. (1986) *The Muse Learns to Write. Reflections on Orality and Literacy from the Antiquity to the Present*, New Haven, CT; London: Yale University Press.

Helman, C.G. (2001) *Culture, Health and Illness*, 4th edn, London: Arnold.

Herring, S. (1999) 'Interactional coherence in CMC', *Journal of Computer-Mediated Communication*, 4 (4), available at: www.jcmc.indiana.edu/vol4/issue4/herring.html.

Hill, E. (2004) 'Some thoughts on e-democracy as an evolving concept', *Journal of E-Government*, 1 (1): 23–39.

Holtz, S. (2002) *Public Relations on the Net. Winning Strategies to Inform and Influence the Media, the Investment Community, the Government, the Public, and More!*, 2nd edn, New York: Amacom.

Huizinga, J. (1950) *Homo Ludens: A Study of the Play Element in Culture*, Boston, MA: Beacon Press.

Inan, H. and Kean, M. (2002) *Measuring the Success of Your Website: A Customer-centric Approach to Website Management*, Frenchs Forest: Longman.

Introvigne, M. (2000) '"So many evil things": anti-cult terrorism via the internet', in J.K. Hadden and D.E. Cowan (eds) *Religion on the Internet: Research Prospects and Promises*, New York: Elsevier Science, 277–306, available at: www.cesnur.org/testi/anticult_terror.htm.

ISO (1998) ISO 9241. *Ergonomic Requirements for Office Work with Visual Display Terminals (VDTs)* – Part 11: 'Guidance on usability'.

ITU (2003a) *World Telecommunication Development Report 2003. Access Indicators for the Information Society*, available at: www.itu.int/ITU-D/ict/publications/wtdr_03/material/WTDR2003Sum_e.pdf.

—— (2003b) *Declaration of Principles. Building the Information Society: a Global Challenge in the New Millennium*, World Summit on the Information Society, Geneva 2003, available at: www.itu.int/dms_pub/ itu-s/md/03/wsis/doc/S03-WSIS-DOC-0004!!PDF-E.pdf.

Jakobson, R. (1960) 'Linguistics and poetics', in T.A. Sebeok (ed.) *Style in Language*, Cambridge, MA: The MIT Press, 130–44.

Jones, S.G. (1995) 'Understanding community in the information age', in S.G. Jones (ed.) *CyberSociety. Computer-Mediated Communication and Community*, Thousand Oaks, CA; London; New Delhi: Sage, 10–35.

Kahn, B.K. and Strong, D.M. (1998) 'Product and service performance model for information quality: an update', in I. Chengalur-Smith and L.L. Pipino (eds) *Proceedings of the 1998 Conference of Information Quality*, Cambridge, MA: The MIT Press, 102–15.

Kahn, P. and Lenk, K. (2001) *Mapping Web Sites*, Hove: RotoVision.

de Kerckhove, D. (1995) *La civilizzazione video-cristiana*, Milan: Feltrinelli.

—— (1997) *Connected Intelligence: The Arrival of the Web Society*, Toronto: Somerville House.

—— and Lumsden, C.J. (eds) (1988) *The Alphabet and the Brain: The Lateralization of Writing*, Berlin: Springer.

Landow, G.P. (ed.) (1994a) *Hyper/Text/Theory*, Baltimore, MD; London: The Johns Hopkins University Press.

Landow, G.P. (1994b) 'What's a critic to do? Critical theory in the age of hypertext', in G.P. Landow (ed.) *Hyper/Text/Theory*, Baltimore, MD; London: The Johns Hopkins University Press, 1–48.

—— (1997) *Hypertext 2.0*, Baltimore, MD; London: The Johns Hopkins University Press.

—— and Delany, P. (1994) 'Hypertext, hypermedia and literary studies: the state of the art', in P. Delany and G.P. Landow (eds) *Hypermedia and Literary Studies*, Cambridge, MA; London: The MIT Press, 3–50.

Langford, D. (ed.) (2000) *Internet Ethics*, New York: Palgrave Macmillan.

Lawrence, S. (2001) 'Free online availability substantially increases a paper's impact', *Nature*, 411/6837: 521.

Lazer, D.M.J. (2001) 'Regulatory interdependence and international governance', *Journal of European Public Policy*, April: 474–92.

Lechner, U. and Schmid, B.F. (2000) 'Communities and media. Towards a reconstruction of communities on media', in E. Sprague (ed.) *Proceedings of the 33rd Hawaii International Conference on System Sciences (HICSS 2000)*, Washington, DC: IEEE Computer Society.

Lepori, B. and Rezzonico, S. (2003) *La réalisation de cours eLearning du Campus Virtuel Suisse Etat des lieux à mi-parcours*, Lugano: NewMinE Lab.

Lepori, B. and Succi, C. (2003) *eLearning in Higher Education. Prospects for Swiss Universities*, Lugano: NewMinE Lab.

——, Cantoni, L. and Mazza, R. (2002) 'Push communication services: a short history, a concrete experience and some critical reflections', *Studies in Communication Sciences*, 2 (2): 149–64.

——, Cantoni, L. and Rezzonico, S. (eds) (2005) *EDUM Project. How to Create and to Manage eLearning Activities*, Lugano: NewMinE Lab.

Levy, P. (1997) *Collective Intelligence. Mankind's Emerging World in Cyberspace*, New York: Plenum Press.

Licklider, J.C.R. and Taylor, R. (1968) 'The computer as a communication device', *Science and Technology*, 76: 21–31, available at: www.memex. org/licklider.pdf.

Liestøl, E. (2003) 'Computer games and the ludic structure of interpretation', in G. Liestøl, A. Morrison and T. Rasmussen (eds) *Digital Media Revisited. Theoretical and Conceptual Innovation in Digital Domains*, Cambridge, MA; London: The MIT Press, 327–57.

Liestøl, G. (1994) 'Wittgenstein, Genette and the reader's narrative in hypertext', in G.P. Landow (ed.) *Hyper/Text/Theory*, Baltimore, MD; London: The Johns Hopkins University Press, 87–120.

Lim, K.H., Benbasat, I. and Todd, P.A. (1996) 'An experimental investigation of the interactive effects of interface style, instructions, and task familiarity on user performance', *ACM Transactions in Computer Human Interaction*, 3 (1): 1–37.

Lister, M., Dovey, J., Giddings, S., Grant, I. and Kelly, K. (2003) *New Media: A Critical Introduction*, London; New York: Routledge.

Lotman, Y.M. (2001) *Universe of the Mind. A Semiotic Theory of Culture*, London; New York: I.B. Tauris.

McCombs, M.E. and Shaw, D.L. (1972) 'The agenda-setting function of the mass media', *Public Opinion Quarterly*, 36: 176–87.

McLuhan, M. (1962) *The Gutenberg Galaxy. The Making of Typographic Man*, Toronto: University of Toronto Press.

—— (2001 3rd edn) [1964] *Understanding Media. The Extensions of Man*, London; New York: Routledge.

—— and de Kerckhove, D. (1977) *D'Oeil à Oreille. La Nouvelle Galaxie*, Paris: Denoël.

Maffesoli, M. (1995) *The Time of the Tribes. The Decline of Individualism in Mass Society*, Thousand Oaks, CA; London; New Delhi: Sage.

Mahmoudian, M. (1993) *Modern Theories on Language: The Empirical Challenge*, Durham, NC: Duke University Press.

Maldonado, T. (1997) *Critica della ragione informatica*, Milan: Feltrinelli.

Manovich, L. (2001) *The Language of New Media*, Cambridge, MA: The MIT Press.

Mantovani, G. (2001) 'Shifts in human-computer interaction: the internet as a mediation environment', *Studies in Communication Sciences*, 1 (2): 137–47.

Martinet, A. (1970) *Économie des changements phonétiques*, Berne: Éditions A. Francke.

Masie, E. (2002) 'Blended learning: the magic is in the mix', in A. Rossett (ed.) *The ASTD E-Learning Handbook*, New York: McGraw-Hill, 58–63.

Masie Center (2003) *Making Sense of Learning Specifications & Standards: A Decision Maker's Guide to their Adoption*, Industry report, 2nd edn, available at: www.masie.com/standards/s3_2nd_edition.pdf.

Maurer, H. (2002) 'What have we learnt in 15 years about educational multimedia?', *World Conference on Educational Multimedia, Hypermedia and Telecommunications*, 2002 (1): 2–9, available at: www.dl.aace.org/10014.

Mel'čuk, I.A. (1970) 'Towards a functioning model of language', in M. Bierwisch and K.E. Heidolph (eds) *Progress in Linguistics*, The Hague: Mouton, 198–207.

Middleberg, D. (2001) *Winning PR in the Wired World. Powerful Communications Strategies for the Noisy Digital Space*, New York: McGraw-Hill.

—— and Ross, S.S. (2002) *The Middleberg/Ross Media Survey. Change and Its Impact on Communications, 8th Annual National Survey*, New York: Middleberg and Associates.

Mioduser, D., Nachmias, R., Oren, A. and Lahav, O. (1999) 'Taxonomy of educational websites: a tool for supporting research development and implementation of web-based learning', *International Journal of Educational Telecommunications*, 5 (3): 193–210.

——, ——, —— and —— (2000) 'Web-Based learning environments: current technological and pedagogical state', *Journal of Research in Computing in Education*, 33 (1): 55–76.

Montagna, L. (2004) *Lavapiubianco.biz. Marketing, business e web*, Milan: HOPS – Tecniche Nuove.

Morris, C.W. (1938) 'Foundations of the theory of signs', in C.W. Morris (1971) *Writings on the General Theory of Signs*, The Hague: Mouton.

Nelson, T.H. (1965) 'A file structure for the complex, the changing, and the indeterminate', in N. Wardrip-Fruin and N. Montfort (eds) (2003) *The New Media Reader*, Cambridge, MA; London: The MIT Press, 134–45; originally published in L. Winner (ed.) (1965) *ACM: Proceedings of the 20th National Conference*, New York: ACM Press, 84–100.

—— (1981) 'From *Literary Machines:* proposal for a universal electronic publishing system and archive', in N. Wardrip-Fruin and N. Montfort (eds) (2003) *The New Media Reader*, Cambridge, MA; London: The MIT Press, 443–61; originally published in *Literary Machines* (1981), Sausalito, CA: Mindful Press.

Newman, J. (2004) *Videogames*, London; New York: Routledge.

Nielsen, J. (1993) *Usability Engineering*, Boston, MA: Academic Press.

—— (1995) *Multimedia and Hypertext. The Internet and Beyond*, Cambridge, MA: AP Professional.

—— (2000) *Designing Web Usability: The Practice of Simplicity*, Indianapolis, IN: New Riders Publishing.

—— and Mack, R. (1994) *Usability Inspection Methods*, New York: J. Wiley & Sons.

—— and Tahir, M. (2002) *Homepage Usability: 50 Websites Deconstructed*, Indianapolis, IN: New Riders Publishing.

Nyce, J.M. and Kahn, P. (eds) (1991) *From Memex to Hypertext: Vannevar Bush and the Mind's Machine*, San Diego, CA: Academic Press.

OECD (2003) *The e-Government Imperative*, Paris: OECD e-Government Studies.

Oliver, R. and Herrington, J. (2001) *Teaching and Learning Online. A Beginner's Guide to e-Learning and e-Teaching in Higher Education*, Perth: Edith Cowan University.

Ong, W.J. (2002 3rd edn) [1982] *Orality and Literacy. The Technologizing of the Word*, London; New York: Routledge.

OPA (2004) *Online Paid Content U.S. Market Spending Report, FY 2003*, 11 May, available at: www.online-publishers.org/pdf/opa_paid_content_report_may04.pdf.

OpenNet Initiative (2004) *A Starting Point: Legal Implications of Internet Filtering*, available at: www.opennetinitiative.org.

Panwar, S., Mao, S., Ryoo, J.D. and Li, Y. (2004) *TCP/IP Essentials. A Lab-based Approach*, Cambridge: Cambridge University Press.

Paolillo, J. (1999) 'The virtual speech community: social network and language variation on IRC', *Journal of Computer-Mediated Communication*, 4 (4), available at: www.jcmc.indiana.edu/vol4/issue4/paolillo.html.

Peirce, C.S. (1931–58) *Collected Papers of Charles Sanders Peirce*, vols 1–6 ed. by C. Hartshorne and P. Weiss, vols 7–8 ed. by A. Burks, Cambridge, MA: Harvard University Press.

Phipps, R. and Merisotis, J. (2000) *Quality on the Line. Benchmarks for Success in Internet-based Distance Education*, Institute for Higher Education Policy, available at: www.ihep.org/pubs/PDF/quality.pdf.

Plato, *Phaedrus*.

Postman, N. (1993) *Technopoly. The Surrender of Culture to Technology*, New York: Vintage Books.

Quintilian, *Institutio oratoria*.

Rappa, M. (2004) 'Business models on the web', *Managing the Digital Enterprise*, available at: www.digitalenterprise.org/models/models.pdf.

Reeves, T. and Laffey, J.M. (1999) 'Design, assessment, and evaluation of a problem-based learning environment in undergraduate engineering', *Higher Education Research and Development Journal*, 18 (2): 219–32.

Rheingold, H. (1993) 'A slice of life in my virtual community', in L. Harasim (ed.) *Global Networks: Computers and International Communication*, Cambridge, MA: The MIT Press, 57–80.

—— (2000) *The Virtual Community. Homesteading on the Electronic Frontier*, revised edn, Cambridge, MA; London: The MIT Press.

Rigotti, E. and Cigada, S. (2004) *La comunicazione verbale*, Milan: Apogeo.

Roberts, M.L. (2003) *Internet Marketing: Integrating Online and Offline Strategies*, New York: McGraw-Hill/Irwin.

Rogers, E.M. (1995) *Diffusion of Innovations*, 4th edn, New York: The Free Press.

Ross, S.S. and Middleberg, D. (1999) *The First Annual Middleberg/Ross Broadcast Media in Cyberspace Study. October 1999*, Middleberg and Associates.

—— and —— (2000) *The Sixth Annual Middleberg/Ross Print Media in Cyberspace Study 1999*, Middleberg and Associates.

Rossett, A. (ed.) (2002) *The ASTD E-Learning Handbook,* New York: McGraw-Hill.

Russell, T.L. (1999) *The No Significant Difference Phenomenon*, Raleigh, NC: North Carolina State University.

de Saussure, F. (1983) *Course in General Linguistics*, London: Duckworth.

Schulmeister, R. (2003) 'Taxonomy of multimedia component interactivity. A contribution to the current metadata debate', *Studies in Communication Sciences*, special issue 'New media in education', March: 61–80.

Shaw, D.L. (1979) 'Agenda setting in mass communication theory', *Gazette*, 25: 96–105.

Sherman, C. (2005) 'Metacrawlers and metasearch engines', *SearchEngineWatch*, 23 March, available at: www.searchenginewatch.com/links/article.php/2156241.

Slatin, J. (1994) 'Reading hypertext: order and coherence in a new medium', in P. Delany and G.P. Landow (eds) *Hypermedia and Literary Studies*, Cambridge, MA; London: The MIT Press, 153–69.

Sloman, M. (2002) *The e-Learning Revolution. How Technology is Driving a New Training Paradigm*, New York: Amacom.

Spar, D. (1999) 'Lost in (cyber)space: the private rules of online commerce', in C. Culter, T. Porter and V. Haufler (eds) *Private Authority and International Affairs*, Albany, NY: Suny Press.

Spence, J.D. (1994) *The Memory Palace of Matteo Ricci*, New York: Viking Press.

Sperber, D. and Wilson D. (1995 2nd edn) [1986] *Relevance. Communication and Cognition*, Oxford: Blackwell.

Sperberg-McQueen, C.M. and Burnard, L. (eds) (2002) *TEI P4: Guidelines for Electronic Text Encoding and Interchange*, Text Encoding Initiative Consortium, available at: www.hti.umich.edu/t/tei/.

Sterne, J. (2002) *Web Metrics. Proven Methods for Measuring Web Site Success*, New York: J. Wiley & Sons.

Steuer, J. (1993) 'Defining virtual reality: dimensions determining tele-presence', *SRCT Paper*, 104: 1–25, available at: www.presence-research.org/papers/steuer92defining.pdf.

Stout, R. (1997) *Web Site Stats: Tracking Hits and Analyzing Web Traffic*, Berkeley, CA: Osborne McGraw-Hill.

Sullivan, D. (2004) 'Major search engines and directories', *SearchEngine-Watch*, 28 April, available at: www.searchenginewatch.com/links/article.php/2156221.

Tardini, S. (2003) 'Keywords as passwords to communities', in F.H. van Eemeren, J.A. Blair, C.A. Willard and A.F. Snoeck Henkemans (eds) *Proceedings of the Fifth Conference of the International Society for the Study of Argumentation*, Amsterdam: SicSat, 995–1000.

—— and Cantoni, L. (2005) 'A semiotic approach to online communities: belonging, interest and identity in websites' and videogames' communities', in P. Isaías, P. Kommers and M. McPherson (eds) *Proceedings of the IADIS International Conference e-Society 2005*, Qawra, Malta, 27–30 June 2005, IADIS Press, 371–8.

Theng, Y.L., Jones, M. and Thimbleby, H. (1996) '"Lost in hyperspace": psychological problem or bad design?', *Proceedings of APCHI '96 [Asia Pacific Conference on Computer Human Interaction]*, Singapore: Information Technology Institute, 387–96, available at: www.cs.waikato.ac.nz/~mattj/lostinhyperspace.pdf.

Tönnies, F. (2001) [1887] *Community and Civil Society*, ed. by J. Harris, Cambridge: Cambridge University Press.

Triacca, L., Bolchini, D., Botturi, L. and Inversini, A. (2004) 'MiLE: systematic usability evaluation for e-learning web applications', in L. Cantoni and C. McLoughlin (eds) *Proceedings of ED-MEDIA 2004*, Norfolk, VA: AACE, 4398–405.

Turkle, S. (1995) *Life on the Screen. Identity in the Age of the Internet*, New York: Simon & Schuster.

UNDESA (2003) *UN Global E-government Survey 2003*, available at: www.unpan1.un.org/intradoc/groups/public/documents/un/unpan016066.pdf.

—— (2004) *UN Global E-government Readiness Report 2004. Towards Access for Opportunity*, available at: www.unpan1.un.org/intradoc/groups/public/documents/un/unpan019207.pdf.

UNICT Task Force (2004) *Second Annual Report of the Information and Communication Technologies Task Force*, available at: www.unicttaskforce.org/perl/documents.pl?id=1385.

Utsumi, Y. (2001) 'Bridging the digital divide through digital governance', keynote speech at the Third Global Forum: fostering democracy & development through e-government, Naples, available at: www.itu.int/osg/sg/speeches/2001/09naples.html.

Weinberger, A. and Mandl, H. (2003) 'Computer-mediated knowledge communication', *Studies in Communication Sciences*, special issue 'New media in education', March: 81–105.

van der Wende, M. and van de Ven, M. (2003) *The Use of ICT in Higher Education. A Mirror of Europe*, Utrecht: LEMMA Publishers.

Wenger, E. (1998) *Communities of Practice: Learning, Meaning, and Identity*, New York: Cambridge University Press.

——, McDermott, R. and Snyder, W.M. (2002) *Cultivating Communities of Practice*, Boston, MA: Harvard Business School Press.

Widdowson, H.G. (1978) *Teaching Language as Communication*, Oxford: Oxford University Press.

Williams, R. (1974) 'The technology and the society', in N. Wardrip-Fruin and N. Montfort (eds) (2003) *The New Media Reader*, Cambridge, MA; London: The MIT Press, 291–300; originally published in R. Williams (1974) *Television: Technology and Cultural Form*, London: Fontana.

—— (1983a) *Towards 2000*, Harmondsworth: Penguin.

—— (1983b) *Keywords: a Vocabulary of Culture and Society*, New York: Oxford University Press.

Winston, B. (1995) 'How are media born and developed?', in J. Downing, A. Mohammadi and A. Sreberny-Mohammadi (eds) *Questioning the Media: A Critical Introduction*, Thousand Oaks, CA: Sage Publications, 54–74.

—— (1998) *Media Technology and Society. A History: From the Telegraph to the Internet*, London; New York: Routledge.

Wood, A.F. and Smith, M.J. (2001) *Online Communication. Linking Technology, Identity and Culture*, Mahwah, NJ; London: Lawrence Erlbaum Associates.

Wyld, D.C. (2004) 'The 3 Ps: the essential elements of a definition of e-government', *Journal of E-Government*, 1 (1): 17–22, available at: www.haworthpress.com/store/SampleText/J399.pdf.

Yates, F.A. (1966) *The Art of Memory*, London: Routledge & Kegan Paul.

Yourdon, E. (2002) *Byte Wars. The Impact of September 11 on Information Technology*, Upper Saddle River, NJ: Prentice Hall PTR.

Zampolli, A. (ed.) (1995) *Survey of the State of the Art in Human Language Technology*, Cambridge: Cambridge University Press.

WEBSITES

AACE – Association for the Advancement of Computing in Education: www.aace.org

About.com: www.about.com

ACM SIGWEB: www.sigweb.org

Alexa web search: www.alexa.com

AllTheWeb: www.alltheweb.com

AltaVista: www.altavista.com

Amazon: www.amazon.com

AOL Search: aolsearch.aol.com

Ask Jeeves: www.ask.com

ASTD Certification Institute: workflow.ecc-astdinstitute.org

BBC: www.bbc.co.uk

BBC World: www.bbcworld.com

Classic Movies: groups.msn.com/ClassicMovies

Clickz Network: www.clickz.com

Corriere della Sera: www.corriere.it

Dmoz – Open Directory Project: www.dmoz.org

Dogpile: www.dogpile.com

EFQUEL – European Foundation for Quality in E-learning: www.qualityfoundation.org

EJO – European Journalism Observatory: www.ejo.ch

Elmundo.es: www.elmundo.es

Encyclopaedia Britannica Online: www.britannica.com

EQO – European Quality Observatory: www.eqo.info

Ferrari Owners' Site: www.owners.ferrari.com

FT.com – Financial Times: www.ft.com

Game Studies: www.gamestudies.org

GBDe – Global Business Dialogue on electronic commerce: www.gbde.org

Google: www.google.com

Harley Davidson: www.harley-davidson.com

HON – Health On the Net Foundation: www.hon.ch

HotBot: www.hotbot.com

HT 2005 – Sixteenth ACM Conference on Hypertext and Hypermedia: www.ht05.org

ICANN – Internet Consortium for Assigned Names and Numbers: www.icann.org

IEEE – Institute of Electrical and Electronics Engineers: www.ieee.org/

IETF – Internet Engineering Task Force: www.ietf.org

Internet Archive: www.archive.org

ISI-Thomson Scientific: www.isinet.com

ISO – International Organization for Standardization: www.iso.org

ISOC – Internet Society: www.isoc.org

ITU – International Telecommunication Union: www.itu.int

Journal of Computer-Mediated Communication: jcmc.indiana.edu

Kartoo: www.kartoo.com

Learning Circuits: www.learningcircuits.org

Le Monde.fr: www.lemonde.fr

Liverpoolfc.tv: www.liverpoolfc.tv

LookSmart: www.looksmart.com

Lugano Tourism: www.lugano-tourism.ch

Mamma: www.mamma.com

Maps.com: www.maps.com

Masie Center: www.masie.com

Microsoft: www.microsoft.com

MSN Search: www.search.msn.com

National Gallery of Art: www.nga.gov
NewMinE Lab – New Media in Education Laboratory:
    www.newmine.org
New York Times: www.nytimes.com
OPA – Online Publishers Association: www.online-publishers.org
Overture: www.overture.com
Project Xanadu: www.xanadu.com
SearchEngineWatch: www.searchenginewatch.com
Spiegel Online: www.spiegel.de
SurfWax: www.surfwax.com
Teoma: www.teoma.com
Times Online: www.timesonline.co.uk
United Nations Information and Communication Technologies Task
    Force: www.unicttaskforce.org
University of Lugano: www.unisi.ch
Useit.com – Jakob Nielsen on Usability and Web Design: www.useit.com
Vivisimo: www.vivisimo.com
Weather.com: www.weather.com
Webopedia – Online Computer Dictionary for Computer and Internet
    Terms and Definitions: www.webopedia.com
WSJ.com – The Wall Street Journal Online: www.wsj.com
W3C – World Wide Web Consortium: www.w3.org
Yahoo!: www.yahoo.com

INDEX

CPSIA information can be obtained at www.ICGtesting.com
Printed in the USA
LVOW12s2040050814

397690LV00009B/20/P

9 780415 352277